MISSOURI
GHOSTS

MISSOURI GHOSTS

And Other Mysteries
Second Edition

Joan Gilbert

*Illustrations and Cover Art
by Adele Graham*

Mogho Books LLC
Hallsville, MO

Missouri Ghosts
And Other Mysteries

Copyright © by Joan Gilbert

2001

Published by MoGho Books
P. O. Box 200
Hallsville, MO 65255

Printed and bound in the United States of America
by Modern Litho-Print Co. at Jefferson City, MO

Second Edition
ISBN 0-9712559-0-3

Library of Congress Catalog Number
2001 126799

Publisher's Cataloging-in-Publication Data
(Provided by Quality Books, Inc.)

Gilbert, Joan.
    Missouri ghosts and other mysteries / Joan Gilbert ; illustrations and cover art by Adele Graham. -- 2nd ed.
        p. cm.
    Includes bibliographical references and index.
    ISBN: 0-9712559-0-3

    1. Ghosts--Missouri. 2. Haunted places--Missouri.
3. Parapsychology--Missouri. I. Title.

BF1472.U6G55 2001   133.1'09778
                        QBI01-201016

Acknowledgements and Dedication

The intention this time was to list every individual
who helped in any way with the book, but again I
haven't the courage to undertake it. Names would
inevitably be left out. As with *More Missouri
Ghosts*, so many people helped in so many ways
that trying to list them all would be a hopeless
undertaking. Therefore, except to Jean Maneke,
without whom it could never have happened,
Adele Graham who supplied the art, and
Mary Jackson who did careful proofreading,
the dedication still must be to:

everyone who helped, by their interest, to inspire
my writing the book;

everyone who shared an unexplainable experience;

everyone who sent clippings or photocopies;

everyone who, as part of their job with a library or
newspaper, took the time to find material I requested;

especially fellow members of Missouri Writers' Guild
and the Columbia Chapter; Missouri Press Women;
most of all, everyone who buys the book and,
I hope, enjoys it!

Preface

Few writers are satisfied with their work as it appears after others have extensively edited it. Most of us are aghast at the covers other people design for our work. We seldom feel a publisher presents us accurately to our readers. Doing it ourselves is the only answer, but that has its problems too; preparing a manuscript for printing is almost as much work as researching and composing, and getting one's product distributed among booksellers can be nearly impossible. But when material has regional interest, that problem is lessened: people like to read about what is familiar to them. When one writes about ghosts, distribution woes hardly exist because as some source, now untraceable, has said, "Everybody wants to see a ghost!" Ghost books sell very well. Statistics say that the books most often stolen from libraries are those about ghosts.

So here is what should be the perfect book, looking just the way the author wants it to look, containing exactly what the author wants in it, plus a great deal of new material, much of which has never been published before. The illustrations are, as television says, "all new!" and there are more of them than before. The first edition of *Missouri Ghosts*, published in 1997, won a first prize from the Missouri Press Women and a second prize from the National Federation of Press Women. *More Missouri Ghosts*, a year 2000 experiment in self-publishing, won the same two prizes plus a first from the Missouri Writers Guild. Only readers of this new edition of *Missouri Ghosts*, can say whether or not it deserves a prize too.

Joan Gilbert, July 15, 2001

Foreword

I have been fascinated with both the history and the hauntings of America for as long as I can remember. There has not been a time when I have not been in search of ghosts, haunted houses and that elusive "something" that we refer to as the unexplained. My own writings have taken me all over the country in pursuit of ghosts and strange history, but growing up in Illinois, I was always lucky to have a place so filled with mystery right outside of my back door ... Missouri.

The state of Missouri is filled with odd happenings, ghostly encounters, unsolved mysteries and most especially, classic ghost stories like the tales of the Lemp Mansion, the infamous St. Louis Exorcism Case, Patience Worth, the Hornet Spook Light and many others. This place is a veritable feast for the haunt hunter and ghost enthusiast!

Until just recently though, these stories were hard to find in print. It required hours of searching through numerous volumes to track down a single Missouri haunting. That was the case until 1997 when Joan Gilbert first collected her wonderful volume of tales, *"Missouri Ghosts."* Finally, after all of this time, the ghost stories and haunted places of the state were all in one spot! And what a spot it was! Joan managed to spin the stories in such a way that my first read of the book was in a single evening. I have since returned to the book many times, always looking over my shoulder as I read it and wondering what might be slipping up behind me!

Now, after following the book with a sequel, Joan has returned to her original material again and has expanded, revised and revisited Missouri's greatest ghost stories! The result of four years of searching for new haunts is now in your hands and you are bound to enjoy this book as much as I did. My only advice is to leave a light on while you are turning the pages because like me, you are certain to wonder if you are really alone!

Happy Hauntings!
Troy Taylor

Troy Taylor is founder of the American Ghost Society, author of several books about the paranormal, and founder and editor of *Ghosts of the Prairie* magazine.

Table of Contents

ix

Introduction

Drifting fog ... threatening thunder ... a crumbling castle or dark old mansion, and nearby a solitary traveler who has lost his way. Then scudding clouds extinguish faint moonlight and the traveler sees ... or hears ... or feels ....

These are standard ingredients of ghost stories, but we usually picture them in Europe, or at least in the parts of our own country longest settled, where the oldest buildings stand. We don't really expect to find spooks in good old Missouri, not beside our lovely streams or in our tranquil woods, not in our cozy little towns or our noisy cities.

Yet we have more than our share of ghostly doings, according to Beth Scott and Michael Norman, who compiled four books of American ghost stories. They wrote that Missouri and Illinois are especially rich in reports of supernatural activity. These two writers believed this was so because many people who settled here brought with them the British Isles tradition of story telling and because, unknowingly or uncaringly, they disturbed burial sites sacred to many generations of Indian people. This must have released multitudes of confused or resentful spirits, judging from the number of Missourians who have a few good tales.

Collecting and sharing ghost stories is a writer's dream because nobody expects documentation. The closest thing we can hope for as proof is when two or more people say they experienced something together and agree to be quoted about it. Most often, people who tell ghost stories make conditions: their names must not be mentioned, or anyone else's name, or the names of their towns. And photographs and supposed recordings of ghostly voices mean little, since they are so easily faked.

Many apparent hauntings, including some described here, could easily be staged by someone clever and agile. Also, it's indisputable that stress, some illnesses and some medications can cause hallucinations of the eyes, ears and nose. So the whole issue of whether or not ghosts exist is like the everlasting debate on whether or not animals have reasoning power and souls. Who can prove the contrary? Nobody has ever dealt with ghosts better than Shakespeare, with the famous line in Hamlet, "There are more things in heaven and earth, Horatio, than are dreamt of in your philosophy."

Missouri has two great unexplained mysteries, the case of Patience Worth and the matter of the Spook Light, visible from near Hornet. Counting Jim the Wonder Dog and real events upon which the *The Exorcist* book and movie were based, we have four enigmas that have attracted to our state — and continue to attract — serious students of the paranormal. Missouri also has, or has had, three residents with national status among psychic investigators and writers in the field. They are Bevy Jaegers, of St. Louis, the late Maurice Schwalm of Kansas City and Dr. Irene Hickman of Kirksville. They can tell us what ghosts probably really are, and what to do when we meet them.

Only one thing more: this book does not pretend to present full or equitable coverage of Missouri's ghosts; it contains only what came to my attention without systematic research. Readers may send their own stories to Mogho Books for possible use in future editions of *Missouri Ghosts* and *More Missouri Ghosts*, or perhaps, someday, in *Missouri Ghosts III*.

Nobody should be timid about contributing, because a recent television comment — unattributed, so far as I could tell — said that 50 million Americans claim to have had some sort of supernatural experience.

I became convinced that the uncharted territory of human consciousness was the next frontier to explore, that it contained possibilities we had hardly begun to imagine.

— Edgar C. Mitchell, Astronaut, 6th person on the moon.

Close to
Home Ghosts

Chapter One

In the Neighborhood

He talked and as he talked
Wallpaper came alive;
Suddenly ghosts walked ....
— Mark Van Doren,
The Story Teller

My mother saw a ghost and always considered it one of the nicest experiences of her life. Repeatedly hearing her story was a cherished part of my childhood. The circumstances: she was lying across a bed one afternoon in the 1920s, crying about some temporary crisis, when she suddenly found herself looking at a favorite aunt who had died years before.

"Why, I thought you were dead!" she exclaimed, amazed to be less frightened than delighted. The aunt said nothing. She only smiled and shook her head, but in such a loving, comforting, encouraging way that her message was unmistakable: "Death is not like you think ... nothing is really so bad ... everything will be fine for you ... don't cry."

The momentary encounter gave my mother strength for her lifetime. I loved to hear details she remembered. The aunt, who had died in old age of a ravaging disease, appeared "young and rested," her expression serene. Her simple, cream-colored garment seemed somehow to be both as thick as wool and as delicate as silk.

My mother's story was one of several I heard as a child
from relatives and neighbors. Recalling them always evokes
a delicious sense of fascinating danger kept safely at bay by
familiar surroundings and the presence of loving adults. The
words "ghost story" bring back our front porch at night,
cousin Lizzie's snug kitchen, the smell of her husband's pipe
tobacco and my urgency in pedaling home from their house
before darkness came.

Our neighbor Minnie's brush with the hereafter was as
happy as my mother's. Hers occurred at the turn of the century when she was barely a teenager. She saw a recently
deceased little brother for a few seconds, trailing along
behind their other siblings.

"He was wearing his favorite hat and carrying his usual
long 'poking stick', bouncing the end of it off the path in front
of him as he always did," she said. "He was as solid as any of
the others. It was broad daylight and the children were coming in because I had called them and they had heard me. I was
not dreaming." To get to the gate, the children had to pass
behind some lilacs which hid them for a moment. When they
came out, Minnie said, "He wasn't with them."

Like my mother's, Minnie's experience gave peace and
strength, seeming to show that wherever they are, the departed can be safe and content. Another neighbor confirmed this.
She told of looking up from her ironing one day to see on the
wall an image of a brother who lived several states away.

"It was like a portrait," she said, "in color, just from the
chest up. He was looking out at me and smiling. He didn't
move or say anything, but he looked so well and so happy,
like in the best years of his life. He looked ready to speak."

Two days later, she learned of his death.

Making A Choice

Here's a story I thought of every time I passed a certain
house, less than a block from my family's home: one night in
the early 1930s, remnants of two families gathered there after
a funeral to consider the future of an infant girl orphaned by
her parents' death in a train wreck.

Nobody present was of an age, or situated suitably to welcome the task of rearing a child, but they had agreed she must not go to an orphanage. As they sat in silence, each no doubt hoping one of the others would take responsibility for her, a faint ringing sound and vibration began and went around the circle, as if someone were moving from person to person, ringing a tiny bell over each head. "A crystal bell," Minnie said, having been present as an in-law. "Or a little glass triangle, a lovely sound, very small, though everyone could hear it and we all looked at each other."

Twice the bell went around the circle and then stopped above an aging, unmarried woman who seemed the poorest possible choice. She had no assets but the house she lived in, left to her by her parents, and her small income from dressmaking. But she agreed to rear the little girl if others would help financially. They promised and kept their promise, and this aunt, older than some of those present that night, was the only one still alive when the orphaned girl finished high school. My mother and Minnie often commented, "Those parents knew who to call on."

A Well-Shod Ghost

Another hometown story came from my mother's elderly friend, known to the whole town as Grandma R. This was an immaculate little lady whose beautiful white hair made aging seem an enviable condition. At the corner of her property was a pear tree whose hearty growth had raised and broken the sidewalk. This was in days before trees were thoughtlessly slaughtered for the sake of neatness, and I'm sure my mother and I were not the only people who ever walked up to Grandma R's at night just to see pear blossoms in moonlight.

Under this tree, just about daylight one morning, Mrs. R told my mother she saw "a ghost or something." She had spent the night, sitting up in the old-fashioned way, with the wife of a man who was terminally ill. Mrs. R was tired, but, she declared, certainly not sleepwalking. She was in a peaceful frame of mind, praying that her neighbor would have an easy departure.

After her encounter under the tree, Grandma R. was not surprised, on returning to her friends' house, to find the husband had slipped quietly away in his sleep. "It must have been his spirit I saw, paused to say goodbye and send me back to be with Martha ... or maybe an angel, come to help him over," she told my mother. "But it didn't have wings." She described the being as not at all frightening; its face was sweet and its eyes looked kindly into hers. "I wouldn't say it was a man or a woman," she said, "but there was a sort of glimmer about it, and blonde hair." There was the white robe one expects for either ghost or an angel, and one surprising item of attire. My mother used to smile at the puzzled way her friend always said, "I noticed in particular — imagine! — it had on white shoes!"

Accusing Footprints

Of all the people in my childhood, Lizzie's husband, Ed, was the best story teller and the most interested in ghosts. He was a blacksmith and children were drawn to his shop, both to watch him work and for the tales he told. Even while holding up one-fourth of a horse, even while hammering red hot shoes into shape, he knew just when to lower his voice, just when to pause and say, "and what do you think happened then?" While driving the big nails in, to keep them handy, Ed held several extras in his mouth. Of course, he couldn't talk then, and we had to wait; this somehow seemed to always coincide with the most suspenseful part of a tale.

It was from Ed that I heard my first disquieting ghost stories, and for one of them there was proof that we could see when we visited him at home. He would show the place on his porch where two footprints were found one morning. Side by side, at a bedroom window, we saw distinct marks of bare feet, as if someone walked through the dew and then stood, peering into the house. No other prints came up the steps or across the porch, but these two never dried up. Scrubbing only dimmed them. They were eventually painted over.

The footprints appeared Ed said, some twenty years earlier, while his aged mother lay dying several blocks away and one of his own children lay fatally ill — though nobody realized this at the time — just inside the window. Cousin Lizzie told my mother she was feeling guilty then, staying home to care for the child, whose illness everyone dismissed, while her mother-in-law undeniably needed help.

My father said privately, just in our family, that Ed probably made the tracks himself with kerosene. Nobody else said such a thing; they just debated possible meanings. Did the grandmother's spirit come reproachfully, to see why her stricken body was being neglected? Or, aware that they would enter the unknown within a week of each other, did her spirit come to accompany the child's? I still shiver, remembering the voices and tones of my elders discussing this.

What Did Dixie See?

Another of Ed's stories is a classic that has been told everywhere with variations. None seems better to me than his. It made me look with new respect at my father's bird dogs, my constant companions. Would they sometime, perhaps, sense danger I couldn't see, and protect me with their warning?

Relatives were clearing out a large old house that had belonged to a recently deceased couple who'd lived there for more than 50 years. The chore had been going on for a week and everyone had long since lost zeal for making sure that everything useful was channeled to the most appropriate individual or organization. One of the workers had begun bringing her dog along for company; she had volunteered to do the attic and found it lonely up there.

The dog was named Dixie, a big old mixed breed who had spent a great deal of time in the deceased couple's house from puppyhood, even to visiting for weeks at a time when his owners traveled. His quiet presence was helpful; he made an island of total relaxation as he snoozed contentedly in a patch of sunlight from the now uncurtained window. His owner didn't see what happened, or the preliminary stages of Dixie's terror. She only turned, hearing a sound from him that she described as "part whimper and part growl," to find Dixie flattened on his belly, trembling, backed against the wall and looking up, to the side of his owner. His eyes were fixed and fearful, as if he were certain of attack.

When she said, "What's wrong, Dixie?" he turned his face, slowly, as with difficulty, and crept a step or two toward her. Then he seemed suddenly to gain courage to scrabble past and down the stairs, rolling part way, as his owner could hear. She went out to find him cowering under the car, shaking violently.

"They said he shook for 45 minutes," Ed told us, relaying this story. "And he would never go back in that house. He was even suspicious of the car for a month or more — he who loved riding and was always ready to go anywhere at anytime. This was a dog I knew and if you ask me, Dixie never was right again."

Nobody else who was in the house that day saw or heard anything unusual, and nobody ever had, so far as the family knew. No tragedies had taken place there. Though all agreed that Dixie was a sensible dog and something must have happened, they did not mention the incident outside their circle, lest they sound silly or jeopardize sale of the house. Buyers of the place loved it, and far from complaining about anything strange, said they could feel the warm family life that had existed there.

My relatives and friends told more stories than these, some of which they picked apart as possible practical jokes, or as delusions of someone who "always was a little flighty" or "under a lot of strain at that time." We were not familiar with psychological terms meaning the same thing and such buzzwords as "wishful thinking" and "suggestible" were not yet in the language. Probably some of our stories could be dismissed that way: a young wife, feeling isolated with her problems is comforted by a loving aunt; a teenager, working through her first bereavement, assures herself that a little brother lost to her still lives happily in another dimension; or, as my father suggested, a domineering husband stages a ghostly visit to influence his wife.

Whatever the truth of these stories, they opened my mind very early to the fact that human certainty has severe limitations. These stories also demonstrated that you can't believe everything everybody says. Other stories — collected over a lifetime and shared here — reinforced those lessons.

Ice Drummer

There is a drummer in the lake,
Under the ice, an Indian drummer
A ghost who swims fast, who loves a joke.
You will hear him only
On cold and sunny noontides,
Doubting your ears at first:
A faint and resonant drumbeat here?
Go to the edge, but be prepared
For a sudden, mighty throb
Right in front of you.
Then he will move off to the side and thrum.
From the other end of the lake, the middle,
The side again, in front of you and away,
Will come single, echoing thumps.

You can picture him so easily:
A laughing swimmer, hair washed across his eyes,
Hugging his magic drum against him
As he rolls and spins through the water.
After tapping softly, quickly, he falls silent
Until you give up and turn away.
Then sharply, loudly, he will thunk
Just where you stood.

But after that, no more
Until you're halfway down the hill.
He may play a tatoo then,
That Indian joker under the ice,
The ghostly drummer in the lake.

Joan Gilbert

Chapter Two

Out In The County

I cannot tell how the truth may be.
I say the tale as 'twas said to me.
      — Sir Walter Scott, *Lay of the Last Minstrel*

One of Cousin Ed's stories concerned a family farther away from our homes, a family he had known well in his earlier life. He felt especially strongly about them, being himself a veteran of World War I, as one of their sons was. It seems a second son in the family, against urgent wishes of his father, who needed his help at home, set off to enlist as United States involvement in the war deepened. He left home before daylight to walk several miles to town, carrying a lantern to see his way across the fields. He'd leave the lantern at the schoolhouse, he said, so the children could bring it home. His family never saw him or the lantern again, and never received a letter from him.

What they did see, on certain summer nights, was a small swinging light, like a lantern in someone's hand, coming across the fields toward the house The first time they saw it, they thought it was the lost son and ran joyously to meet him, calling his name. The light immediately disappeared. This happened through three generations of the family. Any calling out stopped the light at once, but even if nobody said anything, it came only a certain distance toward the house before disappearing.

Questions are obvious. Had the young man met with foul play while still in his own neighborhood? But it was a congenial, tight-knit community and neither he nor his family had any enemies they could think of. If he'd been killed in the war, wouldn't the government have informed his parents? Had he used the army as a ploy just to get away from home and then met with misfortune that made him ashamed, though his spirit kept trying to return? The family couldn't believe he'd be so cruel as to leave them in suspense about his fate if he had any way at all to communicate.

So, is the light this family repeatedly saw just a natural phenomenon we don't understand yet? Actually, unusual lights have been reported at numerous times and in various places. These are discussed in greater detail in a later chapter.

A Misplaced Teen

Another lost person figures in a story carried by either the Waynesville or St. Robert newspaper in the 1960s. It came in the form of a letter to the editor from a couple who remained anonymous. They did this, they said, for the sake of the value of property they'd sold in Pulaski County when they had to move to another state. But they wanted to speak out on something that might be of use to a particular pair of parents in the area.

These people wrote that several times, in the hallway of their St. Robert home, they saw a pretty young girl, blonde, dressed in a short and modern blue dress, walking hastily away from them. Two or three times she turned, seemed to see them, paused, looking confused and frightened, then hurried out of sight. The couple, whose house had been built new for them on a stretch of new highway, wondered if any girl fitting their description had died there. Perhaps she'd been kidnapped or in a car wreck. They said that each time they saw her, they felt overpowering pity and wished they could do something to help.

Later editorial comment said local law enforcement offices had no file on a missing young woman. This is typical of many ghost stories: they give us no conclusion, only a mystery to puzzle over.

Ghostly Treasures

Three Pulaski County stories are standard in that they deal with fortunes abandoned because of sudden death. Two of these stories inspired generations of treasure hunters.

The first centers on an historic building in the Buckhorn community near Waynesville. More than 125 years ago, this was a stagecoach stop and inn, but for the past several decades it has been a private dwelling for a number of different families. At Halloween, 1980, when its owners, Emerson and Marie Storie, were interviewed by a reporter for *The Gateway Guide*, they said they'd heard footsteps when nobody was present but themselves. They also had smelled hickory smoke where no fire existed. Their daughter, in an upstairs bedroom, said she often heard heavy breathing that might even, at times, be called agonized.

In one of the building's tales, three travelers from California arrived on a stormy night and foolishly discussed the gold they'd panned and were taking home. They soon became suspicious of the landlord's interest in them, however, and agreed that while two occupied his attention, the other would take their valises (small hand luggage popular in the 1800s) outdoors and hide them.

The wiley landlord caught on, but steady rain made it impossible to follow tracks or find where digging had occurred. Upstairs he isolated the traveler who had been outdoors and tried to force him to tell where the bags were. When the gold's owner, determined to keep what he'd worked so hard to gain, was not easily coerced, the landlord turned to torture, using a poker heated in the fire. The landlord was thwarted again when his victim's heart gave out under the stress. The other two men, apparently aware of what was going on above, fled into the stormy night. Nobody ever knew whether they were able to retrieve their gold and take it with them. Over the years, many people have dug hopefully around the old stagecoach depot, but nobody in the area has become suddenly rich.

Marie Storie was quoted in the *Guide* as saying "We're not superstitious, but there are things happening here that we just can't explain."

A St. Louis couple named Helde said just the opposite about a home they made in the former Wheeler's Mill, near Crocker. Dorothy Helde declared that they never saw or heard any kind of ghost, not even the ghost of rural life past. Their home was featured in a rural electric cooperative's newspaper in the 1960s for its use of the latest in electric appliances and innovative lighting.

Two ghost stories exist about this peaceful place, nonetheless. The best concerns the Wheelers, who in 1912 were operating the mill as that essential rural service — flour mill and community store. The husband was killed in September of that year, dying suddenly when caught in the belts of some of his equipment. Only a month later, his wife, Agatha, followed him, her death blamed on exposure during his burial ceremony.

Just a few months before their deaths, Agatha received a substantial legacy from a relative, but neighbors "turning out" the house after her death, found no resources of any kind, not even enough cash for the funerals. The couple had made wills, leaving everything to relatives and friends, but nothing of value could be found.

What happened next was described by Eva Marie Woodward, in *Fate Magazine*, in the 1950s. She wrote that her young uncle, Clarence Hamilton, worked for the Wheelers in the manner of many teenagers, after school, on weekends and during vacations. Being childless, the couple took affectionate interest in young Hamilton and he was very fond of them. After their deaths, because he was familiar with the store, Clarence was asked to help take inventory.

On the first afternoon, coming in as soon as school closed, he was astounded to look up from his work and see

Agatha Wheeler standing before him. She was wearing a grey dress that he remembered, one with large white collar and white cuffs. Though she smiled at him in the usual way, he was terrified. Telling the others he was sick, Clarence ran home where he was put to bed and given calming potions.

Next day, at the same time, exactly 4:15, Mrs. Wheeler reappeared to Clarence. This time he was able to stay and work; he just made sure not to look up again. That night his grandmother told Clarence that when ghosts visit us they usually want something. "You should ask Mrs. Wheeler if you can help her," the grandmother told him, "but first protect yourself by saying "In the name of the Father, the Son and the Holy Ghost, what do you want here?"

When the ghost appeared next day Clarence did this, though hardly able to control his fear. The image of Mrs. Wheeler backed away a few steps and motioned him to follow her. This meant not only crossing the whole expanse of store and mill, but also going through a tunnel that led to the house. Once outdoors again, the ghost led Clarence to a newly built stone chimney that had been one of her husband's last projects. Her digging motions and pointing left no doubt about what she wanted.

Clarence sped home, and gathered reinforcements. In only minutes they had unearthed a large Dutch oven, carefully sealed and full of gold, currency and investment certificates. Mrs. Wheeler's debts were paid and her loved ones were rewarded as she had intended. No one ever reported seeing her again.

🐈 The other Wheeler Mill ghost supposedly lost his body there to bushwhackers soon after the Civil War. The story begins with a strange little man's arrival for a night's lodging. He was noticeably nervous and was strangely secretive about his name and where he was bound, rejecting friendly questions of those working or trading at the mill at the time.

In late afternoon, somebody rode in to warn that bushwhackers were in the area. They usually struck mills, good sources of supply and usually harboring a few people who could be robbed. As the mill's owners hurried to hide certain things, and customers fled, the strange guest asked to borrow a shovel. He took his valise and ran outside. The attack came to pass and he was among the fatalities. Belongings in his room gave no clue as to his identity. No amount of searching and digging ever disclosed what he was so concerned to hide.

However, it was said that he haunted the mill for many years, appearing in the west door when the setting sun impeded vision, as it had done on the day of the guerrilla raid. A small man in top hat and frock coat, sometimes carrying his bag and sometimes not, he would rush past a spectator and disappear. Occasionally, if the person who had seen him turned quickly, they got a glimpse of him from the back.

Hoaxes or Haunts?

A last Pulaski County story is surely one of the most far-fetched ghost tales ever heard — or else a blatant joke. The audacious series of events was explored at length in *The Gateway Guide* for October 30, 1975. In supposed newspaper stories dated 1940, 1945 and 1974, authentic local history was set forth along with what had been a persistent story in the Fort Leonard Wood area. An unidentified reporter wrote that soldiers on sentry duty were sometimes found drunk and unconscious on Halloween. All offered the same defense: they had been forced by riotous ghosts, whose language they couldn't understand, to sip hard cider through a straw until they passed out.

The 1940 article told how residents of Bloodland, a town of about 100 people and 40 buildings, learned on Halloween of that year that their homes and town would be taken over to become part of the fort. Gathered for a community celebration when this news was given, the residents were stunned and angry. Theirs was a very old settlement of well established home-loving and hard-working people, mainly of German descent. What right did the government have to do this to them? It was said that because many people had been drinking all day, a minor riot took place.

Then, in 1942, the *Guide* tells us, a soldier named James Klown (clue here?) was court martialed and confined for a year because he was found drunk and unconscious on guard duty in what had been Bloodland. He claimed that while investigating strange noises in the area, he was taken captive and forced to drink hard cider through a straw until he collapsed.

The following year, a soldier named Randall Ellsworth suffered the same fate, but he was not confined and Klown was released. Authorities put the supposedly haunted town off limits for military personnel. In 1974, however, three men together reportedly told the cider tale again and the 1975 newspaper story ended with the question "What will happen at Fort Leonard Wood tomorrow night?"

Probably all this proves that the more complex and imaginative a ghost story is, the more suspicious one should be. Whoever wrote the story in 1975 was no longer at the *Guide* when we inquired in 1997. Nobody now on the staff has any memory of the incidents or any idea whether they were a hoax, but the whole matter demonstrates how easily somebody's joke may be incorporated into folklore. However, the story did exist apart from that anonymous newspaper writer, and he did accurately relay facts about Bloodland's tragic death. No doubt his description was true, too, of all that now remains of a much-loved little town that became nothing but a firing range. Little was left of it, he said, but the foundations of a school in which residents had taken great pride, and a badly damaged and boarded-up Methodist church.

Certainly Bloodland people felt enough outrage and sadness to have stimulated all sorts of supernatural activity, supporting Diane Glancy's speculation in her novel, *Pushing the Bear:* "Maybe, in the end, our acts cause little energy fields that draw their likenesses toward them."

Going to college in Springfield exposed me to a whole new set of ghost stories, some by word of mouth, some from local newspapers, and others from the writing of that famous Ozarks folklorist, Vance Randolph, then at his peak of popularity.

Decades later, from the Internet, came knowledge that a former college classmate, Darrell Haden, had published a book about a unique headless haunt in his native Douglas County. Herewith, then, what the Ozarks taught me about ghosts.

The Ozarks

Chapter Three

Springfield Spirits

I could a tale unfold whose lightest word
Would ... freeze thy young blood ... make thy locks part
... and each particular hair to stand on end,
Like quills upon the fretful porcupine.
— Shakespeare, *Hamlet*

Springfield's most haunted building probably was the Landers Theater, downtown. Built in 1907 for live performances, the Landers saw no other use for many years. By the 1920s, as a vaudeville house, the building was considered to be haunted. As the years passed, it served in every way a theater can, being used for showing movies, then for television filming. Its reputation for being haunted persisted even into the 1960s, when the Landers went back to its live-actors roots, as home for the Springfield Little Theater.

The only story now remaining to explain why the Landers is haunted concerns a despondent stagehand who hanged himself from some of the high rigging above stage. Sources say his body remained there through three performances before his absence — not to mention his body — was noticed. Investigators found no police record of the event, but many such documents seem everywhere to have been lost over the years. All the gentle ghost of the Landers Theater was reported to do was to occasionally walk about on the catwalks. He was heard only by individuals who were working alone when the theater was empty.

Springfield Little Theater's manager, Craig Hutchison, interviewed in the 1970s by Jean Maneke for the Springfield newspaper, seemed unaware of this story. He did say, however, "... this is a hotbed of superstition ... " remarking that many theaters are the same. Their size, big areas of darkness, multiple entrances and exits, and their intricate corridors are ideal for the sightings of real or fabricated ghosts. Hutchison disproved the rumor that the Landers has secret panels and passages. Having been present through extensive renovation, the manager knew that walls were nowhere thick enough to allow anything so dramatic. He conceded, though, that several performers had told him of seeing, from the stage, unsettling sights. Some had complained in rehearsal of feeling as if an observer watched from the wings, with intensity and ill will. The only unusual thing Hutchison had himself experienced was lights that would not always turn off. Some had persisted despite being unplugged and even after the main switch was thrown. He supposed this somehow resulted from the building's being rewired many times. Whenever it happened, Hutchison said he always decided pretty promptly, "Time to be getting home."

Ghosts Affectionate and Otherwise

An outstanding Springfield manifestation was what a newspaper story called "the hugging ghost." This unexplained entity just seemed to enjoy giving exuberant, prolonged and engulfing hugs that caused at least two people to faint from panic. One recipient who didn't faint said it was "sort of like being attacked by a mattress." These events took place in upper hallways of a building that had been business offices converted to apartments or vice versa; the clipping has been lost, but who could forget a story so unique?

A Springfield newspaper column called "Over the Ozarks" once used a letter from Arleen Pomaville of Aurora, telling about a distinctly unpleasant haunted house her great grandparents briefly occupied. The building was far from being what one would expect ghosts to like, just a three-room affair built hastily and crudely to shelter workers. Other identical structures stood in rows with just a few feet between neighbors. Yet only tenants of one particular little house were constantly leaving, saying it was haunted. Pomaville's ancestors, being staunch disbelievers in ghosts, moved in. On their very first night, they were awakened by the sharp sound of ripping paper. It seemed to come from overhead and when they lit their lamp, the noise stopped. Thinking it was rats or squirrels they slept with the light on to discourage such nocturnal activity. Next day they climbed to the shallow attic where they found no indication of animal habitation and no tracks of any kind on the dusty floor.

After a few days of peace, the eerie, unexplained ripping noise began again and was joined by a trick of the water bucket. Its dipper took spells of rising and sinking, into the water, gurgling loudly all the while. The husband eliminated this problem by simply hanging the dipper on a nail.

Not to be outdone, the unseen force began clicking and rattling at the front door, as if trying to jiggle the latch off from outside. This was followed by the kitchen door flying open forcefully and slamming loudly against the inside wall, as if someone had entered very angrily, or a strong wind had blown the door open. Sometimes both door mysteries and the paper ripping went on simultaneously.

The husband — obviously relishing a challenge — once pitted his own strength against the kitchen door. He said the power behind it was far greater than his own. When pushing a sturdy kitchen table against the door didn't help, he nailed a thick leather strap from facing to facing, anchored strongly on each side. To the haunted door this barrier was no more than flimsy twine, so the couple admitted defeat and moved away.

They conceded to neighbors that they'd been losing too much sleep, not that they'd ever been frightened.

The Phantom Flivver

College students in Springfield warned each other that in the area of a small nearby town named Nixa, one must beware of a brand-new looking Model A Ford, which day or night, but mostly night, might suddenly appear and cause a wreck by threatening to collide head on. A sheriff named Frank Jones had been killed in 1932, belief was, at the time, by being forced off the road by "the phantom flivver". (This word was slang in the 1920s for an automobile of little quality or value.) A well-known businessman, Fred McCoy, had told of almost wrecking his car to avoid hitting the fabled Ford.

So long as another vehicle was in sight, drivers were safe, but one had be alert on the Ozarks' narrow, hilly and winding backroads where drivers were often alone. The silent appearance of big and round, but dim headlights could mean danger. Some people who claimed to have seen the ghostly car declared that its horn gave them a derisive "Ahoooooooga" salute as it departed. Nobody ever said they heard an engine.

No explanatory story existed as to why the phantom car patrolled the area. Vance Randolph, in his book *Ozark Magic and Folklore*, said the dangerous car was taken quite seriously by people in the area, many claiming to have seen it. Some said they damaged their own vehicles going off the road to avoid it.

The Sheedy Farm

A suicide, two grisly murders, a fearsome albino protector, seven siblings who never left their parents, a show-place farm allowed to fall into decay: all these are elements of the story told about a pre-Civil War estate near Springfield. The place was first known as Springlawn and was so idyllic that people drove out from town on Sundays to view its beautiful house, many farm buildings, lakes, waterfall and deer park.

One of Springlawn's great attractions was its large herd of lovely Jersey cattle.

After several years, of peaceful ownership, Frank Headley sold the farm to Mike Sheedy and his wife, with their seven children. These nine people all lived out their lives there, the last sister dying in 1979.

In its final years, the farm fell into pitiful disrepair as the three remaining sisters tried to keep it up. Premises took on the appearance of the standard haunted house, almost in ruins, nearly hidden by vines and shrubs gone amok. Some writers say the women hired a large albino man to help them, and that he grew so possessive he turned away visitors at gunpoint. He also was blamed for two hatchet murders done at a nearby little iron bridge; one killing included decapitation, the weapon defiantly left at the scene.

According to Tom Mason, writing in *Springfield!* magazine in October 1985, the bridge began to be called Hatchet Man's Bridge and the farm, Albino Farm. One of the Sheedy sons' having killed himself on the property added to eerie atmosphere of the place and assured its being considered haunted. Mason did not give details of the suicide, but when the house burned in 1988, its legend remained. At the time Mason wrote, stone pillars still stood at the entrance and many people drove north on Farm Road 165 to see them and talk about the Sheedy tragedies, just as people had driven out a century earlier to see a farm so beautiful and productive it could hardly be believed.

Nearby Ghosts

Springfield papers also carried ghost stories from nearby towns. An example: In Ozark stood a house built partly from boards that had been used in a scaffold from which bandits had been hanged. Residents said that in early days of the new house, fluttering and popping sounds coincided with the time of day when the hanged men had met their fate. These sounds stopped at 3 p.m., the hour when the executions was completed.

Ten years to a day after the executions, a clock in that house, a clock that hadn't run for years, was said to have begun ticking of its own accord. It ran through 3 p.m., at which time it stopped and never could be made to go again.

Meanwhile, a neighbor had an experience she felt was connected. While working outdoors, she was approached by a perfectly real-looking young man who asked her about someone who'd hanged himself from a nearby bridge. As she explained that she knew nothing about this, the young man vanished before her eyes.

One of the aspects of spiritualism that has always roused my loudest jeers — the statement that spirits are disturbed by too much light.

Barbara Michaels in *Ammie, Come Home*

Chapter Four

Hill Stories

Some say no evil thing that walks by night
In fog or fire, by lake or moorish fen
Blue meagre hag, or stubborn unlaid ghost
That breaks his magic chains at curfew time,
... Hath hurtful power o'er true virginity.
                    — John Milton, *Comus*

No collector of Ozarks folklore compares with Vance Randolph, who spent about 50 years of his life devoted to the task. His books still are sought after and used as reference. His ghost stories range from only a few sentences to tales long and detailed, and he always gave full credit to those he quoted.

Randolph, who was himself called "dean of American folklorists," often referred to a collector who went before him, Thomas Moore of Ozark, an attorney who in 1938 published a book called *Mysterious Tales and Legends of the Ozarks*. It's interesting to compare Moore's book with *Ozark Magic and Folklore*, the most lastingly popular of many Randolph wrote. This was first published in 1947 as *Ozarks Superstitions*. An example of how the two men complemented each other:

Randolph wrote of a Taney County farmer who kept insisting that his deceased daughter still sang in the woods in late afternoon as had been her custom in life. When derided for saying this, he invited some solid citizens, including a judge and a few attorneys, out to listen. Some of the men said yes, they heard a female voice singing, clearly enough to almost make out words. One said several lines ended in yodeling. Nobody said he heard nothing.

One witness, questioned by Randolph several years later, said he'd not swear that what he heard was a human voice, but he definitely heard something pleasant and melodic and unlike any bird song or other natural sound he'd ever heard. He said that as the men walked together through the area, the singer seemed to come toward them at times, then veer away again. They found no tracks, no crushed vegetation or bruised leaves in the heavy woods, no evidence at all that another person had been near them.

Moore's version of this same thing, several pages long, described underlying events for a tragedy "in the bend of Finley Creek." He said the girl's name was Madelaine and that she probably died because of her father's cruelty. He turned her away in bad weather when she came to him on foot, her baby in her arms, seeking refuge from a failed marriage. Having forbidden the alliance in the first place, he told her she must lie in the bed she'd made and rear her own child. Though other relatives took Madelaine and her baby in, she became ill and died. Her relatives felt that the exposure forced by her father had killed Madelaine.

The girl's mother had wanted all the time to take her back, and their community let the father feel its disapproval. Thus he had plenty of motivation for wanting to believe his daughter was alive in spirit and singing, happy near her childhood home, in this way showing forgiveness. A debunker would probably say he arranged to have someone sing in the woods for witnesses, though of course, even if they all believed it was Madelaine, that would hardly restore her father's reputation.

For a long time, many people visited the site and gave varied reports of what they heard. Some, who had known Madelaine well, declared that they recognized her voice. Others, present with these believers, said they heard nothing at all.

The Smiling Spook

Some of the Randolph tales came from groups which shared experiences. The most inexplicable happened in a deserted schoolhouse named Oak Grove, 50 miles south of Springfield. An actual bushwhacker victim, homeless and mentally afflicted, who had sheltered in the school until his death, was said to haunt the building. Supposedly, he appeared as a bald man grinning at spectators from inside a window.

A group of four or more young men, enroute home from a dance, possibly well-liquored, decided to test this story out and sure enough, saw the "h'ant" sitting at the window. When their civil greetings got no response, one fired six times through the glass. His unknown target sat without moving, facial expression unchanged.

The two bravest boys went inside and came out saying nobody was in the one-room building. Their companions swore that the bald man grinned crazily at them the entire time their friends were gone. They then took their own turn going inside but found only emptiness. More shooting may have taken place at this time, but the experiment was ended by their horses. The consensus among these animals apparently was that they had reached saturation point for strange doings. In unison, they bolted for home.

Some Randolph Short Shorts

Travelers near Rogersville saw, from a little distance, a cabin with smoke rising from its chimney and agreed to stop there for much-needed refreshment. They found the building unoccupied, however, with no sign of a fire having been on the hearth for years.

Mary Elizabeth Mahnkey, a widely read and loved Ozarks newspaper columnist and poet, was also a correspondent of Randolph's. She wrote to him of sighting, through field glasses, a pleasant ridgetop cabin with all signs of habitation. This was near a community called Miney. When she inquired about the cabin, long-time residents of the area told her that no such cabin existed or ever had.

An elderly lady in McDonald County told Randolph of an evening when she sat alone, as usual, in her two-room cabin, doors and windows securely locked against the night. She heard the latch and bolt of the kitchen door lift, and a heavy person in squeaky boots crossed the floor to the water bucket. The rattling dipper meant he was getting a drink, and before he could have walked back out, she was in the kitchen. Nobody was there and all entrances were fastened from the inside, just as she had left them.

On her deathbed, a young woman distantly related to Randolph tried to tell her family the name of a man whose betrayal caused her decline. Unable to make them understand, she was believed to have come back as the ghost who began walking that house at night, opening and closing drawers of an old bureau. Was she trying to lead her family to evidence of her cruel lover's identity? Randolph didn't speculate.

A couple of headless ghosts were listed by Randolph. One haunted the area of a bridge near Kimberling City, gliding about as if on roller skates, or sometimes lying beside the road on very cold nights, groaning horribly. The other was sometimes seen sitting on top of haystacks and would wave at people, then slide down the other side. Nothing was ever there, of course, if travelers went around and looked.

Breadtray Mountain

Sobs, groans and screams from a spot on Breadtray Mountain, a unique formation in Stone County, were explained by Randolph as Spanish soldiers being annihilated by Indians or vice versa. Between him and Moore we get varied possibilities. Chickasaw tribesmen had mined silver and crafted it on the mountain for generations. Then Spanish explorers came along and imprisoned them in their own mine, forcing them to work on as slaves, until the Indians finally found means to revolt and kill their oppressors.

Another version is that when the Spaniards arrived in the area, the Indians greeted them generously, helped them find all they needed for their camp and even provided some young women to do the drudgery. But soon after, when the Indians discovered that their daughters and sisters were being abused, they wiped out the newcomers. Some who have written about Breadtray Mountain said that the sounds were heard by people in groups, all of whom made similar reports.

The late Tom Ladwig, a *Columbia Tribune* columnist, added to this story by precisely locating Breadtray Mountain. He showed it to be now partly inundated by Table Rock Lake, and about ten miles from Reed Springs, near the northern border of Arkansas. Ladwig said that many have searched for the Chickasaw/Spanish treasure and he ended with characteristic humor, warning that if anyone did find the silver, "a great white Internal Revenue Service Man is probably there and watching."

A Truly Complex Tale

One of Moore's stories was about a rotting, multi-haunted mansion somewhere in southern Missouri. People reported firm footsteps that came from the porch down the hall and into a large room with a beautiful fireplace, where the footsteps paused for some time, then departed in a deliberate manner. Inhabitants of this home also heard a weakly crying infant near the back door, and an unfindable creaky chair in which someone seemed to be vigorously rocking. Lastly, some roses on this property took on an odor enticingly like bananas and lured a small boy almost to his death.

The history of the unnamed house, as pieced together by two sets of owners, their relatives, and people who worked there as servants: A Georgian who happened to be an abolitionist came north with his wife and servants and in 1847 built a lovely home. When the Civil War began, he felt compelled to go, and departed with strangely thoughtless haste. He sent his wife back to her parents with some of the most capable and trusted slaves, taking only one wagonload of possessions. He asked the slaves who were left behind to care for the house and the valuables within it as well as they could and to live on the farm's livestock and produce. After the war, which he assured them would be short, they would all reassemble and resume their pleasant life. He had already promised freedom to his slaves as soon as he could arrange for them to go out into the world well-equipped to take care of themselves.

After his wife left, the owner of the mansion sent his body servant to bring up their two horses. While waiting, he re-entered the house, and stood for a few moments in contemplation before a large portrait of his wife that hung over the mantel in the parlor. Then he went back out on the porch, mounted his horse from there, and rode off with his attendant.

The Georgian was killed by Confederates at Pea Ridge within weeks of his enlistment, and when his wife learned of it, she died of grief and shock. According to their will, their property went to relatives from Georgia, but the war prevented these people from taking possession. Meanwhile, the house was ravaged by a succession of guerrilla and military groups who needed shelter, but, surprisingly, they never totally destroyed it. Most of the slaves remained, because they had

nowhere else to go to and most felt loyalty and affection for the absent owner.

At least one tragedy was reported as occurring during the several occupations of the house: a slave with a young baby was clubbed to death in the back yard for breaking the curfew one group of intruders had imposed. Nobody dared go out and get the baby, which lay in its dead mother's arms until it died of hunger and exposure.

The creaky rocking chair, one of the things that most disturbed the Georgians who eventually came into their inheritance, never was explained. Soon the frightened new occupants were all sharing a single bedroom, their dog included. They practically gave the house away in order to get enough money to move to a humbler but more wholesome place. They warned the mansion's buyer that it was haunted, but he was unconcerned:

Apparently this new family, which included two rowdy little boys, was not much disturbed by the ghosts. They first thought the rocking chair was branches rubbing the house or a loose eave trough moving in the wind. Careful attention to these possibilities didn't stop the sounds. The mother said she went to the back door hundreds of times, just in case the crying she heard was a real baby someone had abandoned. When she had tea parties in the parlor and footsteps came into the room, she would laugh and tell her guests, "That's just our ghost. He never hurts anyone." Sometimes she would demonstrate what her children had discovered: if a person stood in the path of the steps, they paused for a moment, but then just continued on the other side of the living barrier.

The banana episode made this family take the haunts more seriously. The boy said the delicious odor came from a particularly beautiful big rose thought to have been brought from the South by original owners. Bananas being uncommon in that time and place, and much coveted by children, he happily devoured several roses. His resulting desperate illness was barely remedied by a combination of doctor's and home efforts. The bush was never reported to smell of bananas again, and Moore did not tell us what became of the brave family or of the house.

Steele's Spin on Ozark Ghosts

Phillip Steele of Springdale, Arkansas, has published several books about historical events and notable people of the Ozarks, and has produced two videos about the supposedly haunted areas. Though most of what he covers is in his home state, the videos, available from Ozark Mountaineer Book Store (417-336-2665), will interest any ghost buff and do contain some Missouri material.

One of the most interesting stories in Steele's *Ozarks Tales and Superstitions,* is about the ghost of something that never was alive, a locomotive's caboose. In the 1930s, he says, a number of respected people in both Arkansas and

Missouri reported seeing a caboose moving serenely over the tracks all by itself. No explanatory story existed, apparently.

Another Steele story is one of those about an Indian maiden who kills herself because she cannot marry the man she loves, but Steele's has an unusually significant twist. In this instance, the girl was named Moon Song, and the man was a Spaniard. Her father forbade their union, almost succeeded in killing the suitor and was going to force his daughter to marry a man of his own choosing. Unable to accept this indignity, she threw herself off a cliff that rises more than 300 feet above the James River in the Breadtray Mountain area of southern Missouri. Her remorseful father had his shaman put a curse on the area, to repel anything that might disturb the peace of Moon Song's spirit.

Accordingly, when white men came, with their determination to utilize all they could for profit, they found some opposition. A strange turbulence existed near the cliff where, unknown to them, Moon Song's body had sunk into the water. Boats entering the eddy were likely to capsize and many fishermen and explorers died at what came to be called Virgin Shoal or The Virgin's Swirl. Up on the cliff, hunters had strange accidents, often fatal. Efforts to integrate this ideally situated bluff into a dam had to be abandoned because so many things went wrong. There were fires, equipment failures, extremes of weather, and accidents to workers. As the Moon Song story became known, problems grew. Workers tended to leave suddenly, declaring they had heard a woman's inconsolable weeping. Nobody could convince them that they heard only the wind blowing through lacy crevices in the eroding cliff. Moon Song's spirit was left in peace.

Steele commented that to this day the curse is blamed for interfering with cameras. Many tourists complain about disappointing results on what they thought would be wonderful pictures, light being perfect, and their new cameras' automatic exposure and focus leaving little to chance. Perhaps some day Wind Song's spirit will find that of her lover and superb pictures can then be taken to show us beauties of the area.

Stories from Students

One other collection of Ozarks ghost stories deserves at least a sampling: in the 1960s an English teacher named Ellen Gray Massey, (now the well-known author of a number of books and an inductee of the Missouri Writers' Hall of Fame), led her Lebanon High School students in a class called Ozarkia, to collect lore of the area. From their work came a magazine named *Bittersweet*, which critics have compared favorably with the *Foxfire* series. Several times Massey's group collected ghost stories, and here are three of their best, used in *The Old Settler's Gazette,* which is published annually in Dixon as part of its heritage celebration:

Travelers who camped near a certain deserted mill were routinely awakened by the sounds of wood being chopped in a nearby grove. The constant noise destroyed their sleep, both the chopping sounds and occasional pauses for sharpening the axe on a grindstone. Randolph wrote of this too, saying it was reported from several places in the Ozarks.

Near Houston lived a farm couple who were expecting a baby, in days long before going to hospitals for birthing was customary. When the time came, the father-to-be set out on horseback with a friend, to get a doctor. They had not gone far down the road before they met a woman dressed in white, walking with a baby in her arms. "We must go back," the husband said. "My wife is dead." He was right. Back home, the wife's mother told him the time of death, and it coincided with the appearance of the woman in white.

A mother working in her garden or in the fields, had put her baby out to play on a quilt nearby. Among its toys was a rattle which it shook with particular vigor that day and the mother was glad; as long as the rattle was going, she needn't stop work to go see about the child. However, when the baby began laughing wildly and continued to do so without pausing, she went over and to her horror, she found her child clutching and shaking a rattlesnake.

Quickly she ran for her tools, and with one hack of a spade was able to decapitate the reptile. It had not bitten the baby, but in only a few weeks the child sickened and died. Outcome is predictable: the sound of a baby's rattle, perhaps blended with the sound of a snake's rattlers, can still be heard in the grass where the snake who did *not* bite the baby was beheaded by a terrified mother.

Chapter Five

Headless in Douglas

> *No, Father John couldn't deny his*
> *people's ghosts. He had never been*
> *convinced that everything could be explained.*
> — Margaret Coel in her novel,
> *The Ghost Walker*

"It was only dusky dark," one of the women said, describing what happened to her and her sister in Douglas County. They were walking together down a familiar road near their homes, enroute to "sit up" with a fatally ill neighbor. Despite the sad circumstances, they probably were intent on each other, enjoying the opportunity to chat. Hard-working rural people of the late 1800s had all too little chance for socializing.

As the road turned to follow Spring Creek, the women were at first startled, then terrified, to see a man step out suddenly from the shadowy roadside and confront them. He was a very strange man: he had no head, and on his shoulder was a Bible. Their story does suggest that it was not large Bible, such as we see on church altars, but one that might logically be carried on one's shoulder. The women did not describe what the intruder was wearing, but saw in his right hand an uplifted lantern, glowing in the near dark. They observed, too, that he fled from them, as they, of course, fled from him, hurrying on down the road. Whatever they had seen made no sound and was not threatening. The headless man simply appeared, then went his way. Had he been as surprised to meet them as they were to see him?

This was far from being the first sighting of something frightening near Spring Creek as the stream neared a small cavern known as Smallett Cave. One of the more bizarre "ha'nts" whom several claimed to have seen, was a man's figure without a head, only a bundle of shoes where his head should have been. Others reported hearing faint hammering from inside the cave, and some said they'd seen light shining out. The light ranged from dim to bright enough to sparkle on the creek's ripples. A more dramatic story, from the few people brave enough to closely approach the lighted cave, was of a silhouetted image on the wall. It showed a headless figure, bent over in the posture of a cobbler (a maker and mender of shoes). One of his hands, holding a hammer, was rising and falling rhythmically as he worked.

These incidents and others are related in a small book called *The Headless Cobbler of Smallett Cave* which was published in 1967. It is the work of Walter Darrell Haden, who grew up, the book's blurb says, "within hollerin' distance of Smallett Cave." Several of the stories he relays came to him from his own relatives. One of the two women whose experience opened this chapter, for instance, was his paternal great-grandmother. Other tales came from elders respected in the community for being level-headed and honest.

Here's one of the most memorable stories: two young men, Walter and Porter Haden, close relatives of the book's author and extra-close companions to each other because they happened to be more than double cousins, were returning home at night by horseback. When they neared the cave and a familiar huge old white oak tree, their horses suddenly stopped and stood like rocks, staring ahead, ears pricked. Riders and immobile horses remained spellbound while "something like a man," as the boys later described it, materialized before them and wavered about, then drifted slowly up and disappeared above their heads. They were totally agreed that whatever this was, it was neither a person nor an animal.

Nobody needed to urge anyone, human or equine, to go home. Walter DeWitt Haden, telling the story to his grandson, WDH, said they were so upset that his father had to untack for them. There was no mention of Porter's former plan to ride on home alone. He spent the night at his uncle's house.

The first Walter's father, Rezin, probably received the boys' story with understanding, for he had his own. No doubt both boys were aware that once Rezin and his tall white stallion, Popcorn, shared a similar fright. As they passed under a tree on the creek road, the animal began "to shy and sidle." Simultaneously, from branches above them, came the sounds of gigantic wings unfurling and flapping off in the direction of the cave. Rezin, who knew there was no native bird larger and heavier than an eagle, honored Popcorn's desire to be elsewhere. Both had heard eagles take flight. Next day Rezin rode back to the site to see what clues there might be. The book does not specify, but no doubt Rezin Haden was looking for remarkable droppings or evidence of the death of an unusually large prey animal, or damage to the tree from something big and weighty resting in it. He found nothing.

Walter Darrell Haden, who wrote the book about his home area, is now an English professor who has taught for five decades, more than half of that at the University of Tennessee at Martin. His resume is an impressive collection of achievements and honors and of teaching and study in other countries. He has written other books and is the editor of two publications.

The Headless Cobbler of Smallett Cave is a scholarly examination of the Douglas County legend, looked at, Haden says, "as human psychological artifact." In his book, Haden explores similar tales of other times and countries to tell us that in many cultures caves and streams are thought to be attractive to disembodied spirits. Headless beings, too, are popular everywhere in ghostly annals, though Missouri has relatively few such claims. WDH also discusses possible explanations for the reported phenomena in Douglas County by reviewing local history that may have given rise to the stories.

First, Haden tells us, he heard vague references, as he grew up, to strange deaths occurring in or near the cave. Bits of data came from so far in the past that they were only hearsay from the elderly. Probably the most affecting tale was of a man who maintained a trading station there and was found dead, his head shattered by a shotgun blast.

Then, during the Civil War, it was said that a cobbler living nearby took his work to the cave in hope of protecting supplies and equipment from marauding guerrillas. Still another possibility was that he was a Union veteran discharged with a disability, so at disadvantage for defending himself. Another spin on the story is that he was a Union sympathizer at risk with either Confederate or "irregular" forces that ranged over the area. Another possibility Haden pointed out is that because of opposing loyalties of the time, he may have been in disgrace with the town. Though his neighbors would have needed his services — preservation of shoes was vital in wartime — they may not have treated him well, so he withdrew in order to continue cobbling for his family and friends.

The bundle-of-shoes-instead-of-a-head stories, Haden feels, could easily have begun because the cobbler commonly carried over his shoulder the footgear he had collected for mending or was taking home, repaired. What more convenient way to carry them? And, of course, a bundle of shoes might be big enough to completely hide a back view of his head.

Actually, probably no more than half of *The Headless Cobbler of Smallett Cave* is devoted to the ghost story and Haden's evaluation of it. He examines world history and geography to find comparable stories and he quotes the speculations of many scholars of the occult. His review includes the retelling of many tales of headless ghosts and examples of other spirits thought to inhabit caves and streamsides.

As he reviews writings from other countries and other eras of history, Haden passes on interesting concepts that will be new to many of us. One example: he remarks that ghosts may be nothing but projections from the mind of the beholder. He asks the intriguing question "What's so different about the 'ghosts' projected by television? Those people are not really there either, yet they are before us, and our senses accept them as being present."

In the end, one fact WDH dwelt on was that the rough terrain in much of Douglas County isolated people from each other in earlier generations and created rather grim vistas, especially in winter. He also pointed out that the predominant ethnic strain of settlers was British; people from England, Scotland, Ireland and Wales have always been lovers of ghost stories and have always been good story tellers.

Haden's conclusion is that superstitious persons living within a few miles of Smallet Cave created, generation by generation, a typical and classic legend, one that is closely tied to the existence of the cave itself. He reasons that the ghost stories probably will all disappear soon, as the cave will. Being located beside a stream, subject to flooding and subsiding water, Smallett Cave was noticeably filling up with silt and sand, even in Haden's youth. He recalls being told that 50 years before he wrote his book, mounted horsemen could ride into the cave. Now, he says, a hiker of normal height must stoop to enter. The last page of his book has a photograph showing how close the unfortunate cobbler may be to having no cave to occupy.

The Headless Cobbler of Smallett Cave was published by Kinfolk Press of Nashville, KY in a first edition of 1200 copies. It now is out of print but can be found by your local rare book dealer or on the Internet. Prices range from around twenty dollars to more than forty and any serious fan of ghost stories will probably find that acceptable. Six pages of bibliography list useful-sounding books that may be equally hard to find today, but worth the search. WDH gives us a proper index, so readers can easily find whatever type of ghostly manifestation, or as experts say, "motif," that interests them most. We must be grateful that Walter Darrell Haden chose to preserve a most interesting and, in many ways, unique, bit of Missouri history.

We will miss our bodies.
We will be restless
for them.

— Kirsten Bakis, character
in her novel,
Lives of the Monster Dogs

Little Dixie's Ghosts

Ghost stories abound in Columbia and Boone County, part of that section of Missouri known as "Little Dixie," having been settled mainly by people from the South. Psychical investigators might tell us it's logical for Boone to be a haunted county since it knew intense emotional conflict during the Civil War. Southerners had worked earnestly with "Yankees" (before that was a derogatory term) for the good of an area they all loved and took great pride in. When war came, people with long-standing good will for each other found themselves sudden enemies, or in relationships desperately strained.

One event that added greatly to the spirit overload was the guerrilla-fostered Centralia Massacre, which in 1864 killed approximately 300 men. A smaller encounter at the Mt. Zion Church northeast of Columbia took at least 40 lives. Frequent guerrilla visits to the area created panic because the marauders' favorite victims were isolated farm families and small, defenseless communities. People lived in fear of losing their livestock and other belongings, of seeing their hard-won homes burned, or of being killed for resisting.

Also, many slaves lived in Little Dixie, frightened and resentful, yearning always for an outcome that would bring them freedom, yet afraid to face a hostile world. Of course these were common feelings over the whole country during the war, but Boone County's plight was especially painful. Ghost stories do seem most prevalent where history has been most dramatic.

Chapter Six

In Town and Near

"Who knocks?" "I who was beautiful
Beyond all dreams to restore,
I from the roots of the dark ...
Knock on the door."
— Walter De La Mare, *The Ghost*

Some writers have referred to Sarah Cave Haden as sad, but recent research makes that judgement questionable. She did lose her life early and she left behind a little girl, a wonderful home, and a husband who was the catch of the county. But during her lifetime, she was probably quite happy.

The story about her had appeared often in Columbia newspapers and elsewhere with provable facts about her husband so most of us accepted it and repeated its inaccuracies. In the first edition of *Missouri Ghosts* I was guilty of this. In *More Missouri Ghosts*, I corrected myself. The young lady, whom we're told married Joel Haden at the age of 17, was not a displaced Kentuckian, but a Boone Countian, a member of a prominent family. Her father probably was William Cave, who owned for a time the historic place named Confederate Hill, which also figures elsewhere in my books. Sarah probably grew up in a beautiful setting with a privileged life. We're told she was very pretty and certainly she married well.

Joel Harris Haden, called by W. M. Switzler, in his *History of Boone County, Missouri* "one of the county's most successful citizens," came to Boone in 1828 at the age of 17. By the time he was 20, he had a fine farm and house. About then he took his first wife, Sarah Cave. It seems to be true that she died in 1835, victim of a typhoid fever epidemic. But before dying, she had given Haden a daughter and this child grew up to marry a Boone Countian and have several children, most of them girls. Joel Haden's daughters married men from the area, so he has many descendants in Boone County, though few of them carry the family name.

The historical part of the story includes Haden's marrying again to a woman who gave birth to two little boys, both of whom died in early childhood. More deaths occurred at Haden House, not for any strange reasons. A total of three wives probably died there, as well as the young sons, and also Haden himself and his mother, who had come to Missouri with him in 1828. If one were intent on creating ghosts for Haden House, there would be plenty to work with.

The contemporary part of the story is that Jack Crouch, who occupied the Haden house with his wife in the early 80's, told local newspapers he twice awakened to find a woman standing in his bedroom door. The first time she looked perfectly real and substantial; the second time there was a haziness about her.

These experiences, and unspecified others, convinced him that the place was haunted, but that did not stop him from converting Haden House, in 1984, to a restaurant which became one of the most prestigious in the Columbia area. Furnished with antiques and appealingly decorated, it reflected lifestyles of Little Dixie's settlers, and the food and service it offered met high standards.

No unusual experience for customers is on record, but many employees, half-afraid, half-amused, blamed Sarah that Haden House had an unusual number of dish breakages, equipment mishaps, and electrical problems. Several bizarre and inexplicable things happened, such as the turntable on a gearless phonograph sometimes spinning madly.

Possibly the most interesting happening reported was to members of a band performing at the Haden House on a regular basis. They left their expensive, elaborate sound equipment stored there, carefully secured, carefully adjusted just as it needed to be while not in use. Nobody but themselves had access to the locked storage area. One day they came in to find everything in crazy disarray, thrown about in a matter that threatened the equipment's well-being. Hardly a switch or knob was as they had left it.

Haden House closed as a restaurant in 1988, stood vacant off and on in the years since, and has been utilized for various businesses.

The House a Ghost Loved

In January, 1988, *Fate Magazine* published, with cooperation of a practicing psychologist named Fred Nolen, a story that can hardly be dismissed as hoax or illusion. Several people went on record in print or on television with supporting experience. Nolen said he lived for a number of years with an affectionate ghost who shared his interest in music and his love for Sutton Place, a condemned farmhouse near the edge of Columbia. Before *Fate's* article, he described his pleasantly haunted life for television station KOMU and *The Columbia Missourian*. Other people who had similar experiences at Sutton House were quoted in the same places.

Nolen was renting the big old place that once had been a fine rural house, property of a prominent Boone County family, but "development" doomed its swelling fields, its woods and picturesque little lake. Giant trees and determined flowers that still bloomed in obedience to planters long dead, would all be bulldozed.

This saddened Nolen and perhaps intensified his enjoyment of the beauty around him. With books, piano, pets and many guests, his was a simple, relaxed life in the deteriorating house. Though other changes went forward in the area, for some reason, destruction of the house itself was repeatedly postponed. Nolen had spent six years there before anything unusual happened.

Otherworldly activity began with what Nolen termed "the classic haunted house things." He heard jingling chains, a soft pounding, small objects rolling about on the attic floor. Sometimes mobiles or tablecloths moved when there were no indoor drafts. Though never indicating fear, his pets often seemed to be looking at things he could not see.

Gradually, Nolen said, he began to feel someone beside him at times. Initially this happened only when he stood looking out and thinking of how much he liked the house and its surroundings; he sensed someone else was reinforcing his pleasure. Soon tactile feelings began. It might be a light, friendly hand on his shoulder as he played classics on the piano, or, for "In the Mood," with its rumbling bass chords, a playfully disapproving ruffle of the hair on the back of his neck.

At last Nolen saw his companion briefly while he was in a state of sleep paralysis. He said she floated by his bed, apparently unaware of him. She was a small, fine-featured young woman with long brown hair parted in the center, falling straight down on each side. She wore something long, simple and grey and "she drifted through the closed door," Nolen said. "I never saw her again."

Once Nolen heard his housemate sing, however. He said her voice was "... crystal pure ... like a heavenly flute," wordlessly repeating the tune he had just played. Another time, two female guests reported hearing her. They were in separate rooms and each thought the other was singing. Others present heard nothing.

A few of Nolen's visitors also saw his apparition. One woman, driving up to his house, glimpsed a girl in an upstairs window. Because his motorcycle was gone, the visitor knew Nolen was not at home, but his guests did not stand on ceremony. She assumed she'd seen a fellow house guest, maybe someone she knew. Going inside, she called out. Getting no response, the visitor looked through every room and found nobody. Later she described to Nolen the same ghostly girl he had seen.

Another friend, Julie, holder of a PhD, a serious student of the paranormal, gave a fuller description. She said she met the ghost in the kitchen. Appearance was much the same, but the person's old-fashioned dress was not completely buttoned and her hair was disordered, as if she'd just arisen and was looking for the day's first cup of coffee. Seemingly startled at the psychic's presence, she backed away through the closed door.

Later, Julie says she was talking with Nolen in the kitchen, and the entity appeared in the doorway, then withdrew quietly, exactly like a person who has inadvertently intruded on private conversation. Nolen saw nothing then, for his back was to the door.

Researching Sutton history, Nolen learned that two women had hanged themselves on the property, one in the barn in 1856 and one from a tree in 1940. He felt sure that his spirit companion was neither of them, but someone untroubled, probably a frequent guest who'd formed an attachment for the place in happy circumstances. He believed she reached out to him because he so strongly mirrored her affection for the house.

When asked if he wasn't afraid of his ghost, Nolen said, "She's a lot less dangerous than people can be." Julie termed her "totally harmless ... a gentle soul, a drifting person."

When, in 1984, after thirteen years there, Nolen finally had to leave, he was asked what he thought the ghost would do when the Sutton house was destroyed. He speculated that she might harass the contractors. Or she might go with the staircase, which she seemed especially to love; he was sure someone would salvage that graceful piece of work.

Nolen said he'd invited the spirit to come with him, but never felt her presence in his new earth-sheltered home, though he played all the songs she liked. His last word was that maybe she was somehow securely in the past. Maybe she would have Sutton Place for all time no matter what was done to it.

A Threatening Encounter

The Columbia Missourian's ghost stories for Halloween in 1994 offered an experience of Floyd Strader, a Columbian whose hobby is documenting old cemeteries. His is a service much appreciated by genealogists and other researchers as well as by historical societies. Strader makes lists of names and dates that are in danger of being lost forever, data that often take hard work and ingenuity to decipher on the oldest tombstones.

Though one might expect a ghostly happening or two for someone who spends much time alone in isolated little grave yards, Strader said he only once met anything hostile, and that was not directly. It came when he took his wife and two sons along on a jaunt that included the Maupin Cemetery near Columbia. The afternoon was very hot, but when he returned to his family, everyone was in the car, quite upset. They had rolled all the windows up tightly and locked the doors. Somebody or something they couldn't see, Strader's family told him, had circled the car, beating on the sides and top and had bounced the whole vehicle up and down several times. They told him emphatically they would never go with him to another cemetery.

Photographs Strader took that day were fine in every cemetery but Maupin; stones he'd photographed there had so many obstructing lines across them that he had to go back later and reshoot. He commented, in talking about this many years later, that as the crow flies, Maupin Cemetery is quite close to Confederate Hill, a Boone County house which is said to be haunted by the spirits of Civil War soldiers and runaway slaves.

Confederate Hill was described in *More Missouri Ghosts* and only one detail about it has turned up since then, apart from the information that Joel Haden's first wife possibly was reared there. David Guitar, Jr., 33, son of the builder of the house, died at Confederate Hill one afternoon from shooting himself with a brother's gun. There never seemed to be any thought, however, that this death was anything more than an accident.

And a Reassuring One

Elaine Kline of Columbia tells of a confirming contact she had from a very close friend, Robin, who had just died. The Klines, in St. Louis for the funeral, were staying in the apartment Robin had shared with her husband, also recently deceased. Both women had been active in groups studying the paranormal and Robin had often said that after she passed over, she'd get in touch with Elaine, if that proved possible.

Accordingly, Elaine watched for a sign, and when lights began going on and off said to her husband "that could be

Robin." He, an electrical engineer, assured Elaine there are many reasons for power fluctuations. While he searched the apartment for something out of order and looked for the fuse box, Elaine, alone in the living room, says she had a visit from Robin.

"It was not full body," she says, "Her legs and feet were not visible, but I could see she was wearing a lavender dress. There was some mistiness to some of the figure, but her face was very clear, and her smile." Though the apparition said nothing, her expression and, Elaine thinks, some ESP, said clearly, "What did I tell you?" and she was gone. Elaine says she felt Robin had effectively proved the truth of positive convictions the two friends held about the hereafter.

Ashland's Ghost Hunter

Until recently, at the Boone County town of Ashland, lived a man named Russ Hawkins, who had a lively interest in the supernatural as well as in folklore and tall tales. He seems the epitome of someone R. P. Shelley wrote of in "Hymn to Intellectual Beauty":

> .... *I sought for ghosts, and sped*
> *Through many a listening chamber, cave and ruin,*
> *And starlight wood, with fearful steps pursuing*
> *Hopes of high talk with the departed dead.*

Hawkins made a point of visiting a number of places reputed to be haunted and he studied such matters enough that his opinion and experience were often consulted by others. Unfortunately, Hawkins seems to have written none of this down, but several friends remember stories he told them. One was short and simple, but has the power to raise ones hair a little.

Hawkins told of being at work in a huge hayfield in summer's blistering heat. He was one of a group of men who saw, almost out of sight across the rolling terrain, another team working with hay wagons and horses. Hawkins and his friends didn't know what to think, since they had understood the whole job of getting this field cut was exclusively theirs, work for two or three days.

After one of the youngest, most energetic workers walked toward the other team, shouting and getting no response, the men told themselves it was a mirage, or that they were all getting dehydrated and close to sunstroke. They drank more water and lemonade, resumed work and saw the ghostly team no more, until they were starting in with their loaded wagons.

Then they looked across the field and saw that the others, also, were pulling out. The field itself soon hid them from sight, and no unfamiliar wagons joined them at the barn. The owner of the fields assured them that nobody else was cutting for him and sent them out next morning to finish up. This included getting in the untouched hay their counterparts had appeared to work so hard on the day before.

Anyone who has spent many days in hayfields might remark that the possibility of being sentenced to an eternity of fruitlessly doing that work would be a good deterrent for any crime!

Hawkins had an even better ghost story than the one involving a hay field. Some say he told it as his own experience, some as another's. But a traveler by horse or bicycle needed water or something else and being in a sparsely settled area, stopped at an unpromising house. Nobody responded to his knocking and calling out. When he looked in the windows, Hawkins said, the traveler felt the house wasn't being lived in, but decided to go around to the back. If nobody was there, and there was some water, he'd help himself. Nobody would mind that.

Behind the house, on the well platform, sat a frail old man in pitiful clothing. His poor color suggested the worst of health, but he was friendly and pleased to have a visitor. He generously offered water. As they exchanged the type of chat people do in such circumstances, the old man suddenly asked, "Have you seen a newspaper lately?"

Startled, the rider said, "Yes, this morning. Is there some particular story you're following?"

"Well, what does it say about Sherman?" the old man asked. "How far has he got? Does it look like he'll really be able to split the South and give it to Lincoln for Christmas?"

Alarmed at what this seemed to say about the mental condition of the person before him, the traveler looked down for an instant to compose the best answer, and raised his eyes to find himself alone. The area was too large for anyone to have gone out of sight so quickly, even at the peak of health and agility. Hawkins considered this a bona fide meeting with a ghost.

One Last Story

One last Boone County story took place not long ago at Wildwood Farm, between Hallsville and Centralia. This is a horse training and rider instruction facility operated by Terry and Lynn Frazee. Lynn says, "I grew up in a haunted house," referring to Skyrim Farm, property of her grandfather, the well-known poet and teacher, John G. Neihardt. Seeing Dr. Neihardt's familiarity with the mysticism of the Sioux and his scholarly experiments in the paranormal, she says, may have sensitized her to things many people don't notice. But some of the strange happenings when the Frazees first bought their property were witnessed by other people besides themselves.

One occurrence seemed to stem from the Frazees adding some bedrooms onto the existing house at Wildwood. To their regret, this closed off some windows that gave a lovely view, but their growing family needed the living space. One morning a young girl who had spent the night with the Frazees' daughters came to breakfast excited about something she had heard in the night. "A window slammed down inside the wall right by my bed," she said. "It woke me up." Nobody else had heard such a sound. The child did not know where windows had formerly been.

But all housemates and builders soon became aware of a contrary door that sometimes would not stay shut and other times would not stay open. There were many such small disturbances, and Lynn believes she knows why. One day she saw an apparition, a man working in the yard around the plants, a small well-groomed man, dressed in contemporary-looking clothing, but not those suggesting a farmer. Something about the earnest solicitude with which he worked made her certain he was the haunting entity, someone who lingered about the place from feelings of love and responsibility. Perhaps he had been stirred with regret that it was being changed.

Accordingly, some years later, when they took the house down, the Frazees gave thought to doing it in a way that would be as inoffensive as possible to a former owner who loved it. Useful parts were salvaged, the residue burned and then buried. Nothing unusual has happened at Wildwood since.

It had arms ... stubs
that were trying
to turn into arms.

— *Barbara Michaels in her novel,*
Ammie, Come Home

Chapter Seven

One House:
Two Names

I waited there for some time, telling the spirits of the place that I came in peace and not as a robber. When ... they had had time to hear me, I went on.
— Stephen Vincent Benet story
By the Waters of Babylon.

In the back seat, the children wrangled, as siblings tend to do on car trips long and short. To stop the distracting noise, their mother said, "Oh, look! See the haunted house?" Quiet descended for a moment and then came demands of "Go slow, so we can see better ...." and "What haunts it?" and "Why haven't you told us before?" For the house was a familiar, ordinarily hardly-looked-at piece of the scenery as they went regularly to visit their grandmother. The long-empty and sadly neglected remains had once been a three-story pillared mansion with a gracious circle drive. Now overgrown shrubs and trees almost hid it.

"Well," the mother, Lorry Myers of Centralia, began, "when I was little they told me that ...." and she paused to give herself time to think. "The owner of the house was a rich horse breeder and a circuit judge and he had a beautiful daughter named ... Camellia .... He was so fond of her that he took her everywhere with him ...." And thus began the saga of the ghosts of Considine House, a place that really does exist at a very small town named Thompson, located between Centralia and Mexico. The story this mother invented has nothing whatever to do with anyone who ever lived in the Considine house, but everyone who hears the tale loves it. Its fame spread beyond Lorry's own household to school groups for which she does volunteer work. Lorry wrote about the house at length for her weekly columns in *The Mexico Ledger* and *The North County News-Leader.* Some of her words:

"Once upon a time, it must have been glorious! Years past, when the windows weren't broken and the porch was still attached. Back when there was no iron gate and smoke rose out of the chimney. Long ago when someone called it home.

"When I was little, I would make up stories about the rich and famous family that surely lived there. I told myself that one day I would live there, too. I would take care of the house, happy ever after with a family all my own. I fantasized about the house back in its youth ... clean with fresh paint, alive with company coming to visit. Ladies with long dresses having tea on the lawn and horses prancing in the fields behind them. I could almost see lace curtains, fluttering on a summer wind. Laughter floating down the lane ...."

Thus many sagas of ghosts in Missouri and elsewhere may have begun. Lorry's contribution to the state's folklore differs from the rest mainly in our knowing when and how it was created. With the others we can speculate. "What really did happen here that gave rise to this legend?" we can ask, or "Doesn't the fact that the story lives prove that more than one person told of some kind of odd experience here?"

As her children clamored for more information about the haunted house, Lorry began talking to elders of the community. Growing up in Centralia, she had never heard of any ghost stories about the Considine house or any tragic event that would support a weird legend. Yet surely such an old place — built before the Civil War — would have seen repeated tragedy.

Two of Lorry's children grew up and left home, but her fascination with the old house remained. She lacked time to do systematic research on the place. Being a bank manager and a free-lance writer with offspring still at home leaves little time for more, especially since Lorry also has committed to volunteer work at the area schools. Some of this involves the enhancement of reading and writing skills. The ghost story was perfect for that. While Lorry hoped to find more facts about Considine House, its fictional past kept expanding in her mind. She decided that the house must have a separate name for her stories. She'd call it Hill House.

The eagerness of school children for more and more details inspired Lorry to give them the story in chapters and to illustrate it with posters on which she mounted pictures of the house and portraits of her ancestors who would have been living when Camellia and her parents lived. She assigned her forebears' faces to those of people in her story.

According to Lorry, here's what happened at Hill House:

Camellia, in accompanying her doting father on trips to town became acquainted, while very young, with a handsome apprentice farrier (horseshoer), named Harvey. He was the son of the highly skilled man who took care of the feet of Judge Arthur Hill's finest horses. For this man, Hank, the judge had great respect. Even though they were worlds apart socially, good farriers were very important to wealthy people and worked closely with them. A good farrier still has special status among horse people. So on this level, Camellia's father treated Harvey and his father as equals and depended on them very openly. He never dreamed that his daughter might take that as endorsement of Harvey as her potential life's companion.

When Camellia announced to her parents that she loved Harvey and wanted to marry him, they were horrified that a manual laborer, a social nobody, would have paid that kind of attention to their daughter. They forbade her to see Harvey again.

Then came events that brought the tragedy to climax. The Hills gave a great party to which every prominent family in

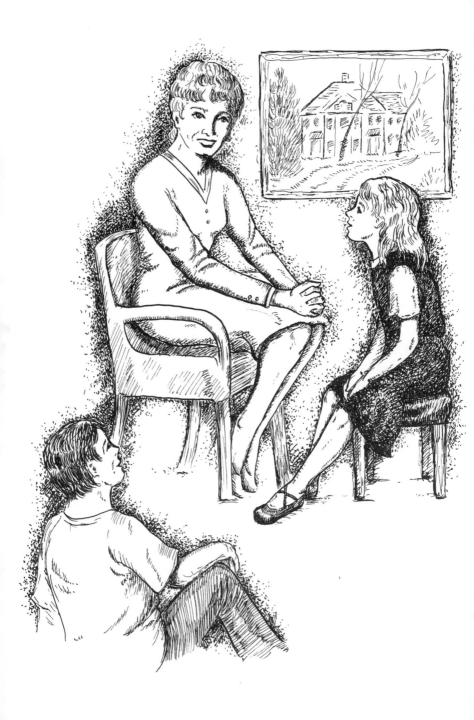

the area was invited. Many eligible young men would be present and the Hills were confident that a suitable match for Camellia would result. Harvey and Hank were present, too, at the barn to take care of any problems that might arise with guests' horses.

Harvey rashly took the opportunity to talk to the judge and lay forth a plan. If they would let him marry Camellia, he promised not to take her from them. He would live at Hill House with her and would take perfect care of all the Hill horses. This was a substantial offer in days when everything — farming, travel and transportation of products — depended on the feet of horses and mules.

Most men in Hill's position would have been glad to have a live-in farrier of Harvey's skills: Hill did, after all, have hundreds of acres of land on which hundreds of slaves produced crops and made bricks and other items that had to be taken to merchants and to the railways and river docks for shipping out to sell. However, Hill already had a servant or two who were good workaday farriers and when he needed something more it was no great inconvenience to go to town. Having his own master farrier could not begin to be worth an undesirable marriage for his daughter!

Furiously, Judge Hill ordered Harvey off the property, but as the young man left, Camellia suddenly approached him on the driveway. She had decided that they must elope and was prepared to leave with him at that moment. Her abrupt appearance startled Harvey's horse and it reared. The best horseman may, at times, be surprised enough to lose control and Harvey did. He fell right under the animal, which frightened it more and both lovers were injured by flailing hooves. Camellia died there in the driveway, Lorry wrote, in her mother's arms. Harvey, with a broken leg and other injuries, was carried into the house but instead of summoning a doctor, Hill had him placed in a small room on the third floor, the servants quarters. Servants were told to give Harvey no attention of any kind and the door to his room was locked. Hill's household focussed on Camellia's funeral and burial in the family plot. Lorry's words again:

"Harvey was not so hurt that a doctor could not have healed him, but no one ever was sent for help. Broken and bruised, he was alone in that room for two days before coming to his senses. He remembered nothing of what had happened, and knew only that he was in Hill House. But where was Camellia? All he could do was scream and scream her name.

"The screaming went on for five days. The family pretended they did not hear the agony coming from the third floor. But the servants heard it, down the stairs, out in the yard ... on down to the barn. On the sixth day there was silence and one week after his daughter was buried, the judge had the third floor room unlocked. The dead man was carried out, thrown in the back of a wagon and buried in a far corner of the property in an unmarked grave."

The judge told his family not to mention Camellia's name again. One sister ran away from home and the other, and their mother, gradually became physically and mentally ill. Many servants left because they claimed to see ghostly figures wandering among the trees, and to hear voices calling in the night as the lovers, each unaware that the other was also a ghost, sought each other.

This is an unusual concept for a ghost story. Most of us assume that once free of the flesh, a spirit can go wherever it wants and find anyone it wants. Lorry's story, questions this. It ends with the lovers hopelessly separated, and with the sad thought that unless someone finds and marks their graves, "they will spend eternity wandering, searching and calling for each other." How could a ghost story be more touching? One quotation, from Theodore Roethke's story, "The Surly One," almost applies:

Ghost cries out to ghost — but who's afraid of that?

The Truth of the Matter

And now comes another mystery which is to many of us just as interesting as the creation of a good new ghost story. So nobody ever died tragically in the house at Thompson —

except for one man who may have killed himself there in understandable circumstances — and there truly were no star-crossed lovers. So why was such a wonderful house deserted to fall into ruin?

A few senior residents of the area told Lorry or me the names of past owners — Sims, Henderson and Locke. They told how the house had looked in its prime: a beautiful staircase and in each room on the first two floors, a fireplace. Mantels were of colored marble, some light green, some rose, others of beige or grey. The house, they said, originally had 23 rooms, lovely chandeliers and carpets, everything one would expect to find in such a place.

According to some, the top floor was a ballroom. Others said it was composed of many small rooms, slave quarters. They knew that a number of outbuildings had existed, but only a few remain.

Tantalizing ideas came forth. "It's said that one of the owners killed himself in another state. Nobody can imagine why he left such a property as this and why a man who owned so much would kill himself."

"One of the later owners rented out rooms to school teachers, handy for them since the school was nearby. That was after the house had begun to go down and wasn't owned by such rich people any more."

"At some point lots of it was divided into apartments and rental rooms, with cheap materials. Doorways were covered up, all its beauty ruined."

"Well, it's past salvage now. There have been holes in the roof for many years; the upstairs floors probably are not safe to walk on. Somehow the staircase got sold and taken away, and the windows were taken out, inside casing and all, to sell the glass. That opened it up still further to the elements. Such a sad shame."

All this was before a real researcher got hold of the story. Julee Tyler of Centralia, a retired teacher and an avid genealogist, knew exactly where to go to find out who had lived in Considine House and what had happened to them. In less than a week, from transfer-of-property documents, from county death records, and from newspapers stored in local libraries and museums, she had retraced the whole history of the house. As she worked Julee reported to us gleefully. "I am so excited! The most fun! I think I have put some puzzle pieces together and come up with the name of the original owner. I think it may have been Sims, and here is why:"

Julee then told of finding a source which said the original claimant to the land was I. Sims, and she thought he was probably the father or grandfather of William R. Sims, a later owner. When William Sims died in 1900, one of his listed surviving children was Mrs. Joe Considine. Elsewhere, Julee found Considine referred to as owner of "the old Sims place. He owns 900 acres, and one of the finest dwellings on it to be found in any rural community in Audrain County." Other sources said the Considine House was called the largest and finest between St. Louis and Kansas City.

One newspaper story described a lovely wedding in which Bettie Mae Considine, Joe's daughter, became the wife of a man named Frank Wales. Later the papers reported on Joe Considine's sudden death in the state of Nebraska. Julee believes, from her findings, that he had invested there in a large flock of sheep. One newspaper said blatantly that Considine killed himself because the Great Depression ruined him financially. Other papers said it was an accident; they said that getting up in the middle of the night to see what was causing a noisy disturbance among the animals, he apparently leaned his gun against the wall or window and it slid down and discharged, killing him. Whatever the cause, Considine was buried in Centralia. His funeral was a very large one and among those attending were his daughter, Mrs. Frank Wales of San Diego, California with her husband and their two sons.

The other suicide, which Julee found an account of in the papers, took place in 1900. Irwin Sims, son of William R. and Polly Sims had been born in the house in 1840. Suffering from a painful illness, he was believed to have killed himself with an overdose of morphine, one of the few painkillers of the day.

In 1932, a family headed by John Henderson was living in the house and it was apparently they who rented out rooms; probably they were responsible for dividing the house up into rental units. Few details about that family appeared in Julee's sources.

The final owner of the house — except for his heirs — seems to have been a man quite famous in his time for increasing human comfort world-wide. He was Sam P. Locke, inventor of the Warm Morning stove. In days when people heated their homes entirely with wood or coal-burning stoves, the necessary procedure was that each night the fire had to be allowed to burn down and then embers were covered with ashes in hope of their lasting until morning so a new fire could be kindled quickly. Usually the embers died overnight and even if they didn't, it took awhile for comfortable warmth from a new fire to build up in the room.

Locke, already a wealthy man from various business enterprises, worked for several years to design his improved stove. It held more coal than other stoves and it kept them alive overnight, kindled more quickly and built up heat faster. At the same time, it worked well on less expensive fuel and burned fuel more completely, producing less waste to dispose of.

The Warm Morning Stove became famous beyond the United States and made Locke a millionaire. A story Julee found in a Mexico newspaper said that in 1943 Locke's stoves were selling at the rate of 2000 a day. His experimental work had been done on the lawn of Graceland, the Mexico house which now holds the Audrain County Historical Society's Museum and the American Saddlebred Museum. Locke and his wife moved from there several years before his death, but not to the Considine House. Possibly he had bought it as an investment, or just to have its acres for his cattle operation.

So we see that the Considine House was apparently a pleasant and satisfying home for a great many people. As to the mystery of its desertion, we can only list the reasons given many times for many other wonderful structures: the cost of upkeep, the few families nowadays which need or want so much space, the high costs of labor and materials for restoration. While some businesses might enjoy the Considine House for its space and the cachet of its historical atmosphere, its location would be inconvenient for most.

On the other hand, buildings of its era were made to last. The Considine House no doubt contains remarkable wood and the most careful workmanship. It probably could be beautiful again and at the time this was written, it was scheduled for auction. Maybe by now someone has taken pity on it and saved it from becoming the only real ghost at Thompson.

A final word from Harold Eastman of Columbia who took a superb series of photographs of the Considine House in its last days: "It seemed to me it was saying, 'I'm still here, in spite of all you've done to me. I am still a house.'"

Ghost that's walkin'
around now was a
pussycat in
true person.

— Margaret Coel in her novel
The Ghost Walker

Chapter Eight

Tableaux, Anyone?

Time. You think it progresses? Leaves things behind? You would do better to think of it in terms of accumulation. If you can.

— Meg Elizabeth Adkins in the
novel *Samain.*

The observer was Judith Retsema of Columbia, owner of the oldest house in Boone County; she had stopped in the middle of Greenwood's pantry because the kitchen held a scene which thrilled but did not really surprise her. Such things happen often enough at Greenwood that nobody gets alarmed any more.

The tableau: in a hardly recognizable room, two black women were working. The older one, tall and thin, was "doing something with bread," Judith says. She wore a tan, homespun-looking dress and bib apron and around her head was a white kerchief. The younger worker, maybe no more than twelve years old, was in blue, with an apron tied at the waist. She was working with potatoes while keeping an eye on a bubbling pot in the fireplace. Both women's clothing was clean and neat but looked worn and faded. We might guess this means Judith had caught a war-time scene, for servants at a showplace like Greenwood would probably have been well attired under normal circumstances.

Though Judith estimated she spent no more than five seconds watching, time seemed to be operating differently on the stage before her. Two men came in, briefly, both dressed for outdoor work. One looked the right age to be the older woman's husband, the other, possibly the girl's father. They were greeted with pleasure and Judith sensed a pleasant "how was your day?" type of communication among them though she heard no words.

The men did not sit down, but departed rather quickly, perhaps to clean up for supper. Judith called to her partner, Pat Rish, to come and see, but even as she spoke, the scene faded. One detail Judith remembered, however, was that the women seemed like a comfortable, accustomed work team, maybe a grandmother and granddaughter, and that all the players seemed secure in their domain. She remembered, too, that there were large quantities of food around, everything in big containers. The women must have been preparing the main meal of the day for a large family.

This particular scene has never been repeated for Judith and Pat, or for any guests in the house, so far as the owners know. They've never seen the same people elsewhere in the house or outdoors. Five people besides them, though, have reported seeing something interesting. Twice it was "a lady carrying a candle" in a downstairs guest room. Judith believed this would be Julia Lenoir Church, daughter of Greenwood's builder, but when she showed guests pictures of Julia, they said it was not. When she showed them pictures of her own grandmother, who never visited Greenwood, they said the image they saw was more like her. This does not seem too unlikely to Judith, since that forebear had told her she would always stay close. The same identity seems likely to Judith for the strongest ghost sighting at Greenwood, "the lady in white."

This has been reported three times. The first was when two women drove slowly by Greenwood, just to see the house, too late at night to go in. As they told it to Judith later: one friend said to the other, "... so beautiful ... " and her companion replied, "Yes, it is a lovely place." The first speaker then said, "No, I mean the lady standing there by the door." The driver of the car saw nothing, even as her companion described a slender woman in a long white dress who was standing outside, her back to the front door, looking west, seemingly unaware of them.

Another sighting was on the lawn in daylight and that person thought the woman's attire might be a wedding gown. The last was more detailed. Judith and some friends in a study group were meeting at Greenwood, and Judith was reading aloud. One of the other women made an awed exclamation and said, "Judith, there's a woman in white bending over you from behind ... she just kissed your hair!" In each of these cases, viewers said Judith's grandmother's picture looked like the person they saw.

The most definite other scene reported at Greenwood was when a guest described small children on the landing of the staircase and Judith says this does concern her. She herself had previously sensed — "sensed, not seen," — she emphasizes, a little girl there in a long, light dress, or perhaps a nightgown. The upper railings are not sturdy enough to have offered much protection and Judith wonders if the feeling of apprehension that accompanied her flash of the presence of a child means one of them did have a fall.

But so far as Judith and Pat have determined, with one exception, Greenwood's history contains no particular tragedy or unhappiness. There must have been some wartime privations and perhaps danger since the house is located near a road over which troops would have moved. But nothing seen there has frightened anyone. The one disturbing event came when a psychic touring the property within the last few years began weeping at one outdoors spot and said someone had been beaten to death there.

Judith and her friends find Greenwood a "place of brightness," a natural site of positive force which offers healing, wisdom and growth to seekers. They believe the area could have been sacred to Indians because of certain uniquenesses. The highest part of their land is one of the highest points in Boone County and overlooks a vast and beautiful landscape.

The topmost point is so level and so rocky that it remains relatively clear and open, almost as if to invite ceremonies. Several people have said, in different ways, "this feels like a holy place."

Judith and Pat and their friends who come to Greenwood as a retreat, feel the hilltop may have been sacred to Indians or even earlier people. They feel it may be the site of a vortex, a whirlpool-like movement of natural force that draws away negatives, giving renewal and strength to people who approach it with that hope.

At first thought this seems a far cry from the property's beginnings, but success and comfort seem to have followed Greenwood's residents. Here's its history:

The house was built by Walter Reiley Lenoir, a North Carolinian of distinguished background (wealthy ancestors were state and national legislators) who came here with a family of six children, twenty-three slaves, eleven horses and several wagon loads of possessions. Lenoir arrived in 1834 and by 1839 had bought 880 acres, then slightly north of Columbia, and had built Greenwood, with all the supporting buildings it needed for farming and for housing his many dependents and animals. Now the city has grown up to Greenwood on the south and the house sits on less than one acre. But its wonderful oak companions remain, some of them, Judith is sure, 300 years old. The trees are protected by a covenant that is part of the house's registry as a National Historic Site.

Members of the Lenoir family were always active in Columbia's social and civic activities. One son, Walter T. became a doctor and another, Slater, made a fortune in the gold fields and then became a prominent "gentleman farmer" and businessman who built the house, Maplewood, east of Columbia. This property now is an historic site and location for the community's cherished yearly heritage festival. Slater's daughter, Lavinia, inherited the house and lived there with her husband, Dr. Frank Nifong. The property now is known by Nifong's name.

The Lenoir family occupied Greenwood until 1881, and it passed slowly through the hands of only a few other owners, most of them appreciative and protective. Warren and Margaret Fuqua, bought the place in 1933, remained for 36 years and in that time did a great deal to restore the house and enhance its future. Though some modern conveniences have been added, Greenwood's character remains. Its six fireplaces have their original carved walnut mantels and most of the paneling and staircase ornamentation is intact. Its two stories are still covered in their original red brick, in a rather severe styling Southerners of its era favored.

From outside, the house looks deceptively small. It is listed as having seven rooms, but if bathrooms and a work/storage area are counted and generous stair landings that were no doubt used as sitting rooms, it has more. The house still doesn't seem like enough for Lenoir's large family, but Southern custom probably meant there were exterior rooms for summer cooking, for guests and for the young men of the household. Little trace of the detached rooms remains, nor of quarters for servants.

We read that Greenwood was one of the most lavish buildings in Missouri when it was built, its 30 windows considered fantastic luxury. An article published some years ago said Greenwood was among the state's 13 most historic buildings. What a terrible shame if it had no ghosts!

Ghosts In Ivy

Certain criteria seem to guarantee the presence of ghosts: picturesque old buildings set amidst massive, ancient trees; marble steps hollowed out by thousands of feet; furniture and books that have survived decades — maybe more than a century — of continuous use; big portraits of solemn people whose importance is now remembered by only a few of those who pass by them daily. Students of the occult seem agreed that huge deposits of human spirit remain wherever intense emotion — triumphant or wretched — has been expended by a great many people, and that under the right circumstances, this radiates out on those within its sphere.

No sites meet these standards of ghostliness better than colleges and universities, especially when we remember that their emotional charging comes not just from students, but also from people of different ages and experience. Teachers, administrators and teams of workers responsible for physically maintaining the institution and taking care of its financial well-being all have passionate desires and numbing dreads and fears to add to the atmosphere.

Only a few Missouri colleges can be explored for ghosts here, and those mainly from the middle of the state, but stories from others are welcome for possible future books.

Chapter Nine

College Town USA

I long to talk
with some old lover's ghost ....
— John Donne, *Love's Deity*

No place could be more ghost-ridden than Columbia, often called College Town, USA because it is home to three centers for higher learning. These are Stephens College founded in 1833, the University of Missouri in 1839 and Columbia College (originally Christian College) in 1851. The two formerly exclusively female institutions have two of Missouri's most romantic ghost stories, the lovers of Stephens' Senior Hall and the lovelorn grey lady at Christian.

Though the Stephens story seems far removed from truth, if it indeed has any factual basis at all, it's still too good to dismiss. Supposedly an Independence girl named Sarah Jane Wheeler was a senior in 1862, living in the school's one residence hall. Somehow she became involved with a Confederate corporal named Isaac Johnson. According to the tale one chooses, Isaac had either escaped from federal forces then occupying Columbia and climbed through Sarah's window in a desperate search for refuge, or he had deserted his post elsewhere and sought her out because of a previous relationship. A third version even tells us that Isaac came to

Columbia to assassinate General Henry Halleck, commander of Union forces then occupying the town. Isaac's mission was to avenge his father, killed by Grant's army in the South. Some stories indicate it was not Sarah the corporal sought, but her roommate, Margaret Parker, of Little Rock, Arkansas.

At any rate, the girls, pitying the exhausted and famished soldier, kept him hidden for several days. Margaret's family had sent two slaves to school with her, their working for Stephens to constitute her tuition. She was thus able to command help in getting food for Isaac and taking care of his other needs.

According to *Haunted Heartland,* by Beth Scott and Michael Norman, Sarah and Isaac fell in love during this short acquaintance. His presence was inevitably discovered and Halleck, alert for problems among Confederate sympathizers, quickly arrested Isaac. The book says he had the young man executed by firing squad under Sarah's window, as an object lesson to other girls who might befriend the enemy, and that Yankees tolled the bell in Senior Hall's tower to emphasize the event. Sarah then rushed up into the tower and threw herself out, or, in another version of the legend, hanged herself with the bell's ropes.

Unfortunately for the story's credibility, Columbia historian John Crighton wrote that Senior Hall had no bell tower in 1862. It was not added to the building for at least a decade.

That fact does no damage to other endings for the story, which include the lovers escaping the college only to drown together in the flooded Hinkson Creek or the Missouri River. Alan Havig, professor of American History at Stephens College and author of a book of Columbia history, confirms Crighton's information and further says that college archives offer no evidence of any girls with those names ever being enrolled at Stephens. He could find no confirmation from newspapers of the time that any such execution as that described for Isaac ever took place.

Nonetheless, students cling to the fun of believing that Sarah may walk the halls of a building recently restored to much the appearance it would have had when she lived there.

At Halloween Sarah sometimes receives the compliment of a vigil, and at least once a team of psychical investigators was scheduled to visit Senior Hall to analyze what one student termed "the unusualness" there. These investigators said in a newspaper interview that inhabiting spirits should be warned ahead of time if huge changes are coming to their abode, with increased human activity to follow.

Results of the investigation were not reported by the papers. Perhaps the visit never materialized. Senior Hall now is used for recitals and music and dance classes, as well as for conferences and other meetings that bring people from afar to the Stephens campus.

One set of facts has been overlooked as good basis for a ghost story: the building that later became Senior Hall went up in 1841 as the home of Oliver and Mary Louise Parker, but they enjoyed it together for only one year before his sudden death. That event must have released some emotional anguish into the building, but is, of course, not as appealing to story tellers as younger lovers.

The college bought the Parker house in 1857, and it became Stephens' first residence hall. Until after WWI, there was no other. When other dormitories were built, starting in 1919, Senior Hall was named and from then on was occupied only by seniors and by notable guests on campus. Possibly empty rooms were rented out at times because history mentions that George Caleb Bingham stayed there for awhile, and later, his wife and daughter. Well-known people who lived or ate in Senior Hall as students or visiting celebrities include Dorothy Thompson, Pearl Buck, Maude Adams, Tammy Grimes, Joan Crawford and Jane Froman.

Christian's Grey Lady

When the Grey Lady began to walk there, Christian College was not the coeducational school it is today, and it would not be renamed Columbia College until much later. Back then its all-female enrollment included many true Southern Belles, since Boone County had been settled mainly by people from the states of Kentucky, Tennessee and Virginia. One of these girls, whose name now seems to be lost to time, was engaged to a young man serving in the Confederate Army. She had vowed to wear only grey clothing so long as he did, and until she could put on her white wedding gown.

When her fiance was killed by Union soldiers in Columbia, not far from the college, we're told the girl immediately jumped from a three-story building called the Conservatory, now known as Williams Hall. Then, in the spirit, she began to manifest herself on campus as a fleeting figure in grey, usually glimpsed only on overcast, foggy or misty days, leaving people uncertain of who or what they had seen. Sometimes, also, she seemed to pass through college buildings at specific times of day, an almost indescribable presence which some people felt strongly and others did not feel at all.

The grey lady was basically benevolent. Sometimes, it's said, students returned to their rooms to find their ironing done. On days that turned unexpectedly hot, dorm windows might have thoughtfully been raised to let in fresh air. One interesting little note on the haunting at Christian College just on the basis of her attire: "grey lady" is a term used in the literature of the paranormal for ghosts of women who died violently for the sake of love.

In 1965, Christian's grey lady apparently did a striking encore, gliding sedately past windows on the third floor of St. Clair Hall, a building that did not exist while she lived. Carrying a candle, she seemingly passed through walls, for all rooms opened only onto a hallway running parallel to the windows and her progress was uninterrupted. Students out in a group, serenading, were amazed to see, on St. Clair's top floor, a white figure with a light slowly moving past the windows of vacant dormitory rooms. A few courageous girls rushed into the building and though they found nothing there, it was only a few days before everyone knew that Penny Pitman, one of Christian's most admired and gifted students, had been "campused," confined to school grounds. She had been found responsible for the frightening hoax, along with a fellow prankster from Texas.

Dean Elizabeth Kirkman, whose office was in a tower of St. Clair, happened to be at work on the memorable night and well remembers the excitement of girls who burst in on her to report "a light on the top floor, going right through the walls!"

"They were very frightened, or pretended to be," she says. Only one clue, never revealed to Pitman, told the dean who to send for. Penny Pitman was, the dean says, "a brilliant student, winner of a trustee's scholarship ... active in athletics and many campus activities, very popular with the other girls, but mischievous ... mischievous!" The dean adds, "I asked her, 'Penny, what were you trying to do? Scare everyone to death?' She grinned and said, 'I guess so.'"

Interview With a Ghost

Pitman, who now lives in St. Charles and restores houses, is not at all averse to sharing how she and her friend achieved their puzzling effect. While one of them walked across one room, the other, identically clad in a big white beach towel, waited on the other side of the connecting wall, candle concealed, until her partner knocked to let her know that her own walk should begin. Then the first ghost scurried out into the hall and past the room being haunted, into the next room. There, she waited for the signal, ready to walk in her turn while the other scurried. Thus they made their giggling, breathless way across the top floor of a building they knew a group of other students would be near that night. They also knew that in the darkness their candles would attract the eyes of any passersby.

Being confined to campus was not, to Pitman and her friend, a big price to pay for the fun they'd had. The college yearbook, *The Ivy Chain*, that year used a Grey Lady theme, with illustrations portraying a ghost whose swirling gown revealed jeans and sandals.

A Few Unromantic Ghosts

Columbia newspaper features written for Halloween often review stories of hauntings from the University's fraternity houses. Some samples: Sigma Phi Epsilon members say their third floor has been haunted by a young woman who lived there when a sorority owned the house in the 1940s. She was Jewish, from Europe, and on learning that her parents had died in a concentration camp, she's said to have hanged herself by fastening a rope to a radiator and jumping from a window.

A floating reddish light and footsteps on the stairs and in a hallway have been features of this haunting, but Tom Schuman, who used the room for a year, said he had "a roommate" who once awakened him with loud feminine giggling close at hand. Nobody could be seen in the hallway or street outside. Now the so called "suicide" room is no more, having been absorbed in a remodeling project. Part of the room became closet, part became hall.

A few added bits about this fraternity house: Steve Petisto, who spent Christmas vacation of 1987 there, says he always locked up properly when he went out and turned off all lights. Often, on returning, he found doors open, lights blazing and showers running full blast. And an alumnus named Mark Merlotti, now a St. Louis attorney, said that one night, after grueling hours of study, he saw, in a mirror in the hall, the image of a girl accompanying him. He turned to look behind, found nothing and then when he faced the mirror again, she was gone. Another member, Ray Lorenz, told the *Missourian* of being awakened in his room one night by a girl who looked "like she was made of ivory" moving toward him. She vanished as he looked, but he said his sleep was destroyed for a week.

In another Greek house, Delta Sigma Phi members report several sightings of the apparition of a petite young woman with "flat, black hair" forming flapper's curls on each cheek. She wears 1920s era pajamas. They think she was named Eleanor and died there of appendicitis when a sorority owned the house. One member, Brent Guglielmino, said he believes he saw Eleanor in the basement once, "just kind of hovering there, back in the corner." He says the girl stared at him blankly and then floated away.

Other oddities reported in this same house included flickering lights and television sets, footsteps and slamming doors. But residents also reported some poltergeist-like activity. Socks flew, they said, and hats fell from racks. Travis Wims said his electric alarm once woke him as usual, when power to the house was off.

The fraternity house with the strongest claim to some authentic ghost stories is that of Sigma Alpha Epsilon. Owners say it was built over the basement of a house that burned in 1907, but had been used at one time to confine mental patients and earlier than that, served as a morgue for Confederate soldiers killed in the area. They list the usual manifestations of electronic devices that behave badly and sudden cold that descends in certain parts of the house.

But strange sounds are said to rise from the oldest portion of their basement and, at least once, a soldier in grey was reportedly seen there. In 1947, we're told, a pledge class locked in below overnight as part of their initiation came up pale and silent. All resigned their pledges, refusing to say why.

The fraternity badly damages its ghostly credibility, by insisting that "Bloody" Bill Anderson's body was in its basement temporarily. The facts are that Anderson was killed in Ray County, near Albany on October 27, 1864, and was buried in Richmond, a few days later. His body was displayed contemptuously in Richmond, propped up in a store window and photographed for posterity. There is no reason why it would ever have been brought to Columbia. Anderson is well-documented to have been only a few miles away exactly a month earlier, however, participating in the Centralia Massacre.

Perhaps some bodies from that tragedy rested briefly in what was to become the fraternity house, but Anderson's could not have been among them, as much as people then would have wished him dead. Had his body been in Columbia, it would be far from a distinction. Serious historians describe the man as a homicidal maniac who went into battle sobbing and frothing, his horse's bridle decorated with human scalps.

Meanwhile, Back at the Farm ...

One of Mizzou's said-to-be-haunted buildings is the last place one would look for ghosts. It's a fairly new utilitarian metal edifice on Bradford Farm, one of the University's sites for various agricultural experimental work. This land was for many years the home property of a prosperous man who did such things as sit on bank boards, ride fine Saddlebreds and endow horse show classes. He and his wife and daughter lived an extremely comfortable and tranquil life on the farm. When he died in the late 1950s, it was not long before his daughter sold the farm to the university. Neighbors who knew the Bradfords say there was nothing in their history to give rise to disturbed spirits. They say that no young person who could have met the dignified Alex Bradford in person would now familiarly speak of the supposed ghosts in their building as "Al."

The people who work on the farm, all of them no-nonsense scientific types, report sounds from impossible places and disturbances around the rest rooms that include a stall door falling down and faucets that turn themselves on and off. Footsteps resonate on metal staircases and radios behave erratically.

One entomologist, working alone, said she was annoyed repeatedly by the sound of flexing metal right outside the door of her lab. Her repeated trips into the hall disclosed no fleeing prankster and she heard no retreating steps, yet the sounds repeated several times.

Out on the grounds, there are sometimes reports of a man fishing in the pond. That sounds like nothing much, but the pond is off-limits, because experimental plantings are all around it. And the person doing the fishing appears to be a person familiar to most, a retiree from the grounds crew, a man who had fished there before the prohibition. Out of respect for his age and service and to avoid unpleasantness, the first person who saw him said nothing. Others, now, just don't feel like they want to approach him because they have learned that the man they thought he was died some time ago. Perhaps, now, he doesn't have to walk on plants as he comes and goes.

The foregoing was all that had been reported from Bradford Farm when I gathered material for the first edition of *Missouri Ghosts*. Since then a *Missourian* reporter has quoted Carl Morris, an agriculture specialist who works at Bradford as saying "a horrible scream," a high-pitched woman's scream has been heard. Several people besides Morris have described chasing around over the building trying to see who is stamping up and down stairs and slamming doors at hours when nobody is supposed to be there. One lab specialist said that his wife will not drive onto the grounds to pick him up from work. Farm employees, the story also said, frequently report finding what they think are Native American artifacts. Perhaps this all belongs in the file reserved for cases of spirits outraged because of alterations to the land that was their home.

No ghost should be allowed to walk
And make such havoc with its talk.
When folks are dead, they should retire.
I have no patience with you, sire.
— Charles Delman,
The Ghost of Hamlet's Father

A long poem titled "Homecoming" appeared a few years ago in a newsletter for people interested in the occult. It was written by William Humphries and it began, "I saw him for the first time/In the shadows by the tree .... he was in a tattered uniform/It looked like World War One."

The speaker, uneasy, hurried away to his dorm, but encountered the person again one late Fall afternoon, when rain forced him to take shelter in a deep entryway. "He said 'Hello' and shook my hand/His grip was strong and cold .... His eyes were tired and old/I knew this was no mortal man ...."

The apparition explained that he enjoyed visiting the campus he had to abandon for war, though everything had changed greatly from when he knew it. He said he hoped he'd meet the student again and then he disappeared.

The conclusion was "So if you're walking to your dorm/On a cool and moonlit night/And you see a shadowy form/In the cloisters near the light ... just be forewarned. It happened so, to me."

I have come back to
let the world know
that what you call being dead
is the most boring thing in life.

— Oscar Wilde at a seance
of the British Society for
Psychical Research, London, 1923

So long as the stories multiply ...
and so few are positively
explained away, it is bad
method to ignore them.

— William James,
American Psychologist, in a lecture.

There is scarcely any other
matter upon which our
thoughts and feelings have
changed so little since the
very earliest times.

— Sigmund Freud in a paper
titled "The Uncanny."

Chapter Ten

More Ivy Ghosts

There needs no ghost, my lord,
come from the grave to tell us this.
— Shakespeare, *Hamlet*

Many ghost story collectors discount whatever comes from college boys, saying something like: "There they are, at the peak of their physical strength and agility, most of them with more than average intelligence, a fondness for pranks and lots of time to play around ...."

But one hardly knows what to do with this story from a woman who visited a certain fraternity house in a certain Missouri college a few years ago and experienced for herself the cold spot she'd been told of in one of their halls. The cold there was so intense she could see her breath. After that, she was inclined to believe what her date and his friends said of other strange happenings in their house, particularly the locked room.

This was a basement room used mainly for storage of surplus dorm furniture. Perhaps the room also was used when needed, as an emergency guest or residence room. Its door was seldom opened, but there came a time when somebody needed to enter and found the door locked. Nobody knew where the key was kept, since the door had not been locked before in anyone's memory.

After extensive futile searching for the key, a locksmith was called and he quickly unlocked the door. But to everyone's puzzlement, the inward opening door could not be moved. It felt as if some super-powerful force held it from the other side.

Since no interconnecting door went into the room and it had no outside window, there seemed no solution but to break the door into pieces. When these scraps were removed, observers found themselves looking at every piece of furniture in the room, piled and stacked against the opening where the door had been. At first thought there seemed no explanation except supernatural activity. So how could a group of people have placed the furniture there and then got out of the room?

"Locked room" murder mysteries are a genre in themselves, cases in which somebody is found murdered in a room locked from the inside and lacking any other means of entrance or exit. Such stories usually turn on one of these solutions: the murderer escaped up a chimney, or through a transom (window-like ventilating opening above a door), or through a concealed trap door in floor or ceiling, or via a secret panel. But the fraternity house room had no chimney, no transom or ceiling trap, and its floor was concrete directly on the ground. Presence of a secret panel seems very unlikely in contemporary basement construction.

A carpenter told me that if the hinge pins were not in place in the shattered door facing, then the door could have been removed in the usual manner from inside, and placed back in position after the furniture was stacked. Most doors have a small strip of outside facing that would have been enough to hold it in place through a little pushing. This facing could easily be removed and replaced for manipulating the door. If such a strip was not included in original facing, one could be cut and fitted into place, then stained to harmonize with adjacent wood. It's doubtful that anyone happened to remove this piece of trim in exploring the problem. It's doubtful that anyone there knew enough about construction to check on whether or not the inside hinges held their pins. It's possible that some door constructions would bypass part of what the carpenter described and would lend themselves easily to a prank. However it was done, the whole undertaking would be a tremendous amount of work, mental and physical. But fresh young minds dedicated to outwitting everyone, might find that a worthwhile lark.

So must we concede that this fraternity seems to have a bonafide case of the unexplainable? Maybe some reader can suggest perfect ways to do a locked room hoax.

Brawny Spooks

Colleges inhabited mainly by men tend to have ghosts more regimented and physically powerful than those found elsewhere. For instance, Wentworth Military Academy in one of Missouri's most fabled towns, Lexington: there, we're told, all the toilets on a floor may flush at the same moment, sometimes while all sink faucets open simultaneously. Doors along a corridor have been reported to slam open in unison and then close one after the other in close succession, so perfectly timed it seems beyond human doing. Yet might it not be easier than we think, given military training and physical conditioning and the patience for dedicated practice?

Here are a few other mechanical ghosts, mixed, in a coeducational school, with more conventional manifestations. A young man who attended Central Missouri State University at Warrensburg only a few years ago, relates the college's most intriguing visitations:

In the 1980s, during stressful exams week, a student named Sarah killed herself on the fourth floor of Houts-Hosey Residence Hall. So many strange things happened there afterward that nobody wanted to live in any third floor room and the building was closed for a time for remodeling. When it reopened, spaces had been altered and rooms renumbered haphazardly, going from Room 8 to Room 11, to Room 3 and so on, so nobody could tell which room had been Sarah's.

My narrator, who lived in Houts-Hosey, was a resident monitor entrusted with various keys and the authority to deal with and try to prevent problems. Oddities he witnessed included a supply closet light that was on almost every time he unlocked the door, despite his care in always turning it off. Nobody else had access to this space.

Houts-Hosey residents, he says, were accustomed to doors slamming down a hallway in quick succession when few people were present and when no windows were open to create drafts. He said that a group playing regularly with Ouija boards reported these devices becoming frighteningly active, but he did not explain further.

In one hair-raising episode, he was with a few others in the building during a school break when the campus was almost empty. Overhead they heard what he terms "a ruckus" that sounded as if a number of people were hastily moving furniture. Heavy objects screeched across vinyl floors. Lighter things, like chairs, were dragged about. Doors opened and closed. The sounds lasted only a few minutes, but when the alarmed listeners got upstairs, they found that in several rooms all furniture had been pushed to the center of the floor. This left them baffled and uneasy. It would have taken many people to do this work in the brief time the sounds had lasted. The students tried reenacting the event and were unable to make the same changes nearly so quickly. Nobody could be found in the completely locked building.

A Wayward Elevator

The most lastingly frightening experience at Warrensburg was shared by several people who got on an old elevator on the ground floor to go to the second. The device had never malfunctioned before, but that night it took them immediately to the basement, where its door refused to open. After a long enough stay there to panic some of them, the car moved again, in response to their frantic, repeated pushing of the second floor button. This time it went to the haunted top floor and paused there for some time, door locked. After a few more erratic starts and stops, it took them back to the ground floor where they gratefully jumped out and ran up the stairs, never again to trust any elevator.

Something else is well remembered by Warrensburg alumnae, quite apart from the college, but of great interest to the students and visited by many of them; a certain tombstone at a nearby cemetery. This stone glows weirdly from a distance, whether the night is black or moonlit, but seems to lose its luminescence as one approaches it. The eerie greenish glow can best be seen when one is not looking directly at the stone.

"Ripley's Believe It or Not" once featured this phenomenon, but without explanation as to what it may be. A first thought might be that the marker is of composition different from the others, even though it looks like them on close-up inspection. Wouldn't we expect all the stones in the older section of a small town cemetery to have come from one local supplier who used the same material for all? A similar stone is reported in a cemetery at Hermann, and in neither case is there any local ghost story that attempts to explain the glow.

In "The Woods"

Shannon Graham of Jefferson City was a student at William Woods College in Fulton in the 1940s. She says the college had a ghost whose presence held something in common with the grey lady of Christian College in Columbia: she was felt, rather than seen. Her movements came at dinner time each evening, when the students and faculty ate together in Jones Hall.

"Promptly at 6:45, total silence and a coldness would descend on the entire group," Graham recalls. "No one needed to look at her watch. Shaky smiles were exchanged, but no comments." The seniors had already made that sure younger girls knew this was the spirit of a student who died at the college before they were even born; there had supposedly been a mysterious accident school authorities would never discuss.

In the years right after the girl's death, Graham had heard, her spirit was sometimes seen as "a small figure with long dark hair and a filmy dress." Graham, a writer who has researched such matters, points out something many students of the occult believe: as the number of people who remember a ghost diminish, it loses its power to function. If that is true, probably few people now at the college have even heard Graham's story, let alone seen or felt any such manifestation. But Graham declares that something was there in her time. She adamantly states, "It was not imagination."

Nowadays, William Woods College has a more modern ghost story, but since the attire for riders and tack for horses has changed little for a century, who knows? Anyhow, a student told me that several people have reported seeing a girl riding in one of the indoor rings late at night.

"This doesn't seem unusual to anyone," she explained. "Because of somebody's heavy schedule — and some of the horses' — it could be the only time they're able to work together. And there's nothing unusual about people seeing them, for there is someone in the barn at all hours of the day and night. Some people who work there, people catching up on grooming or care of tack. If a horse is sick or hurt, a number of people may be visiting him or keeping a vigil. And there are enough of us in the riding program that we can't all know each other."

What's different about this rider is that if observers approach her, or stare at her relentlessly, she jumps her horse over the railing of the ring and disappears. Authorities on the occult might say "this is a typical thought form. Somebody on campus or off, very much alive, is dreaming intensely — awake or asleep — of riding that horse in that ring." Or they might say, "someone recently dead has been reunited with the spirit of her horse and they are simply doing what they always did together." A skeptic might ask, "Are there no riding rings in heaven?" and might be told that early in death, spirits are allowed physical sensation to help them make the transition, so, again, who knows?

If one brought a literature teacher into this mystery, he or she might mention that the American poet, Henry Wadsworth Longfellow, writing of the burial customs of some American

Indians, described their sending horses into the hereafter with their owners. Thus friends and family can visualize a comforting sight on the dismal plains of death, when "the warrior grasps his steed again."

The pupil who told me about the phantom horse and rider said there are other good stories at her school, but what could compare with that? William Woods, nationally noted for its good riding program and high standing in competition, has been operating since 1870.

Unter Linden

Anytime in the past century, students at Lindenwood College in St Charles, might have heard midnight organ recitals or glimpsed a lithe figure in white wafting across the lawn to visit the cemetery. It is the resting place of the late founder of their school, a woman who loved it and her students so much that she told them, as her life neared its end, "I will always be with you. I will always be watching over you and this school."

What the girls heard and saw — which also sometimes included a woman dashing about the campus late at night sidesaddle on a tall Kentucky Horse — was no hallucination of she ears or eyes. It was seniors teasing freshmen. At least there were times when it was; when such a tradition gets started how can we be sure that no playful spirit never takes advantage of the opportunity to make a real appearance?

If ever a person deserved a life extension it was Mary Sibley, wife and daughter of two men very prominent in Missouri history. She was not completely overshadowed by them, for Lindenwood was her idea and carried such weight with her husband that he supported her fully in the undertaking. Mary Sibley was convinced that women should prepare themselves for more satisfactions than those of wife and mother. She preached riding for health, confidence and grace; she said that music enhances growth of the soul. She advocated wide educational choices so that all women could revel in the best of the world's culture, and guide their childrens' educations intelligently, and so they could themselves be admirable conversationalists, and writers, teachers, or whatever else they aspired to be. Her own life demonstrated all this, though she obviously was gifted and privileged from birth.

Born in Kentucky as Mary Easton, she had, by the age of 15, absorbed a remarkably full education, all that was available for women at the time, augmented no doubt, by access to a large home library. She had ridden beside her father on two impressive trips, the first from Kentucky to Missouri when the family moved here, then from Missouri to Washington City, which became Washington, DC. Her father was Rufus Easton, who served as the second representative to Congress from Missouri Territory after having been its first postmaster, first U.S. Attorney, and first judge. He also went to Washington to lobby for Missouri's 1821 admittance as a state.

At 15 Mary married a man more than twice her age and of national prominence. He was George C. Sibley, who had surveyed and resurveyed the Santa Fe trail and otherwise distinguished himself in military and political service. As factor and commander of Fort Osage, he took his young bride to live in what were then the wilds of Jackson County. The legend is that it required two boats to move her, which is probably a great exaggeration, but she did take along her expensive horse, her grand piano, masses of clothing and books and probably a great deal of furniture provided by her parents for her new home. Sibley made Ft. Osage an example of how Indians could be treated fairly in trading and the couple remained there until the fort was closed in 1822.

Mary had long held her dream of a girls' school and when her husband won a St. Charles estate called Linden Hill in a court settlement, he presented it to her. In 1853, on a small scale, they started the first college for women west of the Mississippi. Girls and parents loved what the Sibleys did and the school became very popular. It still carries on Mary Sibley's principles. Surely, with such a caretaker in residence at Lindenwood in spirit, no ghost would dare do anything tasteless or unduly frightening. Here are a couple of the existing stories:

During a fairly recent summer when the campus was almost empty, Sibley Hall was being exhaustively renovated. There was no reason for anyone but workmen to be near it and they came and went by the front door, taking care that no other doors were unlocked. One day between the noises of their own equipment, the men heard feminine voices on higher floors, from time to time. Accompanying the voices were loud clunking sounds like drawers being opened and closed and screechings of what the men thought were trunks being dragged around.

At quitting time, one or two of the workers went upstairs to make sure the ladies could get out and knew to be sure and lock up well. They found nobody there, no furniture and no trunks. A search of all floors, all vacant, gave no hint of how those sounds could have been made. Just as they could not understand how the women had got into the building without passing by them, the carpenters could not understand how they had got out.

A second story seems related to the staged ghost appearance at Christian/Columbia College. A Lindenwood staff member named Norman was working in the college book store in 1982 and its windows gave her a full view of Sibley Hall. One winter evening, close to the 7 p.m. closing time, she looked across and saw something most unsettling. A white clad figure was gliding back and forth in front of windows on the unused third floor. Were the rooms like those at Columbia college, without interconnecting doors? Norman didn't say; possibly she was not familiar enough with the building to know. But she described the figure as "vivid" and "floating" and seemingly lighted from within. Norman did know that particular floor was not wired.

Even though she was at a safe distance away and inside another building, Norman said she told herself thankfully that she could soon close up and go home. She says that when the campus security guard made his nightly check she told him what she had seen and he brushed it off casually, saying he'd heard the same story many times before.

Lindenwood may have a couple of undiscovered ghosts, for Elijah P. Lovejoy, the crusading newspaper publisher martyred to the cause of abolishing slavery, was a close friend of the Sibleys. Driven from St. Louis with his conscience-stirring newspaper, he set up his press in Alton, Illinois. One night after an abolition lecture in Missouri, he was threatened so bitterly that Sibley is said to have taken him to Lindenwood for refuge. Maybe the editor was hidden in the legendary tunnel under the school which some say had been constructed for the girls' safety in case of Indian attack and which others say never did exist. In any case, after a few days passed and Sibley deemed it safe for Lovejoy to go home, he gave his friend a horse for the trip. Lovejoy left by night. What a wonderful excuse for a haunting that would be!

Then, after an anti-abolition mob murdered him in Alton, Lovejoy's heavily pregnant wife came to St. Charles to the home of her own parents. No doubt she was in the Sibley home during her period of mourning. A young woman who taught at Lindenwood wrote of what outrage Mrs. Lovejoy's friends felt for her. Between them, the Lovejoys must have exuded a great deal of emotion in Lindenwood. Perhaps they have their part in whatever haunts the college.

Playful and Pitiful

In fleshly life, Roberta Steel was a joke-loving, endearing friend and companion and a conscientious student. She didn't deserve the death fate gave her when an explosion from a nearby gas storage facility set her dorm on fire at Northwest Missouri State University (Maryville) in late April of 1951. After 19 months of treatment which included repeated skin grafts, Roberta thought she was well enough to resume attendance at the college she loved. She re-enrolled at Maryville in fall of 1952 but just two months later, at Thanksgiving vacation, had to give it up. Roberta lived only a week longer.

The restored building which had always been called just Residence Hall or The Girls' Dorm, was renamed Roberta

Hall and the gallant student's memory was honored with a large portrait of her over the mantel in the hall's parlor.

In the fifty years since her death, Roberta's mischievous spirit has been blamed for a multitude of strange happenings. Most of the incidents reported are rather standard as ghost stories go: lights, radios, televisions and water faucets activate and deactivate themselves, doors open and close. Nothing blamed on Roberta has seemed ominous or has even seriously inconvenienced anyone, but the spookiness factor caused at least one girl to move out of the residence hall and never return.

Tami Tomblin said that what happened to her just filled her with apprehension that something worse might follow. She and a friend were studying together while listening to the radio. Its volume kept fading and the friend finally said sternly, "OK, Roberta, turn the radio back up!" Instantly the volume was restored, louder than they previously had it.

"I never believed in Roberta before," Tami told a newspaper writer. "I had not put an iron burn on my rug or anything. But there was just something so eerie about that room that night. I couldn't stop thinking about it. I didn't want to be there any more."

The iron burn she referred to is a half serious tradition the girls developed soon after Roberta's death. They put a scorch spot on their throw rugs with an electric iron and told each other this action would keep spirits out of their rooms. The tradition probably has died by now, since irons are no longer standard dorm equipment and because the school's administration persistently discouraged the practice.

Though Roberta, if she is there, is not an ingenious or troublesome ghost, she seems to have a few unique twists. Lights come on in unused and locked dorm rooms and it's said that each year on her birthday, the commemorative portrait falls to the floor. One resident told a newspaper reporter of going to the basement to get something from a meeting room. She found the door locked and could hear a piano playing within . When she knocked on the door, the music stopped but nobody responded to her repeated knocking and calls.

The most beautiful thing
we can experience
is the mysterious.
It is the source of all
true art and science.

—*Albert Einstein*

Chapter Eleven

Jason's Collection

True science will not deny the existence of things because they cannot be weighed and measured ... if a phenomenon does exist, it demands some kind of explanation.
— Sir Stanley Jevons, *The Principle of Science*

Two chapters about college ghosts are quite enough, you think? Wait until you see the collection of one alum of Central Methodist College in Fayette, Howard County. He is Jason Roeder, manager of a Columbia book store and here is what he wrote:

"This idyllic, picture-perfect liberal arts college has much history, including buildings that were built pre-Civil War. Almost every one of these has its ghost story. Even Holt Hall, a dormitory built in the shape of a cross, has whispers of a shadowy silhouette holding a dozen helium balloons. Many residents of Holt believe themselves to be safe, citing the shape of the building, but from time to time someone awakens to see the dark figure at the foot of her bed.

"Howard-Payne, a large dormitory on the southern edge of campus, has the distinction of being CMC's most haunted building. Sometime around the turn of the century, a violent snowstorm hit mid-Missouri. A girl was rushing back to Howard-Payne, seeking to escape the storm, when a brick fell from a poorly constructed window sill. It struck her on the head, killing her instantly. Now, on nights when snowfall is extreme, she can still be seen attempting to reach her room.

"In 1926 a student named Mary Kirk disappeared from the campus. It was thought she had simply returned home, but when her parents were contacted, it became obvious that she was missing. Her dorm room was kept unoccupied, her possessions untouched, in case she returned. The room was, of course, locked. One month after her disappearance, a maid entering to dust found Mary's room completely ransacked, with possessions strewn everywhere and all of the furniture smashed and splintered. Had a person broken in and done all this destruction, it would have been a noisy operation. No one in the hall, however, reported having heard a single sound coming from the vacant room.

"That day the room was again tidied, furniture replaced and the door was boarded up. But next morning, muddy footprints were found starting at the stairs and leading to the room. The dean ordered the boards removed and it was found that the footprints continued into the room and contents had once again been vandalized. Prints of muddy bare feet were all over the floor, yet it had not rained in the area for three weeks. Mary's possessions were sent to her parents' home and the disturbances ceased.

"The fifth floor of the north wing of Howard-Payne is also considered haunted. To this day, nobody is housed in the small top floor area because according to campus legend, a girl, distraught over her boyfriend's infidelities, hanged herself in one of its rooms. No one has slept there peacefully since. Whether this legend is true has never been proved, but some strange occurrences have taken place on the fifth floor of Howard-Payne North. From time to time, all showers will be found on with the shower room door propped open. The entire hall will be so full of thick steam that visibility is reduced and the area becomes very hot. It has been said that walls occasionally bulge slightly and then retract, almost like rubber.

"The most disturbing story I have heard about the fifth floor, however, took place in 1989 before renovation of the building. Four members of a Methodist youth group, at CMC for a work camp, slipped away to explore the building. On the fourth floor they found a door behind which was a narrow staircase leading up to the dreaded fifth floor. The stairs were completely carpeted with dead pigeons and detached feathers. The brave group picked their way through the rotting remains and found that the entire fifth floor was likewise covered. They found no area where the pigeons had been nesting and no place where the birds could have come in from outside. After almost an hour of searching, no broken windows or holes in the plaster were found. All windows had been nailed shut and paint over the nails was old and peeling.

"A sudden and terrifying interruption ended the group's search. An exposed pipe that crossed the ceiling suddenly bent down with a loud screech. It was as if a great weight had been placed upon a single point of the pipe, making a V shape in the process. The boys ran in terror from the room and down the narrow staircase. They immediately told their camp counselor what had happened, and he went to check for himself. He was unable to verify their tale, however, for when he found the tiny door on the fourth floor of Howard-Payne North — the one that led to the narrow stairs — he could plainly see that the door had been nailed shut years before.

"Within sight of Howard Payne is the administrative building of CMC, Brannock Hall. It was built before the Civil War and is said to have housed Union soldiers during that conflict. On a clear, warm summer night, a dull-witted young soldier was tending to the horses that were stabled in the basement of the building. One animal, startled at the sound of distant cannon fire, kicked over the soldier's lantern. Oil spread out over the straw and flames quickly followed. The soldier, too confused and frightened to attempt to put the fire out, simply ran from the building. Many horses burned to death and it is said that on clear summer nights, strange flickers like firelight can be seen in the basement windows of Brannock Hall and the almost human-sounding screams of the horses can be heard faintly, like an echo of the tragedy that occurred there."

In the Stacks

"The campus library holds vague tales of a very nasty spirit in a storage area called "the old stacks". Only yellowing bound periodicals are there, now, with the main collection of books housed in the newer addition to the library. Magazines dating back to the 1800s are in the old stacks and little else. The place is dimly lit, strangely constructed and usually vacant. Huge thick gray tiles make up both floors and ceilings. Many students refuse to go into the old stacks; even those who have heard nothing about history of the place instinctively fear being there alone.

"The story goes that a young man with no ties to the area hired on as a general laborer during construction of the building, which was many decades ago. Only a few days after he started work, a crane that was lifting a tile to its place on the fifth floor broke. The tile fell endways and split him in two. The unknown young man was buried in an unmarked grave and nobody knew how to contact his next of kin. Nobody even knew his last name.

"A few weeks later, a federal marshall came though town looking for an escaped fugitive who had killed six people, been convicted and then killed one more person in his escape from prison. At first, no Fayette citizen could tell the marshall anything, but when he showed a picture of the escapee, several people positively identified the slain construction worker. The marshall had the corpse exhumed and sent back to the county where the crimes had been committed.

"As the story goes, many strange sounds and smells were reported in the library after this time. Some students complained of feelings of being watched and others reported an overwhelming sense of dread, followed by chills. Still others simply lost track of time and stumbled out of the stack several hours after entering them.

"For many years after, only librarians were allowed to enter the stacks. Students would request a certain volume and the librarian would go back into the dismal place and find it. No reports of hauntings came from this period and after a while, the stacks were opened to students to browse. Although reports of these events dwindled over time, strange occurrences are reported sometimes, even to this day.

"A common story on many campuses and in many dorms is that of a student who committed suicide in his or her closet. CMC is no different, though the reported suicide in McMurray Hall has never to my knowledge been substantiated. However many strange events have occurred in room 323 in the western back wing. In the fall of 1993, before the general student populace had moved in, only two people were in the building, the residence hall director and a resident assistant. The assistant was asked to make sure that each room had the required furniture and that other workers had turned lights off. He said that the lights were still on in 323 when he let himself in with his key. 'Both closet doors were open,' he said, 'though I distinctly remembered them having been closed before. As I backed out of the room and reached over to turn off the light, I found the switch already in off position. Then a hissing sound, like the rushing of steam passed by my ears on both sides. I stepped back out of the room and the door slammed in my face.'

Musical Ghosts

"The music department also has its share of ghosts, haunting the conservatory, the recital hall, the band room and even the meeting rooms of the music-oriented fraternity and sorority.

"Many years ago a band director, leading his musicians in a concert, lifted his arms to cue in a trumpet passage known as 'The Devil's Entrance'; he collapsed on stage and was found to be dead by the first person to reach him. According to legend, he still appears occasionally on clear, cool nights, strolling toward the church. He wears a concert tuxedo and sometimes is whistling lightly. As observers get closer he may say, 'It's a nice night for a concert, isn't it?' His picture, hanging near the band room, supposedly—completely on its own—always returns to its proper place if it is moved."

Editor's note: At a book signing last year someone gave me a variation on this story, saying the conductor is hurrying and has a frantic expression on his face. He anxiously asks "What time is it?" as if panicked of being late. In plain sight of everyone on campus is a large clock in a tower. Does this mean that ghosts cannot see the material objects in our world? But back to Roeder:

"A piano teacher is reported to haunt the conservatory and especially the recital hall. When a frantic student is practicing for an important recital, her hands will sometimes be felt atop those of the student, helping him or her to play the piece properly.

"However, she does not like to be taunted. Several years ago a somewhat intoxicated female student entered the recital hall late at night to practice. She sat down on the piano bench and said loudly to the room, 'I really have to learn this tonight, so don't give me any trouble!' Almost as soon as the words left her lips, one of the huge pipes from the pipe organ fell across the end of the piano. When inspected later, it was discovered that under usual circumstances the pipe could not have been moved without first being raised up off a peg and it was heavy enough that this action would have required two strong people to lift in unison.

"In late October of 1996, a student was crossing the campus at about three in the morning when he looked up at a conservatory window and saw the face of a woman looking back at him. He saw no body at all, only the visage looking sternly down. Months later, walking through the Conservatory, he noticed a portrait on the wall of one of CMC's most famous piano teachers. This would have been either N. Louise Wright or Opal Hayes. Whichever, he said the face was the same he had seen frowning at him on that early October morning.

"Another student related a story to me about his experience in the recital hall. After giving what he felt to be the best performance of his life, he was looking about the room, smiling and bowing to the audience. However, he suddenly became terrified. There in the balcony, which had not been unlocked and opened that night, stood a long departed and much beloved teacher. She was smiling gently and clapping as well. After leaving the stage with some difficulty, he passed out in the green room. He never entered the recital hall again."

The teacher in this story, Jason later told me, was Dr. Wright, a Fayette native who died in mid-March of 1958 while giving a piano concert to a packed hall. She was 79 and had taught at CMC for 55 years, for much of that time serving as dean of Swinney Conservatory. She also was renowned for her composing, some of which was in the popular genre. A piece of sheet music for her song, "Lovin' You" made up the Winter/Spring 2001 cover of Talon, CMC's magazine. Inside was a long feature about Wright and Hayes.

The concluding paragraph of Roeder's paper:

"Central Methodist College has much more to offer than just ghost stories. If you ever get out that way, visit the remarkable Ashby-Hodge Gallery of Art or historic Lynn Memorial United Methodist church. Just remember that, like many older colleges across the country, CMC has its fair share of ghosts."

Big Town Ghosts

Though we think of ghosts as preferring isolation and silence, metropolitan areas seem to have special attractions for spirits, especially Missouri's two largest cities. From their beginnings, both St. Louis and Kansas City brought together people of widely differing ethnic and religious backgrounds, varied talents, skills and ambitions. Both cities had vital roles in Western expansion; both saw fortunes made quickly and elaborate houses erected to shelter generations of families. Many of these families made vital Missouri history; many of them saw great success and great tragedy. How could Missouri's' biggest cities fail to have some of the best ghost stories anyone could hope for?

Chapter Twelve

St. Louis

A voice in hollow murmurs through the courts,
Talks of a nameless deed.
— Ann Radcliffe, *The Mysteries of Udolpho*

A *St. Louis Globe Democrat* article for Halloween 1978 listed seven St. Louis buildings with a reputation for being haunted. Another undated clipping stars six entirely different houses and discusses ghosts connected with the Missouri and Mississippi Rivers. Anthologies of ghost stories always include St. Louis. The Lemp Mansion has special fame, being one of *Life Magazine's* "Nine Most Haunted Houses in the U.S.," a designation given in 1980. The Lemp family is dealt with at length in another chapter of this book. Meanwhile, some other interesting sites and stories:

Daddy's Girl

A sad little story in the a 1989 *Post-Dispatch* told of a child who wandered staircases for many decades in a luxurious home known as "The Castle," in the Central West End. Her plaintive cries of "Daddy! Daddy!" were attested to by several people. She was thought to be the ghost of Jacob Goldman's youngest child, Hortense, who had died shortly before he built and moved to the new mansion.

Despite his wealth, Goldman had been able to do little to compensate Hortense for losing her mother at the age of four. When the little girl herself sickened only two years later, he was equally powerless to save her. Goldman was said to have doted on Hortense, and to have suffered greatly at her loss.

The father's story had other sad aspects. He was a German who came to this country as an almost penniless teenager before the Civil War and somehow managed to make a fortune in cotton in the southern states. When Goldman came to settle in St. Louis he owned half of the world's largest cotton company but because he was Jewish, was nonetheless barred from building in the rich and fashionable areas, Westmoreland Place and Portland Place.

Goldman bought a large tract between Kingshighway and Euclid, naming it Hortense Place. Several well-known people built lavish homes there, including Albert Lambert, heir to the Listerine fortune, later honored by having the airport named for him. Goldman's own Carthage-stone palace contained the biggest ballroom in the city, and invitations to dance there were highly coveted. He spent $35,000 to furnish the house, a fortune at the time, and remained until 1930 with his three other children from the wife he had lost in 1894. Whether or not the family heard Hortense's cries was not part of the story; perhaps she was contented there until her family left the house.

The next owner of The Castle was Henry Miller, who modernized it according to standards of the era. It was his servants who first discovered presence of a little girl searching the stairs for her father. Sold again in the 1940s, and converted to a rooming house, The Castle began to decline; in the 1960s vandals damaged it badly and took away its chandeliers and mantel pieces. In the 1970s, however, the house was renovated and became a private home once more. Whether or not Hortense continued her search through all this, she was active again in the 1980s, when guests heard her questing voice and remarked to their host that they'd not known he had a child. He had none.

This touching story is unusual in that Hortense seemingly followed her father to a home where she had never lived and clung to him there. Most ghost stories center on a place, rather than a person.

An Awful Story

The Scott and Norman book, *Historic Haunted America,* tells of a family named Furry who bought a pleasant two-story frame and brick house on Plant Avenue in Webster Groves and experienced terrors later studied deeply by psychical investigators.

The earliest event was Mrs. Furry waking at about 2 a.m. with the unpleasant feeling of having been shaken. This happened repeatedly. Once she was wakened by what sounded and felt like a strong hammer blow on the headboard of her bed. Then, each day about sunrise, she began hearing the footsteps of children running up and down stairs, rapidly and confidently, as if on familiar ground.

The couple slept in separate rooms and she mentioned none of this to her husband for some time, certain he'd not have heard the sounds and would not believe her. But as oddities continued and grew more unpleasant, Mrs. Furry decided she had to leave. When she told her husband, he admitted having heard some strange things himself, but supposed they were natural to the house. Soon thereafter, he saw a translucent shape in his bedroom and as it drifted out, he followed it to one of the children's rooms.

The children began making reports of their own, one of a woman "who hits me with a broom, but it doesn't hurt." In spite of all this, the Furrys stayed in the house for several years. When they sold the place, they had related their experiences to nobody.

The next occupation was in 1965 by a family named Whitcomb, who only rented the house. Mrs. Whitcomb, who was interested in the supernatural, later said she sensed a strangeness there from her first entrance. She said she was not surprised to see misty human-like shapes and to feel unexplainable drafts of cold air.

The only manifestation to really disturb her was a baby's crying. When her children began asking questions about running footsteps on the stairs, Mrs. Whitcomb undertook to research the house, starting with neighbors. They told her it had belonged to a man named Henry Gehm, who was involved with circuses. For reasons not fully explained, they'd concluded that Gehm kept assorted valuables in his home. They thought that the disturbances probably were related to his spirit's guarding these or searching for them.

This didn't seem to fit very well into what was happening, but Mrs. Whitcomb began keeping a journal of events. Author Norman comments that these were some of the most varied ever recorded in one place. Included was a musty odor that came and went, as well as footsteps in the attic heard by all family members at the same time. Often one of the Whitcombs felt a strong urge to go to the attic and once there, usually found things out of order, different from their last visit. Sometimes storage boxes and trunks were open, with contents strewn about. Most affectingly, a doll house outgrown by the Whitcombs' youngest daughter once was pulled out into a more accessible location and the dust around it was full of little bare footprints.

Other happenings were routine for haunted houses: lights went on and off, objects flew through the air, the Whitcombs' neatly organized desk drawers were stirred into chaos. But not all activity was destructive. Once a defunct old music box they'd kept for sentiment's sake was suddenly and permanently repaired.

Further questioning of neighbors convinced the Whitcombs that no outsider pranks were involved. The only possible conclusion seemed to be that they were sharing the house with a discarnate family resentful of them, wanting them out. On the day the Whitcombs obliged, it was to the accompaniment, even as they carried their own possessions down, of children running at furious speed up and down beside them on the stairs and by the sound of voices, something they'd never heard before.

The *National Directory of Haunted Places,* by Dennis William Hauck, varies from Norman and Scott by saying Henry Gehm was a German immigrant who built the house in the 1890s and lived a reclusive life in it until he died alone there in the early 1950s. Among experiences Hauck listed for later residents were sounds like birds hitting window panes and a ghostly lady in black who moved about surrounded by a white cloud. He refers to a family named Walsh, saying they saw the black lady and also a small blonde girl. In March of 1966, Hauck says, Gehm's ghost appeared to Mrs. Walsh and directed her to a secret chamber, possibly once the location of his treasure, but completely empty when she looked in.

A Diaphanous Gown

A more recent and modish apparition was reported several times in Room 304 of the Chase Hotel in St. Louis, starting in 1980. A typical experience, shared by a salesman for a *Post-Dispatch* Halloween feature: he entered his room one night to find a lovely young lady with glamorously arranged red hair standing at the window, looking musingly down at traffic below.

When she turned and smiled hazily at him, he assumed she had somehow arrived at the wrong place and he tried, pleasantly and politely, to dismiss her. She neither replied nor moved as he explained that he needed rest and privacy. Eventually, embarrassed and angry, he phoned the desk, only to hear, "... no problem; she'll probably be gone when you turn around." And indeed she was.

Not all who saw this charming apparition were men traveling alone. Women were visited too, and at least once a couple the newspaper described as "a well-known entertainer and his wife" saw her. Sometimes the ghost just stood near the bed, smiling. Sometimes she made her exit through a closed door.

Nobody at the Chase could offer any explanation. Nobody knew of any young woman who had lost her life there, but the hotel was built in 1921 and few people associated with its early years were still employed there 40 years later. The staff only knew that all who saw the phantom commented on her beauty and a gown variously described as white chiffon or as "... filmy ... full and fluffy ... like a showgirl ... glittery ... sort of transparent but not really revealing ...."

Some St. Louis Short Shorts

🕊 Newspapers in 1908 and for years after, reported a West End ghost, near Easton and Kingshighway, which began just as "a big noise" and later became a veiled and black-gowned lady who languished along a staircase and played poignant tunes on the piano.

The landlord denied her existence bitterly, saying someone just wanted to devalue his property. But a tenant said she'd heard enough odd sounds such as footsteps where nobody was walking, to make her spend most nights with friends and relatives. When interviewed, she'd slept in her own apartment only four nights of the past fourteen. What she'd heard from the piano, she said, was at times almost a tune, but usually sounded more like a cat or parrot walking over the keys.

🕊 Another West End home, on Maryland Avenue, was visited in January of 1967 by Joan Foster Dames of the *Post-Dispatch* staff. The owner had reported footsteps of an invisible climber going to the third floor and a mournful upstairs presence that made people's hair bristle. The family's Chihuahua, Ginger, was often upset for no reason anyone could see, but the spirits were at least apparently harmless.

Thorough research of the house revealed no past tragedy. No previous owner claimed to have experienced anything strange. But house guests sometimes complained of being pushed out of bed, so the couple spent an experimental night on the third floor. The wife slept well, but her husband said he was awakened several times by someone punching him. Dames took a light view of all this, mentioning how many times the couple referred to their dog's reactions to the spirit they called "Old Chap." Dames concluded, "A Chihuahua is not what one usually calls 'a reliable witness.'"

🜄 A childish apparition whose audacity included appearing at a child's party finally exasperated the long suffering mother of a certain St. Louis family. She had felt sympathy for the little ghost even though its appearances usually were followed by troublesome bloodstains on the carpet. But one day when her own children were elsewhere, and upstairs romping got too loud, according to *Post-Dispatch* writer, Jim Creighton, the mother ended it permanently, without knowing she could do so. She shouted angrily "You're dead! You're dead! Go away!" Creighton's experts told him this was a case of the child not knowing she was dead until informed of that fact. This is a variation on what psychic investigators tell us to do and something to remember, perhaps, for ghostly encounters!

Also Near St. Louis

Hella Canepa told an interesting story she discovered in researching the resort hamlet, Castlewood, near St. Louis. A wealthy man contracted to buy a luxurious house there on bluff top acreage with a wonderful view of the Meramec River. He soon decided, "... this house is haunted ... full of ghosts."

As Canepa quoted him: "Things happen all day long, strange noises I can't locate, objects inexplicably moved to crazy places, my dog yelping or growling for no reason, intense creepy feelings, a sudden draft or stench from no apparent source. I keep a horse out there and it won't come near the house ....

"But the really bizarre stuff starts at night ... I'm awakened by the same three notes played on a violin. Can you imagine? It's loud, right in the room with me. Then it's gone and there's nothing but silence again.

Of course I can't get back to sleep. I get up and go to the kitchen or bathroom ... and the 'parties' start. All of a sudden, sounds of laughter, music, lively conversation and activity surround me. I look all over the house but can never find where it's coming from before it stops. This also happens when I come home late at night."

A psychic who visited the house told the man she felt "an unbearable sense of horror and impending doom." She was sure that somebody — maybe several people — met their end there suddenly and violently. She suggested that he move at once. He later learned that the house was built on the spot where a hotel had burned more than fifty years earlier. If Capena researches this further, she may find that many people died in the fire, or that nobody was ever sure whether all bodies were found.

What are ghosts for,
if not to do the duty
Of warning us to make
the most of beauty?

—Robert P. Tristram Coffin,
"The Grieving Wind."

Chapter Thirteen

Kansas City

At night I fly over the housetops
And stand in the bright moony beams.
　　　　　— Stevie Smith, *The Heavenly City*

Among Kansas City's best-known haunted places are the castle-like Epperson House on the University of Missouri-Kansas City campus, areas of the Radisson Muhlebach Hotel, Loretto School auditorium, and the Spanish Chapel in the Nelson Art Galley.

Kansas City also has one particularly detailed and unique story, about a house that sheltered a family happily for decades, yet when the parents were gone, seemed to turn unkindly on their daughter. This story appeared in *The Star Magazine* in 1987, in a Halloween article by John Hughes.

The Hostile House

Neither past nor present owners of the house wanted to be identified, so Hughes gave the name "Maggie" to the daughter. Her father had died peacefully, but Maggie's mother then killed herself, by asphyxiation with the car exhaust.

While recovering from these traumatic events, Maggie had two friends with her, one at night and the other by day.

Neither woman was a drug addict, she said, and neither had any interest in the supernatural, but one said she saw Maggie's parents and was instructed by the mother to go out and buy Maggie a dogwood tree. Maggie took this as a direct message, for shortly before her mother's death, the two of them had discussed whether or not a dogwood from further south could survive in Missouri. This was the trivial sort of exchange nobody would bother to share with anyone else and Maggie hadn't.

The other friend, on a day when Maggie was away, heard a noise in the garage and when she went to check found the car motor running, all doors locked and no ignition key. Among other things Maggie found she could not live with: books and other objects rising from their places and falling loudly to the floor; her dog sitting up in bed and moving its head to intently watch something that seemed to be moving across the room; the fragrances of food in the kitchen on the day of the week Maggie's mother had always shopped for groceries; doorknobs that turned when nobody was there. A friend asked about the woman she'd seen primping at a hall mirror; another friend said she heard faint cries of "Help me! Help me!"

When Maggie had a group of psychic investigators in, they said they found nothing of significance, though one of them accurately described Maggie's grandmother whose disposition had been unpleasant. After they left, Maggie and a friend were terrified by two loud crashes, each hard enough to shake the house. They called the psychics, who interpreted this as proof of presences and a sign of anger at being investigated.

Buyers for this house reported no disturbances for several months, but did eventually call and ask Maggie for the psychics' phone number.

The Epperson House

The Epperson House, originally built in the early 1920s by a couple made wealthy from insurance and meat-packing investments, was truly a showplace in its prime. It cost $450,000 to build, and besides having 54 rooms, featured romantic turrets, tunnels and trapdoors. The Eppersons were noted for generous financial support of Kansas City's most worthwhile civic and cultural efforts, but also for doing something most unusual in their private life. They adopted a woman only a few years younger than themselves, a person of great musical ability. Was their intent to insure her of wherewithal for pursuing her talent? The story doesn't say. It does say she died at only 47, of supposed complications from routine surgery. Both the Eppersons lived into unusually old age.

A group of psychics led by the late Maurice Schwalm, who was prominent in investigation of many Kansas City haunts, felt indications in the Epperson House of drama involving a woman. As relayed in local publications, these included a possible abortion, someone fleeing via ladder, a bad fall down the grandiose staircase, and someone slashing her wrists. One investigator found an entity strongly resentful of intrusion.

As for what people of the present see and experience at Epperson House, now a part of the University of Missouri-Kansas City: students and staff working in the building have always insisted they felt an oppressive atmosphere and many report mildly frightening sights and sounds.

Probably the best testimony of all comes from a university patrolman who was quoted in May, 1979 in *The Kansas City Star.* He said that one night after cruising the area, he parked for a short time and in the small, quiet hours, was suddenly impacted from behind by another vehicle. He heard all the sounds of collision, broken glass raining, metal crumpling. When he got out to look there was no other car and no damage to his own, though his neck ached. Closer scrutiny showed that his car had moved about eight inches, leaving skid marks.

On another occasion, he and a fellow officer were doing their usual 2 a.m. walk-through of the building, turning lights on and off to illuminate their way as they went, thus being separated most of the time by the length of long hallways and large rooms. One light would not turn off and just as the officer nearest it commented on the strangeness, the other saw, behind his friend, an arm in a blue sleeve reach out and flip the switch.

"Who turned that off?" the patrolman asked, turning in puzzlement. "I didn't try to tell him then," the other told the *Star's* reporter. "I just promised to explain when we were outside and we got there as fast as we could." It was these two men's problems with their disbelieving colleagues which led to Schwalm's group being invited to investigate. Schwalm said an improvement in atmosphere probably would be noted just because resident spirits had been given an opportunity to express their feelings. This seemed to be the case, at least when the *Star* story appeared.

The Muhlebach Blonde

The young woman who haunted a restaurant in the Radisson Muhlebach Hotel was quite attractive, yet the sight of her caused one new busboy to run out the door never to return. Her presence seemed to set off troublesome activity in the kitchen and elsewhere. She dressed always in blue, in fashions of the 1930s and 1940s and she must have spoken to someone in her earliest appearances, or been known to people who lived or worked at the Muhlebach.

One employee, a tarot card reader, said for a *Star* story in April of 1985, that she had seen the entity six times and had communicated with her telepathically. She said this pensive visitor had been an actress who researched her roles by watching people in public places. It had been her misfortune to have an affair with a gangster who killed her. This spiritual trauma put her on an endless search for an earlier lover who had been kind and protective.

Some of the problems the blue lady's appearances seemed to stimulate included unreliable behavior of lights and other electrical equipment and such events as heavy trays of hors d'oeuvres rising off counters and crashing to the floor.

One of the cooks told the *Star* he'd never think of spending any time alone in the restaurant.

KC Shorts

🐾 Apparitions, strange sounds and erratic stage lights have been reported by students and teachers at Loretto School Auditorium for years, and some even said they saw the shadow of a hanged nun. In 1979 so many problems occurred with the light panel that psychics were invited in.

Their conclusion: the spirit of a woman, formerly a top-echelon administrator, was disturbed at plays she considered too free-thinking for a Catholic private school. This was not nearly as exciting as the previous assumption of a connection with three students who died tragically on stage in 1909 in burning Halloween costumes. The school was located elsewhere then, so this latter story was a bit of a stretch.

🐾 The Spanish Chapel's ghost, Schwalm suggested to the *Star* reporter, might be 14th century martyr, Jacques DeMolay, drawn to this location because some of his ashes somehow got incorporated into some of the chapel's art objects. Ron Taggert, senior curator at the gallery, was quoted by the *Star* as saying he never had seen or felt anything eerie or interesting and has always felt annoyed that whatever haunts the chapel ignores him.

An Untrue Story?

The Vaille Mansion, built in Independence in 1881, and serenely welcoming guests today, has no recent accounts of hauntings, according to Terri Baumgardner in the *Star* in fall of 1996. But the reputation of the house was once so ominous that neighbors crossed the street rather than pass in front of it. The ghost, which children said they'd seen in windows, was said to be that of Sylvia Vaille, who died only a few years after her husband built the impressive home for her. He was so unwilling to let her go that he supposedly buried her on the front lawn in a glass-topped coffin set flush with the ground. Protests of those who lived nearby soon forced him to give his wife conventional burial, Baumgardner wrote.

People working with the house today say they can find no evidence or documentation to support the truth of this remarkable burial. What they do tell us makes the house sound enticing to visit. Renovated about 15 years ago, it now looks much as it did when new and written of as the grandest home in the country. Among its riches: 30 rooms in three stories plus a four story tower; nine marble-faced fireplaces and three crystal chandeliers reportedly designed for the White House, but rejected there; ceiling murals painted by European artists. One of these, the story goes, was in the Vaille couple's bedroom, a reclining nude with Mrs. Vaille's face, and was thought scandalous at the time.

According to a 1985 newspaper story the builder of the house, Col. Harvey Merrick Vaille, made his fortune from investing in the Erie Canal and in a mail carrying service of the Santa Fe Trail. This story, incidentally, called his wife Sophia, rather than Sylvia. It says that the house originally stood amidst a 1,500 acre farm and that its immediate surroundings were beautified with a lake, greenhouse, fountains and arbors. Later history of the house included use as an inn, then as a sanitarium and asylum. It is, as one might assume, listed in *The National Register of Historic Places.*

A Haunted Jail

Also reported in Independence was an 1859 jail which has one cell so thoroughly haunted that the casual visitor can pick it out. Gay Clemens, site director, told Baumgardner that when anyone asks him which cell is haunted he invites them to go and see if they can tell him. Seldom is anyone wrong. He says, too, that guards and inmates have reported nausea and chilling in this building, as well as sounds of inexplicable footsteps, growls and gasps. He also described a physics' thrusting his arm into the cell through its bars and his hair then standing up as if from electrical charge.

The cell became haunted, we're told, in days when the custom was for a town's main law enforcement officer to have his home in the same building as the jail. Marshall Jim Knowles died there trying to stop a fight between prisoners with opposing sentiments during the Civil War. Dennis Hauck's *National Directory of Haunted Places* says though, that the disturbed and disturbing spirit is possibly a deputy marshall killed in a jailbreak in June of 1866.

The foregoing is only a small sample of what could be written about Missouri's metropolitan ghosts. Surely no cities anywhere can claim more variety. Two books written within the last few years of the century just past, give much more background on the haunts in our big cities. These are *Spirits of St. Louis,* by Robbi Courtaway and *Mo-Kan Ghosts* by the late Maurice Schwalm.

Ghostin'
On The River

Chapter Fourteen

The Haunted Delta Queen

There are still reports that late at night
an invisible boat shoots by the docks,
lifting them high with its wake.
— D. W. Waldron

Before exploring Delta Queen's ghost story, we need to do a little scene setting, looking at the boat's history which is unforgettable even if there were no disembodied spirit aboard. This vessel has spent 55 years on the rivers of mid-America, much of that time sweeping up and down through Missouri. One of the countless articles written about The Delta Queen points out that millions of miles of water have passed beneath her hull.

But her life began on the famous River Clyde in Scotland where a multitude of other famous boats and ships were built. Her hull and that of her sister, Delta King, were constructed there in 1924 and 1925 by a company renowned for remarkable work. The heavy galvanized metal plates were fastened together with bolts rather than rivets, so they could be disassembled, their parts numbered and sent across the ocean to the boat's owner for reassembly.

The two boats were finished in Stockton, CA and put to work as luxury overnight transport on the Sacramento River. From 1927 to 1941, the sisters plied back and forth daily from opposite ports, Sacramento and San Francisco, never in port together, but meeting and hailing each other every night.

In about 1941, with tourist trade diminishing, a decision was made to take the sister boats by sea and stream to New Orleans where they could be fitted out for use on the Western River System. They would be towed along the coast, through the Panama Canal, along the Gulf Coast and so to the Mississippi and New Orleans. When World War II began, The Delta King had already been sheathed around with wood to close up her open decks and make her seaworthy for this journey.

Then the Navy requisitioned the matching boats to work as ferries, taking troops — as many as 3,000 at a time — back and forth to and from military ships anchored in San Francisco Bay, and to serve as barracks. After the war, for reasons not given in anything I could find, the Delta Queen was sent to New Orleans as formerly planned, but she went alone, carrying her sister's engine in her hold, to be used as needed for spare parts in a new life. The ravished Delta King then was used as a stationary historic site for the city of Sacramento.

The Delta Queen quickly became the most beloved cruise ship on the inland rivers. Her historic decor and touching history are not the only reasons; many people had an emotional investment. For instance, WWII veterans who had known her in California were intrigued with the idea of taking their families on board the Delta Queen for vacation trips. So were people who had, for decades, seen her passing through their home towns, or had at one time worked on her. Many couples take repeated honeymoons on the Delta Queen.

A highlight of her career came in 1979 when President Jimmy Carter took his wife and daughter on a cruise from St. Paul, Minnesota to St. Louis. For the occasion, the Delta Queen had a large sign appended which read, "Steamboat One." Princess Margaret of England and many other celebrities have traveled to points in the United States from which they could board the Delta Queen.

The extent of public love for the Delta Queen was demonstrated in 1962 when our government issued new safety regulations for cruise boats carrying large numbers of people: they must be of all-steel construction. This seemed to doom the cherished vessel, but so much public outcry arose that she was spared. The owners made extensive adaptations to increase her safety and the government granted the Delta Queen a special exemption. She is, after all, registered as both a National Historic Site and a National Historic Landmark.

One reason this boat is declared to be thoroughly haunted is that her very being takes people back; they feel they have stepped into the past. Three times each year, the Delta Queen, The Mississippi Queen and The American Queen, last three paddlewheelers left from the 11,000 that once swarmed our rivers, stage races. These are a far cry from those of more than a century past in which captains taxed their engines to the utmost, risking the lives of their boats and all aboard to see who could go fastest. The races still are dramatic and colorful, another strong taste of time travel.

This is not all the background we need for proper appreciation of Delta Queen's remarkable ghost, however. We have to know a little about that lady herself. She was Mary Becker, born in 1869 and married to Gordon C. Greene in 1890, the same year he established a steamboat line. The newlyweds lived on various riverboats and during a period when resources were low, Mary learned to pilot, saving them the cost of employing a co-pilot. She said in interview that seeing a woman in charge of a riverboat was such a novelty that she always took the night duty, to avoid being a spectacle.

Mrs. Greene nevertheless went through the certification process to be qualified to operate a ship alone. She was — if not the very first — one of the first women ever to do this and so deserved her nickname, "Captain Molly." We're told that in 1903 Mary Greene beat her husband in a steamboat race and that when the World's Fair was held in St. Louis the following year, she was entrusted to take his newest boat, The Greenland, there for display. No doubt, they also provided short cruises for fairgoers.

The Greene line owned more than a dozen boats when, in 1946, they bought the Delta Queen. Mary, by then long accepted as a pilot, could steer the boat with little comment whenever she wanted to or needed to. She became very fond of the craft, watching over its whole operation. Despite being rather fussy, she was not resented by the employees, but became as well loved in her niche as the Delta Queen was in hers. Mary Greene had the logical mind and toughness required to be an exceptional business person, yet was described in a *Fate* magazine article as "five feet of femininity." She became stout as she aged, but never lost the friendly, fun-loving personality that won so many people to her. As a widow and retiree, Capt. Molly made the Delta Queen her permanent home, seldom going ashore. The *Fate* writer says that two nights before her death, she was dancing with the crew. Mary Greene died on board her beloved boat in 1949, at the age of 80. "But only her body died," employees have said. "She never left. She's still here." Here are some examples of why they're so certain:

🐾 An officer of the boat told of awakening from a deep sleep one night with the irresistible sense of being summoned urgently. Though nothing sounded, smelled, or felt unusual, he made a tour of the boat's vital areas and found a leaking pipe that would have caused serious problems had it gone unnoticed for a few hours longer.

🐾 A photographer taking souvenir shots of tourists in the salon, fell backward, very distraught, and told people trying to help him, "She's alive ... she's alive in that picture frame!" A large portrait of Mrs. Greene that had been a part of the background for hundreds of pictures he took, had suddenly changed, he said. The woman in the picture altered her position to look directly at him and made further movements inside the frame. He was so traumatized that he had to go to bed, and some say he never worked on the boat again.

🐾 One couple credit Mary Greene with matchmaking their marriage. There are several versions of this story, but the essence is that a young woman, newly hired as purser, one night came to the first mate in great distress. She'd received a phone call from one of the staterooms, from an elderly woman who said she was ill and needed help. This woman identified herself as one who had visited the purser's office that day and the young woman remembered her appearance, though not her name.

When the purser reached the designated room, however, it was empty, obviously unoccupied for that particular cruise. "She must have told me the wrong number, in her panic," the purser told the officer. "How will we find her quickly?" As the two of them went together back through corridors to the room, the girl stopped in amazement. "That's her, there in that picture!" she said, stopping to stare at a large portrait on the wall. "That's the lady who visited me earlier today, and she's the one who called me."

"We don't need to go any farther," the officer said and explained who Mrs. Greene was and that many strange things happened on the boat. None of them had ever brought harm to anyone; they seldom were even frightening.

The new purser was so shaken that the officer remained with her for some time. Because of this shared experience, a relationship developed between them, and eventually, marriage. All versions of this story say that the couple often joked to people that a ghost brought them together. As captain of a boat, Mary Greene had been authorized to marry people and had performed many such ceremonies, so who can say with certainty that the couple was wrong?

🐾 Another tale, repeated often with variations: A woman who worked on the boat as an entertainer, so had to return to her own quarters after most people had already retired, disliked the eeriness of having to go alone through long corridors of closed doors. Probably most of us have experienced this at some time on ships or in hotels. The performer said she was often heartened to see a fellow nightowl hurrying down the hallway before her. The elderly woman was always wearing a floor-length green cloak, as if over formal attire. What unnerved the entertainer was that after they turned a certain corner this fellow traveler had always slipped silently into her own room and disappeared, never, apparently, needing to pause to get out a key and fit it into a lock.

Then one night the mystery was solved. The green-cloaked one disappeared in mid-corridor, before the eyes of the woman who had so greatly appreciated her company. Having heard the stories about Mary Greene, the entertainer knew she had been taking courage from the presence of a ghost.

Mary Greene's helpful spirit and her protectiveness for the boat and its passengers is said to characterize most of her appearances, with perhaps a bit of playfulness thrown in now and then. For instance: a tour conductor on the boat said she had several times noticed in her group a woman dressed in outmoded clothing. Since there was no logic in the same person repeatedly joining a tour that offered identical sights and data, the conductor began to worry that this woman might be a stowaway — possibly mentally ill — living on her own on the Delta Queen. Once the puzzled tour conductor realized that her strange tourist could be the ghost of Mary Greene, the appearances stopped.

So be warned: if you board the Delta Queen, you may have an odd experience. It is unlikely to be anything but pleasant.

For those who like stats: The Delta Queen is 285 feet long and 60 feet wide, with four decks and seven watertight compartments. Her wheel is 29 feet tall. She accommodates 178 passengers and requires a crew of 80. New Orleans is her home port.

River towns have special atmosphere bestowed by their heritage of being early sites of settlement where history was made and where residents followed colorful occupations. And most of us are awed by the hypnotic presence of that endless procession of powerful water — coming from elsewhere, going elsewhere — amazing our senses just as it did those of our forebears, and of people famous to Missouri's history.

Chapter Fifteen

Streamside Spirits

.... fantasies ... of calling shapes and beck' ning shadows dire,
And airy tongues that syllable men's names.
— John Milton, *Il Penseroso*

Boonville

Boonville is a classic river town, settled in the early 1800s, serving as Cooper County seat since 1818. Founders were largely Kentuckians and Virginians, with many German immigrants among the town's earliest settlers. For decades, Boonville hosted flotillas of steamboats bedecked as ornately as wedding cakes. The town was a point of departure for pioneers heading west.

The streets of Boonville are lined with wonderful old houses that saw it all, occupied by generations of people who left their mark on Missouri. Such houses must have ghosts, of course, and be remembered for them even when those houses themselves are gone. One of the best stories of this kind appears in many anthologies as "Aunt Eternity's Curse." It is about a Virginian named Howard Thornton Muir whose home was rated among the most elegant mansions in Missouri. His horses and carriages and uniformed servants, his lavish entertainments were the grandest in the area.

Like all the powerful people of his time, however, Muir was helpless against health hazards. When his treasured daughter, Nancy, suddenly fell desperately ill, difficult travel and slow communication gave no hope of getting medical experts to her quickly. She had a fast-working malady familiar in those days: Monday, blooming health; Tuesday, chills and fever; Wednesday, delirium; Thursday or Friday, death.

The frantic family tried every home remedy they and their neighbors knew, every suggestion of local doctors. Nothing helped. The distraught father turned in panic to one of his oldest slaves, regarded by her companions as a possessor of magical healing powers. He did this reluctantly, because Aunt Eternity had more reason than just slavehood to harbor hostility for the family. Not long before Nancy's illness, the girl said she caught Aunt Eternity in some act of minor dishonesty, one version of the story says stealing a guest's silk scarf. The old woman, who had painfully, with a lifetime's work, achieved a position of importance and relatively easy tasks in the household, was demoted to the most menial and difficult, losing all the prestige she'd had among other slaves. She never stopped insisting on her innocence.

No doubt Muir cautioned Aunt Eternity forcefully about what would happen to her if she tried to take revenge on Nancy, and the old woman seemed to sincerely try to save the girl's life. The illness, however, was a hopeless one and Nancy died. Apparently Muir and his wife accepted the inevitable at the time, but in the next few weeks he brooded more and more about their loss and one night, possibly when drinking, he began to wonder if Aunt Eternity might actually have brought the illness upon Nancy.

He went to the old woman's cabin and beat her to death. In true ghost story tradition, she cursed him as she died, him and his house and all his relations. And true to tradition, calamities came upon them, one by one. In only a few years Muir was a ruined man, his family gone and his wonderful property in someone else's possession.

The story is not specific as to when the haunting began, whether in Muir's own day — reducing the sale value of his house — or much later. But as everything fell into decay, people of the area reported numerous strange happenings there, including sounds and lights inside the house. The most choice manifestation was a languid, pale young woman who sometimes wandered the overgrown flower garden that had once been so beautiful. Sometimes she was seen leaning against the dry fountain and singing sadly.

This story has been told and retold. It appeared in the book *Haunted Heartland,* a widely read anthology of 1985, and many articles have featured it. *Columbia Daily Tribune* columnist, Tom Ladwig, went so far as to point out the exact location of Muir's home site, in southeast Boonville near the I-70 exit.

The late Ladwig would have exploded the story if he could, for he was a great lover of humor and irony, but he didn't know that the Aunt Eternity story is apparently a fabrication. Some researchers cite evidence that the story was created by a respected Missouri historian just as an experiment to see how far it would go. Shall we consider what this tells us about ghost stories in general? Or maybe just about some of the most detailed and logical-sounding ones?

The Spectral Carriage

Bob Dyer, a well-known Boonville writer, historian and folklorist, often performs in concert a ballad he wrote from data originally collected by Charles van Ravensway, one of his most respected counterparts. It retells a Boonville area story that seems based on truth: an aging couple living in a crumbling mansion on the bluff overlooking the settlement of Overton Landing and the Missouri River obtained a fortune by killing a stranger who took shelter with them. Their victim had been carrying enough money to fulfill their best dreams, for her a black silk dress, for him a fine carriage. The wife died, soon after, however, and was buried in her coveted and ill-gotten dress. The husband, now wealthy, remarried and as the last of his wedding guests departed, according to Dyer's song: "There came a phantom black carriage, and a woman in

a black silk gown ... " the young wife watched from the window as "the man got in and the carriage disappeared ... "

The song continues, "It's been a long time now since it happened. There's nothing left now of the house on the bluff or the town. But people still see the carriage, and a woman in a black silk gown."

Dyer wrote that his song stemmed from a Boonslick folk tale first published in the 1930s, a tale with elements numerous people confirmed. Overton Landing stood across the Missouri River from Rocheport, and was a steamboat dock that gradually declined as so many others did. Dyer believes that "the house on the bluff" mentioned in his song may have been the family home of the woman, now deceased, who originally told the story. It still stands near Wooldridge, long abandoned, and he says it has "a distinctly haunted quality about it."

Bob Dyer is the author of several books, some pertaining to the Civil War in Missouri, others to Jesse James. His recording *The River of the Big Canoes,* includes "The Phantom Black Carriage."

An Innkeeper's Tale

Another interesting Boonville story was told on TV channel KOMU in Columbia in October 1994. Called "An Innkeeper's Tale," it concerned a woman who was caring for an aged father in a small-town hotel she operated. The man was convinced that he could not sleep if his feet were covered up. He said this constriction made relaxation impossible for him.

For a long time the daughter slipped in every night and covered his feet, unable to bear the thought of anyone, especially an elderly person, sleeping in that condition. But because her father so often woke up and protested angrily when she went in, and because his feet were always uncovered in the morning anyhow, the daughter finally stopped trying. She feared her father's anger would do him as much harm as the cold, and decided maybe he was safely conditioned by a lifetime of sleeping that way.

When the daughter began to find his feet cozily tucked in each morning, she questioned him and he said wearily, "Oh, I've given up. That woman you send in here every night just keeps doing it and pays no attention to anything I say."

The television account ended with that statement, and we can hardly do better for an unexplainable little situation.

Arrow Rock

Arrow Rock is another place so rich in history one doesn't know where to start. With settlement beginning in 1815, it became a flourishing commercial port with a stable population of 1,000, augmented each year by thousands of travelers and river workers. People following the Santa Fe Trail stopped at Arrow Rock and some famous Missourians lived there, attracting many visitors. Famous residents included the painter, George Caleb Bingham, and Dr. John Sappington, whose research was vital in conquering malaria. Arrow Rock also gave Missouri three state governors.

The town now has shrunk to only about 70 residents, but still attracts thousands of visitors. Between March and January, it teems with craft shows, festivals and historical tours. Its repertory theater, The Lyceum, is active during that period, along with many antique shops and excellent restaurants and a dozen bed and breakfasts, some of which are in restored historic homes. Arrow Rock is always in the process of doing more restoration. Naturally, this is a place ghosts cannot resist.

A favorite spot, apparently, is The Old Tavern, built in the early 1830s by slaves belonging to a Virginian named John Huston. The tavern still operates as a restaurant. The Old Tavern's present manager, Bunny Thomas, has lived there for four years and says, "I love it, and have never been afraid, but some people won't go upstairs." Her daughter, she says, would never stay in the building alone at night and a teenager who mopped up for them quit, saying that when every other room was empty and he was in the kitchen, he could hear eating and talking in the dining room. He even heard his own name called out.

Bunny has heard her name called out too, from the front when she's in the kitchen and vice versa. Once, she says, she was greeted as she came through the swinging door into an empty dining room, by a male voice saying in flirtatious tones, "Well, hello there!"

Her most memorable experiences, though, came in 1981, when she worked as floor manager and was given an upstairs apartment to live in. The very first night she saw smoke in her bedroom and went downstairs in panic, only to find no sign or smell of fire anywhere. Creakings and various other sounds were so constant that Bunny began keeping the radio on all night to drown them out.

One odd and interesting event starred an old dog whose owner had died. Though nobody officially adopted this animal, he was not a stray; he was the town dog, eating at several places, petted by everyone. His habit was to visit the tavern's back door every night for whatever he might find there, and he would hang out for awhile with Bunny, then go on his way or perhaps sleep near the building. Bunny never brought him inside and he never seemed to have any desire to come in.

One night they had finished their usual routine and Bunny had gone up to bed. At some point she was wakened by the sound of scratching on her door, but supposing it was just one of the ghosts, she turned the radio up louder and went back to sleep. Next morning, when she opened her apartment door, the town dog uncurled himself from the hall carpet and greeted her.

"I always try to figure out how things could have happened," she says, "but I never could see any way he could have got in. If he had his own entrance, why did he use it only that once?" And she adds that her employers, who sometimes play pranks, had promised her solemnly that they would never do anything to frighten her if she would take the job. "I believe them," she says, "I've never had any reason not to."

Another odd occurrence involved an element of The Old Tavern's decor, a display of historic documents. One time a visitor whose ancestors had lived in Arrow Rock found something pertaining to his family and wanted to photograph it. Light inside being inadequate for his camera, Bunny went outside with him to hold the paper where proper exposure would be possible. When the picture was developed, it showed not the printed material, but a picture of a log cabin. There was no such structure within the camera's range.

Ghosts seem to dwell also in some of Arrow Rock's private homes. One of these, among the town's oldest, has a small upstairs room the present tenant uses for sewing and as a guest room. Some of her guests decline to sleep in it. One is a daughter — a tax accountant — who refuses to even enter the room alone. Another is a black Labrador Retriever belonging to the householder's son; though the man has slept there without incident, the dog, who shares his room everywhere else, resolutely stays in the hall.

The owner says she never saw or felt anything in the room, but her daughter once reported something substantial crowding against her in the doorway, as if someone was rudely pushing past.

St. Charles

St. Charles, too, is a highly historic town. It was our first state capital and the place where leaders met to do work necessary for gaining statehood and then to create a state constitution. Many famous men traveled to St. Charles to participate in these important efforts. Many people who became vital to Missouri first stepped onto its soil from riverboats docking there. The town is rich in lovingly preserved and restored buildings and one group of them clusters in the Southeastern part of town as shops offering a variety of wares and services. Here are a few of the incidents reported by John R. Dengler for *St. Charles Life,* things that happened on his property and to his business neighbors on South Main Street.

🐿 An employee came tearing down the stairs of The Farmer's Home, a former inn which now houses both Dengler's home and his tobacco store; she said someone touched her gently on the shoulder. Once, for about four days, a French-speaking entity played tricks with cigarettes, hiding them or floating packs in the air; on the fifth day of his visit, a baby was heard crying and then quieted by soothing French words. Sometimes heavy-booted footsteps pace the halls and stairs of this house, and sometimes the enticing aroma of green beans and ham wafts from what was the ladies' dining room a century or more ago. A daughter of the Dengler family was once startled by a hearty and very close-by male laugh when she was alone in the guest room.

History of his house, Dengler says includes ownership first by a Frenchman, later by Alexander McNair, the state's first governor, a man who had 27 tanning vats on the property. Another tenant was a woman named Lizette Wayne, whose eight-year-old daughter died suddenly there. Surely every human drama imaginable has been played out among all those who stayed for brief or extended times during the many years while the building was an inn.

🐿 One of Dengler's neighbors often sees poltergeist-like movements of merchandise in her shop. Sometimes these are seen by customers, too, and once an explosive sound from the ceiling sent everyone present to the floor in terror. No cause for this sound was ever found.

🐿 Aimless movements in a place called The Button Shop suggest to the owner a bored child who goes about flicking display racks into motion and doing anything else it could think of for a little action. This proprietor found that she could stop the annoyance by saying sharply, "Quit that!"

🐱 Donna Hafer, owner of a restaurant called The Mother-
In-Law House told Dengler a strange story of how
mishaps seemed constantly to occur on the north side of
her building: spilled water and coffee — sometimes on
guests — food that was unaccountably hot when it should
be cold or vice versa, disappearances of supplies and
equipment.

A psychic advised redecorating with happier colors to
overcome a negative imprint made by the spirit of the
builder's mother-in-law, who had spent much time sitting
in her rocker in that area, feeling forlorn and unwanted.
She was hurt, no doubt, that her son-in-law's condition
for her living near her daughter was that she have entirely separate quarters. Hafer was also told to try to extend
love to this lonely spirit. These suggestions seemed to
solve the problems.

Dengler speculated that all bizarre happenings might
stem from the 1789 St. Charles Borromeo Cemetery that
once occupied nearby land. Moving its bodies — those
that could be found, considering that many had been tran-
sients buried without stones — to another cemetery a
mile or so away may have left some disturbed spirits.

A Capital Tale

More Missouri Ghosts, published in 2000 by Mogho
Books, set the small precedence of declaring that any ghost
story told by a Missourian is therefore a Missouri ghost
story. Otherwise, a great many tales and legends, not to mention
current experiences, could not be mentioned. This one, from
a Jefferson City resident, falls into that category.

The family, a much extended one, had assembled in
Arpin, Wisconsin, for the funeral of Lynne Loschky's grand-
mother-in-law. After the services and a wonderful dinner, a
group of about twenty people packed themselves into a mod-
estly sized living room to see a slide show. Their hostess
wanted to share her recent trip to Germany. All the chairs in

the house being occupied, Lynne was among those sitting cross-legged on the floor.

As on any such occasion she was thinking, as we all do, of family members already gone from the circle. For her, memories of her late father-in-law, Lester, were especially poignant. Their rapport had been instant and had constantly deepened over the years of his life. She still grieved for him several years after his death at only 58. In Lynne's own words, here's what happened, along with the showing of pictures:

"To my delight, the show that Rene gave us was wonderful. She had chosen her slides with care, and had obviously practiced her narration. Within a couple of minutes, she had us under her spell. Somewhere during the early part of her presentation, I became aware that Lester was sitting right next to me. This seemed not a shocking or even a surprising event. Instead, it was as if I had been hypnotized into forgetting that he ever died. Like me, he was sitting with his legs crossed. His familiar silver-rimmed glasses were on his nose. His perpetual pen was in his shirt pocket. His standard grin took up most of his face. Together, throughout the slide show, we talked without speaking a word; I knew he was enjoying the pictures as much as I was.

"When at last the final slide was shown, Lester, observing me trying to get out of my sitting position, gave me his arm. Just as the lights were turned back on I, too, saw the light, emitted a loud cry and fled the room. I was aware for the first time that I had just spent the past half hour with the ghost of my beloved father-in-law."

Lynne concludes, "In a life full of wonderful memories, I have never again had anything so eerie yet fascinating happen to me. And the fear of death, in my case, is a thing of the past."

Whose else, that motion and that mein?
Whose else that airy tread?
For one strange moment I forgot,
My only love was dead.

— Amy Levy, in the
Mile's End Road

Ghosts
In a Row

Hannibal, Paris, Marceline, St. Joseph: four towns in an almost straight line across the state and each of them has one or more good ghost stories. St. Joseph's has been popular for decades among the most serious psychical investigators and Marceline's ghost has the almost unheard of distinction of supposedly killing people. Hannibal may be exclusive nationally, in staging a tour of its ghosts and haunted places.

Chapter Sixteen

This Town
Loves Its Ghosts

That affable, familiar ghost,
which nightly ....
gulls him with intelligence ...
— Shakespeare, *Sonnets*

In October of 1996, an organization called Hannibal Main Street held its first Ghostly Gala, a trolley-car tour of the town's oldest buildings and the sites of historic structures no longer standing. This tour included a review by Kirstin Hildahl-Dewey of Hannibal's traditional ghost stories and a few new ones invented just for the occasion.

From their seats, participants could look out and see embellishments of these tales. Included were a pale, period-dressed person hurrying across the street, a silhouetted figure in a lighted window, then two figures engaged in what appeared to be life and death struggle. This just-for-fun approach does not obscure the fact that Hannibal residents describe some unexplained and unexplainable manifestations.

Jerry Adkins operates a hardware store which apparently has a benign resident ghost. Whenever something goes wrong, employees say, "It's Percy again!" They're referring to Percy Haydon, the man who in 1919 established a hardware store in a building now incorporated into Adkins'. Haydon made a great success of his business by working hard, including night hours. He was much appreciated in the community for his wide selection of merchandise and his fairness with customers. Adkins says, "He was a little gruff on the surface, but actually very kind-hearted." Adkins remembers him as a heavy-set man "always chewing on a stogie."

The way Haydon demonstrates himself now, probably not deliberately, is by footsteps overhead in a loft where merchandise was and is stored, and, sometimes, footsteps on stairs to the ground floor. There also are occasional problems with the lights; they may turn themselves on again after being shut off, sometimes repeatedly in a short period of time.

The most striking event came one evening at closing time when Adkins and employee Jeanie Waters had locked doors and were doing final work with the cash registers. They were startled by a hearty sneeze very near them and at face level. Their first thought, Adkins says, was that despite their careful check, someone still had not left the store, though that of course would not explain why the sneeze seemed to be right beside them. They found nobody. The store has no cat, but Adkins says what they heard was much more than a cat sneeze.

Another time, another employee named Jeanie was checking doors in remote reaches of the store which actually is made up of three buildings, some from before the turn of the century. She returned upset, Adkins says, because someone, from very close to her whispered urgently: "Jeanie! Jeanie!"

Though Percy has never hurt anyone, it took Adkins awhile to get used to him. In his earliest encounter with the footfalls, Adkins assumed intruders were upstairs and called an employee to come with him to take a look. "You're going to think I'm crazy," he apologized when he phoned, but stairs to the loft are right by the office door where Adkins worked. "Nobody could have come up or down without my seeing them," he says. "I've never been one to believe in ghosts," he adds. "I'm not a superstitious person at all. That night, I honestly thought someone was in the store. Afterwards I didn't know what to think."

When the footsteps come down on the first floor, Adkins says he usually goes home. One night, however, from inside the rest room, he heard quite a lot of walking around, and thought an employee who had a key to the store was playing a joke on him. He decided to reverse the surprise and when the footsteps paused near the restroom door, Adkins — picturing someone looking around for him — slammed the door open suddenly, expecting to make that person take a gigantic jump. Nobody was there. No steps had gone away from the door. That was one of the nights when Adkins postponed his work for daytime hours.

Restorer's Hazards

Experiences of Jean and Scott Meyer, their employees and their partner, Jeff Trevathen, are not as mild as Adkins', though nobody has been hurt. This couple's business is River City Restorations, specializing in restoration of historic buildings. They have experienced a number of small mysteries, but the most memorable, Jean says, came one night when she was reading in bed upstairs, alone in their own home, then undergoing extensive renovation.

Suddenly she was shocked by two almost simultaneous crashes from the room right below her, very loud, heavy noises. She thought immediately of two massive pocket doors that had been taken from their niches for refinishing. They had been leaned up against a wall and Jean was horrified, imagining an intruder downstairs had blundered into them and been crushed. She phoned Scott to come home because she was afraid to go downstairs alone. Together they went through the whole house and found nothing amiss. The doors were just as they'd been left and no new tracks showed anywhere in plaster dust that coated most of the floors.

More than once, the Meyers have had employees who declined to work alone in the old houses, some saying they felt or heard something strange. The most remarkable story came from David Anderson, who says he went alone to the Ebert-Dulaney house one night after working hours to use some of the equipment for a home project of his own. Hearing a car stop outside and its door slam, he thought a friend had noticed his truck outside and stopped to visit. When the back door opened, he called out and then started to the hall to greet whomever it was and reassure him about the plywood that had been put across hall joists when flooring was taken up.

Before he could get there, Anderson heard the rumbling steps of someone walking across the plywood, but these sounds stopped just short of his own door. He found the hall empty, and there had been no retreating steps. There was no inside doorway nearby that an intruder could have stepped into for concealment. Looking out the back, Anderson saw a neighbor carrying in groceries which explained the car sounds, but there was no way that person could have entered the old house, walked the length of its hall and then got out so fast. Anderson says, "I put things away and went home."

The House on Maple Street

This is how Hannibal residents refer to an impressive antebellum house with an interesting history. The house is not considered haunted, exactly, just strange. Candace Klemann, who has visited there often, has experienced "something like a current of energy that affects some of the back rooms and the back yard." She says some people quickly leave these areas, saying they are nauseated or intensely apprehensive.

"I think it's something natural," Candace says, "Like earth energy or power rising from an underground stream, maybe something that somehow catches and holds emotions from the past."

Candace has an interest in the paranormal and has been present when sensitives tried to analyze the place. Though local history offers no details of tragedy, these people felt that the house has seen great fear and suffering, events witnessed by black people, though not necessarily directed at them. Klemann says the psychics described a group of men, soldiers, perhaps, out of control, drinking and doing destructive things, being abusive to women.

The house on Maple Street was occupied during the Civil War by a Commander Greene, who was in charge of some of the Union troops in the area. The strong Confederate sympathy around Hannibal probably made his family less than comfortable. It was rumored that he had something to do with the underground railway, supported by strong abolitionist sentiment in Quincy, Illinois, just across the river. Also, Mrs. Greene supposedly taught runaway slaves to read and write, and might also have given refuge to escapees using the underground railway. Did unpleasantness arise because of all this, maybe something life threatening or even fatal to the Greenes?

Connection to another part of the house's history might be suspected by the reaction of Klemenn's son-in-law when he was doing dry-wall work there. He decided not to work alone anymore because he had, first, a sensation of being watched with great interest, then the feeling that something determinedly wanted him to come upstairs. This pull was so strong that he was inclined to go, in spite of his fear, but he fled the house instead.

Though the young man knew nothing of it at the time, this upstairs emphasis could be related to a local story Klemann has heard. An elderly man spent his last months in an upstairs room, bedfast. He perhaps considered himself a prisoner, and he may have been, in some way. Probably no experience with the supernatural is more upsetting than the thought that from another dimension someone is pleading for help or trying to command us to perform some task left undone. Klemann speculates, "Maybe now that the house is happily occupied by a family, the ghosts can rest and release their hold on the premises."

Not Really Haunted

The beautiful 30-room mansion, Rockcliffe, is a mecca for all who visit Hannibal. Its owners say it does not actually have any ghost stories, though they concede that before restoration it certainly looked the part. Neighbors considered it haunted but never said specifically why.

A showplace in its prime, Rockcliffe was called one of the finest houses in the US, but it stood empty for 43 years on its hill overlooking the river. When I visited Rockcliffe twenty years ago, I asked a tour guide if it had ghosts. She laughed and said, "Maybe a protective spirit of some kind, for during its empty and unprotected time, it didn't get nearly as much vandalism and damage as it could have."

Some of Rockcliffe's remarkable features: Tiffany chandeliers and windows installed by the great artisan himself; many marble-hearthed fireplaces with hand-carved mantels; self-storing storm windows that drop down into the walls; a refrigerator room, with wooden-doored compartments enough to handle food for huge entertainments; a schoolroom with dais for the teacher's desk and a series of roll-down maps that still remain; balconies from which the original owner, John Cruikshank, could watch his lumber being shipped out by rail to go all over the nation.

Though the present caretaker, Mary McAvoy lives in the house, she says she has never seen, heard or felt anything unusual. Psychics who have visited Rockcliffe say they sense a discontented female presence, a safe guess, considering that many women worked at Rockcliffe as servants!

Mark Twain and Ghosts

We might hope, in Rockcliffe, to feel a little of Mark Twain's presence. Clemens is said to have stood on its gracious staircase before the large Tiffany window and addressed a group of 300 Hannibal people who came out to honor him. This was in 1902 when he visited his hometown, in his prime and at the height of his fame.

Clemens claimed not to believe in ghosts, and was even quoted by one of his biographers: "As you know, I'm not one of those spirit people." Yet his writings indicate a mind not totally closed on the subject, at least during part of his life.

Anyone who has read much by or about Clemens remembers from *Life on the Mississippi* his account of the vivid dream which not only foretold his brother Henry's death, but accurately revealed many details about it.

Though Clemens spent most of his life outside Missouri, he was born in the small town of Florida and grew up, to the age of 22, in Hannibal. Since he traveled a great deal, he may have never spent so many years in any other one place.

Clemens' writings immortalized Missouri. He is not only the state's most famous literary son, but many critics feel that time will decree his *Huckleberry Finn* to be the greatest American novel. Surely it's appropriate to include here Clemens' supernatural experiences.

Two of his essays have "mental telegraphy" in their titles and tell how frequently ESP seemed to work for the writer, with no effort on his part. He often received, in an unexpected way, he said, just the data he needed for research. Often he ran into someone in a most unlikely place, when he'd been trying to figure out how to get in touch with that person. Letters so regularly crossed in the mail for Clemens that he established the custom of just not mailing many of his, confident he'd not need to. He delighted in keeping his family apprised of how often this worked.

One of Clemens' experiences would be considered by psychical researchers as a perfect example of the Doppelganger (German for "double goer") Effect: a person appears to be in two places at the same time. Another explanation for the following story could be that Clemens saw the apparition of a living person or had an instant of seeing something before it happened.

Clemens wrote of being at a crowded reception preceding one of his readings and in the crowd seeing a friend from the past, a woman who lived at such a distance he would never have dreamed of seeing her that day. She was dressed attractively, as always, and he took special note of her outfit, hoping he could make his way to her before his performance started. He was not able to, but when he finished, she came up to shake his hand and ask if he remembered her. He told her

of seeing her earlier, and she said "Oh, no, I wasn't at the reception. I regretted missing it, but only got here in time to hear you." And there she stood in the dress and hat he'd so carefully studied earlier.

Clemens' most decisive experience came in Redding, Connecticut at Christmas time of 1909, less than a year before his death. His daughter, Jean, then in her young adulthood and the next to last remaining member of his family, died suddenly during an epileptic seizure. Clemens, ill himself, and in shock at his loss, was not able to accompany her body for burial in another city where her mother and sister lay. He stood in the window and watched her coffin taken away on a snowy night and then went into the bathroom where she had died. One of Clemens' biographers, Albert Bigelow Paine, says the writer described a vague notion of telling his daughter goodbye where her life had ended. Clemens said that in the room, always well-heated and cozy, he felt an abrupt cold current of air that chilled him badly. There was no place for a draft to enter and this one was only momentary. Clemens told Paine he considered it an acknowledgement from Jean.

In his autobiography's account of Jean's death, Clemens said that he intended to stay in the house, because he was sure he would feel her spirit there. He told of visiting another place, then empty and in poor repair, where he had lived earlier in deep happiness when his family was complete. He said, "... to me it was a holy place and beautiful. It seemed to me that the spirits of the dead were all around me and would have welcomed and spoken to me if they could."

They were very different women. One wore black and one wore white and one wore a frilly blouse and hair combs. But they have something in common; all proved to be of such lasting interest to psychic investigators that they are known of far beyond Missouri.

Chapter Seventeen

Memorable Ladies

What? And did the thing appear again tonight?
— Shakespeare, *Hamlet*

Paris: Tall in Black

The Paris ghost existed for some 70 years, according to annals of the occult. She first appeared, we're told, soon after the Civil War when most women in Monroe County and elsewhere over the whole U.S. wore the black of mourning and, as fashion decreed, brimmed, concealing bonnets, often with veils. Also, strangers were commonplace everywhere then, as people displaced by the war sought family members, and wives and parents traveled to battlefields, searching for the remains of loved ones.

First Paris resident on record for seeing the lady in black was a young mother, calling her children in for supper. She thought only that this was someone she didn't know, a woman noticeable because she was at least six feet tall. The next night, at about the same time, the same mother and her husband, together, saw the stranger, who shook her cane at them, apparently feeling they were staring rudely. The husband said something was wrong with the woman and they decided to keep their children closer to them.

Soon many Paris residents were talking of the lady in black and were pooling stories. She often brandished her cane at people, and some said she walked a little above the ground, which is why she seemed so tall. Some said that from a distance her face glowed behind the veil, others that she had brushed against them as she sped past in the dark, skirts rustling. Some claimed she had peered in their windows, so everyone began to close curtains and lock doors, few venturing out at night alone for the whole winter.

With spring the unwelcome woman in black no longer walked and everyone was relieved, but when fall came around again, she reappeared, and for many years this was her pattern. She never hurt anyone, but the sight of her was unsettling even to men who considered themselves brave.

The sightings stopped for good in 1934 when a 90-year-old resident died, a woman taller than average, but far from being six feet. She'd been abandoned by her lover at the age of 19 and had lived a bitter, solitary life thereafter. A journalist who lived in Paris for several years did most of the writing we have about this episode in the town's history, and he suggested that the rejected spinster was the frightening lady in black. He described her as "coarse and angular." Apparently it did not occur to him that the spectral figure might have been a man, or that in a small town, residents would have thought at once of the tall and eccentric woman they all knew. Perhaps her usual appearance and demeanor were so different from the ghost's that they could not imagine her going out to frighten people. In any case, this seems to truly be an unsolved mystery.

Marceline: Lethal in White

By heaven, I'll make a ghost of him that lets me!
— Shakespeare, *Hamlet*

In 1887 when Marceline was little more than a "stomped down cornfield," according to Clifford Funkhouser, a *Marceline Press* writer, the Santa Fe Railroad decided to build a division point there for routing trains to Chicago. This change brought many strangers together rather suddenly in a place unprepared — in such ways as law enforcement — for increased population. The Linn County town gained a reputation for roughness, for being a spot where, Funkhouser said, nobody thought much about it if someone died violently.

The story is that a certain railroad man killed a woman he'd been living with and also killed her baby, disposing of their bodies down a dry well. Old timers were sure that the bodies rested on the site where, in 1895, a cafe called "The Hole in the Wall" operated.

A woman named Marian Roberts worked there as cook for 20 years and she related strange events to Funkhouser. First, Roberts said, she met problems in getting employees to go into the cellar for supplies. Many left their jobs abruptly saying they heard a baby crying below, and a female voice pleading. Then came reports that a woman in a white dress sat there, glaring.

For awhile, nothing more than this happened, but in 1900, an engineer named Wise was preparing for unexpected duty, filling in for someone who could not work. The cafe's owner, Eva MacDonald, cooked him an early breakfast before the cafe opened for business, and they were talking in the kitchen as he ate. Suddenly, between them, the trap door to the cellar flew open and the woman in white stood there, pointing angrily at Wise. A waitress who had entered the room fainted, and Wise was so upset that he wired the railroad's roundhouse and asked to be relieved. He had to go, they told him; nobody else was available to take the train to Kansas City.

Less than an hour afterward, the train wrecked near Rothville and Wise was killed. About a year later, his brother had a similar experience, his death occurring in a wreck at Bosworth, twenty miles from Marceline. The next victim was a brakeman who saw the woman in white and before an hour had passed, died in a fall from the top of a boxcar on the Rothville Hill. The train did not wreck that time nor the next, when a trainman who had seen the apparition died on the ground, crushed between two cars.

In 1910 the ghost added something to her repertoire, or she was used as an excuse for murder. An engineer who told of meeting the woman in white left for his train anyhow, but came back into the cafe asking for help, saying the ghost had shot him. He had four bullets in his body, and in the 24 more hours he lived, insisted his assailant had been the woman in white.

That incident is much simpler than another recorded in the Marceline paper. An engineer named William Beach said he'd seen the woman in white, but successfully defied fate, he thought, making his run and returning home safely to Ft. Madison, Iowa. He went upstairs to take a bath and was found dead there with a bullet in his head. It had come through screen and window glass, angled down, from a position impossible from outdoors unless the shooter had been on a high ladder. Funkhouser wrote that the snow under the window was undisturbed, with no sign of tracks, human or ladder. Neither of these two murders was ever solved, at least when the newspaper stories appeared.

The last episode blamed on the woman in white was in 1917, when a brakeman named Fletcher made fun of the ghost and descended to the cafe basement, "to have a talk with that lady." He emerged pale and shaken, unwilling to discuss what he'd seen and eager to get out of the cafe. Later that night, however, possibly drinking with friends, he regained his spirits enough to promise to attend the train-men's New Year's Eve dance, "dead or alive." Enroute to Ft. Madison, he fell under a car and lost both his legs. He died in the hospital there at about 7 p.m. which is when his roommate in Marceline came rushing into the street declaring he'd seen Fletcher's ghost.

Soon after that the cafe burned and not much later, Mrs. Roberts died. Some who have tried to analyze this story suggest that she was an unknowing channel for activity of a spirit that was finally satisfied with the revenge it had taken and accepted the fire as being decent burial. Resentment on this score is, of course, considered one of the strong motivations for ghostly manifestations.

St. Joseph's
Famous Scratched Cheek

*I am willing to accept the possibility that the spirits of the
dead might try to communicate with the living, if there was an
urgent need or a strong commitment.*
> — speech of a character in Barbara Michael's novel,
> *Be Buried in the Rain.*

This remarkable happening must have been exceptionally well documented at the time, perhaps by many people's vouching for the honesty and stability of the family involved. Most serious reviews of credible paranormal events include this classic Missouri story.

A St. Louis man identified only by initials sat in a St. Joseph hotel room one sunny afternoon in 1876, smoking a cigar and happily recording orders from a successful sales trip. Gradually, he became aware that he was not alone, and looking up, found his younger sister seated beside him, one of her arms resting on the table.

The girl had died in a cholera epidemic nine years earlier, yet she looked natural and pretty, exactly as when he last saw her in life. Mr. F. G. said he felt nothing but joy at seeing his sister and greeted her lovingly. She smiled sweetly and disappeared before his eyes. The whole incident was so brief that it was over before ink had dried on his paper. Still, F. G. took in several details. The girl's blouse was familiar to him, as were her breastpin and hair combs. To his puzzlement, there was a slight scratch on her right cheek, near her nose.

The more he thought about all this, the more alarmed the man grew. How did her cheek get scratched? It had not been that way at her funeral. What did the visit mean? There had to be some purpose in her appearance. F. G. cut his business trip short and went home to tell his parents.

Upon hearing his account, his mother said she accidentally touched her daughter's face with a pin while preparing her body for burial. She concealed the mark with powder and mentioned it to nobody, not even her husband.

The mother died suddenly two weeks later and Frederic W. H. Myers, a noted psychical researcher, wrote this in his book, *The Human Personality and Its Survival of Bodily Death:* "A clear case of a spirit's feeling her mother's approaching death ... the son is brought home in time to see his mother once more, by perhaps the only means which would have succeeded. The mother can face the hereafter sustained, knowing that her daughter loves and awaits her."

🐦 St. Joseph has another ghost story that has made the books. The building which served as headquarters for the Pony Express is said to be haunted, presumably by the one young horseman who lost his life in the short existence of a daring undertaking. Riders were at such great risk from weather, injury, robbers and Indians that the operators of the system callously wrote "orphans preferred" in their recruitment ads.

Jerry Ellis, in his 1994 book, *Bareback*, described his own private retracing of the Pony Express trail. He said he made special arrangements to spend a night in the old depot, but aside from a hissing space heater that he at first thought might be a ghost, he heard and saw nothing.

🐦 After the first edition of *Missouri Ghosts* appeared, a fellow member of the Missouri Writers Guild sent me data that gives St. Joseph claim to being one of the most haunted towns in any state. It fills a chapter of *More Missouri Ghosts,* published in 2000.

Ghostin' Down the Border

Chapter Eighteen

Grave Dowsing

I think it's really not the method used, dowsing or tarot cards or whatever, but the person using them. I think if you have the talent, you use the medium suited to you that puts you in touch with that Other Dimension, that focuses you.
— Adele Graham in a letter

Two Cass County women were walking slowly around in separate parts of a country cemetery, each holding two pieces of wire, forearms horizontal from their waists, eyes intently forward, when a deputy sheriff stopped and asked what they were doing.

"We're dowsing for graves," they told him and explained that as volunteers for a local cemetery association, they were looking for unmarked burial spots. As happens often with these two, Brenda Marble and her sister, Debbi Lehr, had been asked to help locate the long-ago burial places of some people whose relatives wanted to find them and put up stones. The two women routinely locate such sites because the occult-sounding practice of grave dousing helps them not only to find graves, but to determine whether a buried person was male or female and, usually, their approximate age.

Like most, the deputy was extremely skeptical, so the women showed him how to do what they were doing. Despite his holding the wire wands tightly and resisting their movements, the procedure worked well enough for him that Brenda says he departed saying, "This didn't happen! This just didn't happen. I'm not telling anyone back at the office about this!"

The tools Brenda and Debbie use are made from coat hangers cut off just before the twist and carefully straightened out as much as possible. Three or four inches of each straightened out hanger is turned at a right angle to make a handle. When carried at waist level, as Brenda suggests, arms parallel to the ground, the ends of the wires will seek each other and cross when the dowser is over a grave. They uncross when the dowser steps off the grave.

Brenda's most dramatic proof of success came in an assignment in the summer of 2000 from a funeral home which suspected the location of three unmarked and unrecorded graves and wanted to be sure. Brenda quickly located them, and told the gender of each buried person, genders confirmed by the family involved. They were skeptical enough to ask the funeral home to dig down far enough to confirm, and they did. Two wooden coffins were found exactly where Brenda's dowsing rods had indicated, and the third site was then accepted as accurate.

So what is all this? Most of us know that dowsing is an age-old art or skill or talent, referred to throughout recorded history, with many instances described. But we associate it exclusively with locating water and minerals. To a much smaller degree, dowsers have claimed to be able to locate lost items and veins of precious metal. Until the last few years we heard little about dowsing for graves, but Brenda's research shows this is part of the art's long history. There has just been much more demand for the other kinds of dowsing.

In earlier times, good supplies of water were essential for travelers and pioneers. A person who could by dowsing or "witching" locate underground sources of water was highly valued, even though he or she might be looked on with awe bordering on fear. Successful dowsers were often suspected of obtaining their talent by "unnatural" means. Even today, many people consider dowsing a practice of witchcraft, but Brenda says she is certainly not a witch and doesn't know a dowser who follows anything but conventional religion. She herself is an active church member, as are all her family.

"This is just, like so many other things, beyond our understanding at the moment," she says. "Some law of nature is at work here and we are fortunate that dowsing was discovered and passed down all these centuries, just as we're fortunate we somehow learned to use electricity without understanding everything about it." Brenda feels that as breakthroughs of knowledge continue, much that is today considered "occult" and probably unwholesome, will eventually be understood and used freely to enhance our lives.

It may surprise many readers to know that there are so many dowsers in the United States that a national organization exists for them, and has existed for 40 years. It is called The American Society of Dowsers, Inc. and its headquarters are in Danville, VT. It currently has almost 4500 members. This organization holds annual meetings and publishes material of use and interest to dowsers.

ASD was mentioned in *Ozarks Mountaineer* magazine, in Fall of 1997, in a substantial article on the subject of dowsing as an Ozarks tradition. The author, Radine Trees Nehring, described her own experience when a dowser gave her a forked branch from a peach tree and showed her how to hold it. "Thumbs up and out," she said, "fingers folded toward me. I gripped the forked ends of the branch so tightly my knuckles turned white." As she began walking toward a known vein of water, she said the branch turned downward, as strongly, "as if a rope tugged it," and she concluded, "It isn't the kind of experience one forgets."

The OM illustrations for this article showed dowsers working in different ways. One woman held her dowsing rod at shoulder level, at arms' length, palms of her hands down, her face serene as she walked along. One man held his with palms up and elbows bent, the rod at chest level. His expression suggested that he was having trouble holding on, as his small tree branch strained forward.

Among the society's statements, which OM quoted and with which Brenda agrees completely: every human is born with the ability to dowse and most children exhibit easy sensitivity until their mid-teens. Approximately 12 out of every 100 adults retain this sensitivity and most others can recall it through receptiveness and practice. ASD holds classes in dowsing and the success rate among pupils backs up their stats. Brenda says that 90% of the people she has coached in this skill have been able to do it.

More about the equipment and technique? Though Brenda and many others use wire, dowsing rods are now being manufactured from many materials, including plastic. Rods are available with costly ornate handles and carrying cases, a far cry from the traditional dowsing tool, a branch of very flexible wood such as peach or willow. This original tool is held by the ends of the two branches and the thicker center section then moves in response to the nearness of water. The severed branch, one might almost think, is seeking water for its own preservation, and that is no more far-fetched than the common miracle of tree roots physically searching in darkness through the soil for water and making themselves longer and longer so they can reach it. Could we say, then, that trees are dowsing? They apparently know exactly where to send their newly forming roots.

In a book called *Learning the Art of Dowsing — Divining,* Thomas J. Milliren wrote that dowsing might be considered a collaboration between the conscious and subconscious parts of our minds. This seems to mean that as in most of our quests, the conscious mind says "We need ...." and the subconscious mind compiles data and performs experiments until it can say "OK, here it is."

A few of Brenda's answers to our questions:

Do you prepare in any way for dowsing, like do you pray or ask for any kind of protection as some ghost hunters say they do?

"I often pray afterwards when I've been successful. One of my most satisfying assignments was searching for the unmarked grave of a baby who was born unexpectedly as its parents traveled. Because of the mother's serious condition, and need to be taken to a hospital elsewhere, they never were able to visit the burial spot or to know exactly where it was. With spotty data from people who knew a little about where others had buried the child, I was able to find it.

"When I saw what it meant to that mother to be able to mark her baby's grave, I was just very humbly grateful to God for giving me an opportunity to be of help."

By contrast, one of Brenda's most intriguing cases probably will never be openly recognized. As part of a psychic investigation team's visit to a troubled rural household, Brenda's dowsing indicated that the very old structure was surrounded by almost 150 unmarked graves. These were arranged in an orderly way and almost all of them held males. Nobody in any era would deliberately build a house in a graveyard, but history of this place was not well known. Because the graves are farther apart than in most cemeteries, Brenda guessed this is a military cemetery, where many graves had to be prepared in a short time, requiring teams of diggers who worked standing back to back and thus needed more room than in a situation where people are buried one by one, over a period of time.

Subsequent research revealed that a Civil War battle or two had been fought nearby and that Union soldiers had been encamped — possibly on the very property — while, among other actions, enforcing the infamous Order Number ll in October of 1863. Brenda reasons that the house could have been used as a military hospital or morgue while its owners were in exile. Possibly the owners never were able to come back, or perhaps no trace of the mass burials remained a few years later, when the place could be occupied again. Or it could be that some family was so desperate to resume their life that they gladly accepted living in a cemetery. The possibility for speculation here is endless, but Brenda feels the subject is best left alone for the peace of those living in the house. Appendix C explains Order No. 11.

How do you tell if the person in a grave is old or young, male or female?

Brenda says the wires cross when she is over a grave. By going backward or forward until they uncross, she can tell where the person's head and feet are and thus determine approximate size. The number of steps it takes before the wires uncross tell her whether the body below belonged to an infant, a toddler, an older child or a young teen. There can, of course, be uncertainty about small adults. She explains that each dowser has to determine the length of his or her steps.

"Gender," Brenda says, "is determined in one of two ways, and I usually use both as a double check. If I balance one wire on one extended finger, it will move clockwise for a male and counter clockwise for a female. Or, I can hold one wire up above my head, horizontal to the ground, and it will dip at the head for a female, at the feet for a man."

Can you find cremated remains?

"Not if they've been scattered."

How long does it take to get good at this?

"I think that depends on how much you practice. You should go where there are marked graves and try, being careful not to look at dates on the tombstones until you have seen what you can get. You need to do a lot of this. You can also practice on living people; the wires act just the same." Some say that dowsing rods are reacting to disturbed soil, some to gasses emitted by decaying bodies. Brenda believes, because rods react as they do to living people, it's a matter of magnetism, that perhaps death does not completely destroy this elemental of life.

Did nothing scary ever happen to you in relation to this?

Brenda tells of one time when she was helping to mark some graves where a trench had been dug down three feet and she was standing in it, within two feet of the contents of a marked-off grave. "My wands reacted very strongly. While I was measuring the grave, they swung around behind me and I could not pull them back. Another time, in the same place, they came up and wrapped around my neck. I felt this was an act of anger. I don't know if it was because the graves had been disturbed or because something was upset about being under a parking lot. There was unpleasant emotion at that site because the graves had been discovered in a place where it would be inconvenient and expensive to move them. I was very much resented for having brought the bad news that the graves were there. Greed was behind all this and usually is, when people disregard the sacredness of a cemetery, I always wonder how they think it will be when they get on the other side and meet the spirits of those they have dishonored."

Here's one last experience of Brenda's told in her own words.

"We did an investigation recently where my dowsing proved beneficial to ghost research A friend purchased some repossessed land that has a house on it. He had heard for years that the place was haunted and asked us to do an investigation before he destroyed anything. It was known through genealogy that the original homesteaders' family cemetery had once been located on the land, but no one knew exactly where. Before selling outside the family, they moved their direct ancestors to an established city cemetery, leaving all other bodies behind. I believe that family cemetery had also been used by neighbors and perhaps for slave burials. I decided to dowse the portion of the five acres my friend had bought. Sure enough, there they were. The existing house had been built right among between 55 and 68 graves.

"I am speculating that sometime before the house was built, some owner of the land razed the cemetery and did not tell the buyers that it had ever been there. I think this unfortunately happens more than we know. People are hesitant to buy land that has a grave yard on it and some sellers are more concerned about the dollar than the sacredness of a cemetery. I really don't think the spirits mind someone living beside their resting places, but I do think they are upset to have a home built upon them.

"Anyway, throughout the years, according to stories passed down by various owners, that particular home had considerable paranormal activity. Most instances were pretty commonplace, such as items being knocked off tables, lights coming on and off and the TV turning itself on and off. Someone living there in the 1970s had claimed to see a misty white blob. In the summer of 2000 the historical society received a request for history of the house because the tenants then were hearing a man's voice and growling noises. It was this family's hurried departure, abandoning a lot of belongings, that resulted in the property's being repossessed. My friend and his wife decided to tear down the existing house and build their own home elsewhere on the property."

The method by which people travel through the fabric of time is not for us to understand. We have no business delving into this.

— Mary Kilbourn in a 2001 letter to *The Centralia Fireside Guard*

Souls are not bound by time in the same way that living bodies are ... they are able to exist in what we would understand as two places at once. Also, a soul can move either forward or backward in time ... in addition, there is what we might call sideways motion ....

— Kirsten Bakis, in her novel, *Lives of the Monster Dogs*

A famous physicist whose name I can't remember — so is he that famous? said that there is no past, present or future, it's all happening now. So maybe someday we'll be able to pass among it all. I don't feel bad about not understanding, because the guys who proposed it don't either.

— Adele Graham in a letter

Chapter Nineteen

Dowsing the Past

The point is that our time does not exist
to the sixth sense. Forward of backward
make no difference. In the sixth sense's
world, there is only the eternal "now."
　　　　　　　　　— T.C. Lethbridge.

On the Missouri border opposite and north of Brenda Marble's home, lives another dowser whose findings are as interesting as hers, though very different. Chester Clark, from the small town of Nelsonville, in Marion County, was pictured in a spring, 2001, issue of *Missouri Life* magazine with a short story about his search for a certain stagecoach inn near Palmyra. Using metal wands or rods, similar to Marble's, Clark seeks to verify the sites of vanished buildings, of trails and military campsites.

Like Marble, Clark uses wands of his own making. His material is baling or coat hanger wire, with the same type of right angle bend Brenda makes to provide a handle on one end of each wand.

Clark's quest near Palmyra is fascinating because the land's owner knows the building stood on his property a century or so ago, but has no idea of its exact location. Not a trace remains of its foundation and intrigue is increased because no road now comes close to the area where the owner believes a good-sized building stood. Any stagecoach inn would necessarily be on the edge of a much-used road.

Here's how ML described Clark's work: as he walked along, the ends of the two wands, held out parallel before him, sometimes crossed and uncrossed, and when this happened his fellow dowser, Bob Fuqua, planted a flag. Observers could soon see a rectangle taking form on the soil. Clark says that he "senses" some details about what he is seeking, but he gives these no great weight until he can confirm by research that each impression is correct. Clark speculates that the stage coach inn's foundation could be under ground, farther than one might expect. There is nothing supernatural about this idea; the field has been under cultivation for many years. On the other hand, the foundation, as such, may never have existed. The building might have rested on large rocks, strategically placed. Or a solid foundation could have been deliberately broken up and moved from the field, pieces perhaps hauled some distance away to be used in other construction.

Clark came to dowsing by an unusual route. As a young person he had been interested in it and tried the standard forked peach tree branch. Having almost no success, he gave up the idea and spent a busy life as electronics engineer. About 25 years ago, he established a plumbing and wiring service and a man who worked with him once used dowsing to locate the pipes they needed.

Clark, thoroughly scientific in his outlooks by that time, laughed at these efforts until he saw that they worked. One evening after the man left, Clark tried the wands in an area where he knew pipes existed and to his surprise found that the tools worked for him, very well. He experimented with other types of dowsing, with enough success that it occurred to him to try to find lost sites of buildings and of activity pertaining to the Civil War era, one of his strongest interests.

"It is sort of shocking," he agrees, when people spontaneously say something like "You're one step from time travel!" and "If you find these sites, aren't you afraid you'll find the people who were there? Are you worried about what doors you may open?" Clark will deal with that if it happens, but meanwhile he's just enjoying seeking information of interest to him. Many Civil War buffs appreciate his efforts and tell him of sites they'd like to see him dowse.

Finding artifacts has not been a big part of Clark's agenda, but of course if others find them where he's dowsed, he'll welcome the confirmation of his work. "I've not been on an archeological dig," he says. "I hope to do that this summer. I hope we can dig at Palmyra and see if we find any foundation down there."

Clark doesn't buy very far into the usual material about the supernatural. "I have an open mind," he says, "But I'm careful what goes into it." He does admit, however, that sometimes revelations about the sites he's seeking come to him, hours or days removed from the dowsing.

"I'm not sure but what there's some source of information, some type of knowing that we don't understand fully yet," Clark says. "The universe is created in a wondrous way and we've not yet discovered all of it."

Has dowsing for the past changed Clarence Clark? "Oh, yes, the realization that the universe may include a automatic memory system which includes universal consciousness ... this realization has really changed my perspective and increased my desire to understand how it could all be possible."

Times goes, you say?
Oh no! Alas!
Time stays. We go.
Anonymous

Ghosts and ghost stories
have existed through the ages,
and they are present
in every culture
and every society.

— *Lester Golden, psychologist*

Chapter Twenty

A'Ghosting
We Will Go

If ghosts are anywhere,
they must be everywhere.
— Sue Gerard, Missouri author

Ask the Web to show you ghost hunters and you'll be overwhelmed with choices. You'll even find a firm called Rent-A-Ghost, which presumably provides ghostly effects on request. Ask just for Missouri Ghost Hunters and you'll still have several to choose from. Over the years, many Missourians have made dedicated efforts to find out more about the paranormal. They have worked in different ways and for different purposes. For instance, the main focus of The St. Louis Psi Squad, founded by Bevy and Ray Jaegers, has been to help people extend their own senses and abilities in order to live more fully, but they also have often given law enforcers substantial assistance. Another St. Louis-based group, known as PROBE, was the first, or one of the first, to use high-tech cameras, sound and heat-sensing equipment to try to establish the existence of unseen forces and beings. Currently several Missouri groups offer Web sites.

One of the most interesting and unusual of these is Missouri Ghost Hunters Society, headed by Brian and Linda Lile of Butler, in Bates County. Its Web site has won 20 awards for excellence among its counterparts, and MGHS has also been featured on television. The Liles became full-time psychical investigators in 1997, when Brian retired because of work related injuries. They "went public" that same year, taking on team members and offering their services to people who requested aid.

This group is surprising for the religious background — Assembly of God — of its founders, and for Brian's occupational background, two decades in law enforcement. Their church is one of the most conservative and most adherent to Biblical teachings, and Brian's having been a lawman deepens his drive to work in a realistic way. It gives him no patience with anyone who would use the paranormal to take advantage of others, as is a common practice among some fortune tellers: "Oh, I see terrible danger all around you! Visit me three times a week and give me extra money to buy special protective candles and I can keep you safe!"

The Liles characterize themselves as "God-fearing people with belief in the Bible and in following God's rules. We do not practice witchcraft or black magic or worship evil and would never support those who do." Linda's interest stems partly from having lived, as a child, in houses that were said to be haunted.

The couple feel no conflict between their religious beliefs and their fascination with what many churches strongly reject as "the occult." As their Web site points out, the Bible gives a number of accepting references to ghosts. One came from Jesus himself, when his friends recoiled from him after the resurrection, "terrified and affrighted, and supposed they had seen a spirit." He invited them to touch him and said (King James version, Luke 24:38-40): "A spirit hath not flesh and bones as ye see me have." Another reference is to Jesus' walking on water, when the disciples "supposed it had been a spirit and cried out" (Matthew 14:48-50, Mark 6:48-50).

So what statement of purpose comes from all this?

"Our mission is to prove that there is life after death, to gather evidence and to investigate that evidence in a scientific manner. We yearn to understand the so-called paranormal and to know exactly what happens after the soul leaves the body." Among other stated purposes: "We strive hard to help the public understand that ghosts are not what you see on television ... we want to assist, in whatever way we can, people who request help because they are troubled in their home or work place by what they feel is supernatural activity ... we are dedicated to the history of our country and to helping preserve historic sites, cemeteries and battlefields."

Among the public education offerings of the much-awarded Web site is entry to many other such sites and a forum where visitors can compare experiences. The Liles also give basic, classic ghost-hunting admonitions, similar to those of many other psychic investigators; essence of their advice:

🐦 Don't experiment with seances and ouija boards; these can be portals for evil spirits.

🐦 Remember that there are always physical dangers when you are out at night in abandoned buildings, things as mundane as rotten flooring and unstable stairs. There may be squatters, human or animal, who will resent your presence. Outdoors, there may be bad footing, unseen obstacles, animals or plants that are dangerous when blundered into. In either setting be prepared for property owners or police to approach you.

🐦 Wherever you go, be sure not to disregard trespassing signs and be sure to leave behind you no added damage to the premises, and no debris. It could even be a good idea to gather up and take away some of the trash others may have left.

🐦 Always take plenty of fresh batteries for all your equipment.

🕯 Never go out ghost hunting alone. Take at least one and preferably two or three companions. Be sure somebody else knows where you are going and when you expect to be home and if you don't phone at that time, to send help.

The Missouri Ghost Hunters Web site (ghosthaunting. com) includes a series of very appealing photographs with unusual content; Brian then explains what happened, either inside the camera or from outside lighting, to produce the sort of effect that psychic investigators constantly offer as proof of having met a visible ghost. Investigators may sincerely believe in their pictures, but these are quite unconvincing to most viewers and can cause people to disbelieve everything else an investigator might say. MGHS does them a favor to point that out.

Another offering of the MGHS Web site is surveys that gather and share public opinion about the paranormal. Though some of these polls have relatively few respondents, they still show trends. For instance, one recent finding was that 62% of respondents believed in portal haunts, and 62% believed that orbs (luminous round spots that appear in some investigators' pictures) are souls of the once living. As to whether or not a ghost can harm anyone, 38% believed this depends on the kind of spirit energy present, 22% believed with no reservations that ghosts can be physically dangerous and 22% believed that in some circumstances they can be. Only 3% felt confident that ghosts present no risk at all.

The part of the MGHS Web site that most visitors will read most avidly is the forum where ghost tales are exchanged by visitors. Many stories are from outstate, but a couple of Missouri's are unique and memorable. One is about a farm house in Monroe County which had, among its odd qualities, a door that sometimes opened, knob turning of its own volition when someone reached out toward it. Another Show Me tale was of a Kansas City cat, ordinarily cuddly and quiet, who occasionally seemed to go insane with fear of something only she could see. A few people, however, said they sensed a dangerous presence in the room where the cat's uncharacteristic behavior occurred.

The part of the Web site contributed by the Liles themselves will disappoint many because, as Brian says, they are not out to entertain. The supposed symptoms and causes of hauntings — the human interest that folklore is made of — get only a few lines in their reports; the bulk of space is taken up with careful recording of weather conditions, the equipment used and where it was placed, and, sometimes, sensations of the investigators.

Their six-page report on two visits to one Cass County cemetery is an example. This spot was reputed to be a portal, a place which allows passage into our world by beings from elsewhere. Strange odors, wisps of mist or smoke and even unusual animals have been described by other portal investigators; some claim that snatches of music or human voices mean a portal is open. Many investigators feel they have captured such effects. The Liles felt their photographs indicated some activity, and Linda experienced a difficulty in moving her legs that alarmed her enough to demand to go home.

It's easy to understand the interest in portals that so many investigators take, right now. Humankind has for centuries wondered whether places exist which permit spirits to enter our world and into which we might fall. There are several stories, supposedly documented convincingly at the time, of people who disappeared from view, but could be heard for hours or days pleading for help from behind an obviously nearby but invisible and impassible barrier.

The belief in portals apparently is tied to part of the ancient Celtic celebration of a new year, the time when household fires were replenished, and souls of the dead were thought to be able to visit their families and former homes. Special offerings were made at that time to honor the returned spirits and, in case they harbored any ill will toward their survivors, to placate them. Here's a charming poem by Katharine Tynban Hinkson, called "All Souls" which describes that night:

The door of Heaven is on the latch
Tonight and many a one is fain
To go home for a one night's watch
With his love again ...
They sit down and they stay awhile,
Kisses and comfort none shall lack;
At morn they steal forth with a smile
And a long look back.

The November Christian celebration of All Hallows, when departed saints were honored, grew to incorporate some of the earlier festival of Samhain or Samain (pronounced Sow'in) in order to attract Britain's native people to Christianity. Church officials delegated the most popular features of Samain to the night before their own celebration, All Hallows Evening, or Halloween. These practices included wearing costumes and masks to mislead any ghosts who might be seeking vengeance. Samhain traditions involved, as well, certain foods and games. Until the past few decades the holiday was spelled Hallowe'en, the apostrophe indicating that part of "evening" had been left out. This conforms to pronunciation of earlier times and it simplifies what would otherwise have had the cumbersome title of "the night before the All Hallows celebration."

In the matter of portals, the Liles have gathered evidence they consider valid, but they are far from satisfied with their work. They realize that what convinces them will not convince skeptics; ever more conclusive evidence must be found for the existence of unbodied intelligence. The Liles know that any kind of investigation requires a great deal of time and patience. Their tentative conclusions may not be accepted until the same type of evidence is collected by many different people.

The Liles realize, too, that some disappointment is inevitable. For instance, Brian and Linda and a few members of their team took the time and trouble to visit the Joplin area where the world-famous "spook light" is said to appear almost every night. They spent about eight hours there and nothing happened, though many of the people who shared their vigil insisted that the lights appear reliably and that they, themselves, see them often.

The trip was not a total waste, however, because the Liles were able to correct for others inaccurate Internet directions for finding the place. And they noticed one thing that could have bearing for all future seekers of the spook light: ditches in the area are full of debris left by crowds that assemble there nightly. Brian suggested not only that visitors refrain from adding to this problem but that they take a few garbage bags when they visit the spook light and gather up all the trash they can and take it away.

Brian said that people living near the scene told him how much they resent the littering and how much they wish the road would be closed to everything but through traffic. He warns that if enough people whose homes are near the road feel this way, we might all lose the privilege of witnessing something incredible. This is the kind of practical insight that is essential to continued psychical investigating, yet one seldom sees such topics approached by those in the field.

But apart from all the problems investigators face and despite what they may find that will be rejected in annals of the so-called supernatural, the Liles believe their quest is worthwhile. They believe purpose and truth exists behind what is, by most people today, still dismissed and derided. They feel that it is essential for us to try to understand, and then to use new findings in a positive way.

Here and There

Not all stories fit neatly into a category and it's not possible to have enough chapters to accommodate them all; others, by location, fit into no existing chapter. So here, organized a bit differently from the rest of the book, are some we might call miscellaneous except for the fact that they include some of our most interesting.

Chapter Twenty One

And Everywhere

Aurora's harbinger; at whose approach,
ghosts wandering here and there
troop home to churchyards.
— Shakespeare, *A Midsummer Night's Dream.*

In Maries County

Two stories from Maries County, near Vienna, one very old and the other, fairly recent, told to me by people who experienced it:

The oldest story stars an elderly man who never had subscribed to any religious belief. This made him the favorite target of a certain circuit rider (preacher who went from church to church by horseback on a regular schedule) who felt obliged to save the soul of every non-believer. The old farmer always tried to be polite, but finally lost patience with the persistent minister and said, "I'll tell you what. If you can prove to me that there's any form of life after death, I'll be baptized." This not only quieted the evangelist for the moment; he never came back. The farmer and his wife congratulated themselves on being rid of a nuisance until the community eventually learned that the preacher had died. Then the couple felt a bit guilty.

One evening as the elderly couple sat on their porch at dusk, the preacher came riding up the lane, wearing his usual wide-brimmed hat. His satchel, as always, flapped from the saddle horn. "They were wrong about him dying," the wife said. The minister dismounted and stood at the gate, as if ready to raise a loop of wire holding it shut. Then, instead, he just looked at the couple with a big, triumphant smile and turned back to his horse. Man and animal gradually faded to invisibility. The story teller did not know whether the aged agnostic went to church as a result of this visit.

The other Vienna story concerned a house that had belonged to a couple named Gib and Hettie Helton. Gib was a fiddle player and passersby were accustomed to hearing his music. A number of them claimed they still heard it, throughout the many years his widow lived there alone.

These reports did not disturb a young man named John Malone, who bought the old house, four rooms, two-over-two, with a lean-to kitchen. Preparing to marry, he reworked the house extensively, enlarging it and, among other things, he replaced the steep, narrow corner staircase with a wider one more conveniently located.

While working on the house, Malone lived in it, and told his family of hearing a number of inexplicable sounds from upstairs. Nothing seemed menacing, but despite repeated investigations, he still found no causes. What he heard most often was the latch working on the now non-existent staircase door, and the sound of footsteps going up or coming down.

"It's old Hettie going off to bed," he would laugh to his bride, Kathryn, when she came to share the house with him. Kathryn Malone, who now lives in Jefferson City, says she never heard that particular sound. She heard a few others, but nothing that seemed dangerous to her or their three daughters. The girls, sleeping dorm style in a big upstairs room, related a few puzzling little happenings. Once it was covers rising up on a bed. Once it was what the girls said "looked like a pillowslip floating around." Once it was an old man who spoke to them. The only adult who felt alarmed there was Lois Malone, John's mother. She said she dreaded baby sitting in the house because it had sounds "like someone throwing boxes around upstairs."

The couple lived in the seemingly haunted house without mishap until their family was reared, Mrs. Malone's father having spent his last days and dying there, too. After a number of years with other owners, the house burned.

A Sinister Hill

Knob Noster's curiosity is best reviewed in *Haunted Heartland* which devotes a long story to the fearsome stranger who came to the area well before the Civil War and lived like a hermit up on "the knob," the hill from which the town gets its name. When he visited the stores for supplies, he spoke no unnecessary words and seldom looked anyone in the face. Something about him frightened almost everyone. Children needed no urging to keep their distance.

Surprisingly, this man had a slave who was very pleasant and friendly and — to the town's relief — usually did the hermit's trading and errands. People commented that they felt sorry for anyone who was slave to such a person as the hermit and when the black man stopped coming, wondered if his owner had done him in. When the old man resumed his own shopping, someone became bold enough to ask what happened to his nice servant. He didn't answer and after that appeared less and less often. At last people were sure he had died or moved away.

Then came a summer of drought so terrible nobody cold think of much else. The damage to crops and livestock hurt the community beyond anything anyone had ever seen. When relief finally came, it was through an equally remarkable storm. Nobody could remember such torrents of rain, such terrifying thunder and lightning. Only a few had even the nerve to look out their windows at it, but some who did reported seeing, between the blasts of lightning, a dim, swinging light, like a lantern, slowly descending the knob. "It's the old hermit," they told each other, "Maybe his house got struck or maybe he just got too scared to stay alone."

After one especially close and long-lasting barrage of thunder, the observers looked out again and saw no little light. Had their unpopular old neighbor been hit by lightning?

Next day a few men ventured up the hill, and writers Beth Scott and Michael Norman say they found the unloved fellow dead, with no sign of being injured in any way. Yet his face, the story says was "so contorted with fear that everyone staggered back in horror." After that, on stormy nights, residents of Knob Noster declared they could see a faint, swinging light during pauses between lightning flashes.

A Vengeful Wife

Angry spouses are rather common in ghost stories, but Missouri has one with a unique twist. *Haunted Heartland* used a Kirksville story that began in 1873 with the death by consumption of a woman named Harriet Burchard. She had been a most possessive wife, considering her husband so attractive he could hardly be risked out of her sight. Burchard accepted this with flattered amusement and never gave her any cause to distrust him. Everyone said he was kind and attentive through her illness.

However, he waited only five months before marrying again. He chose a younger and prettier wife named Catherine. One day, about three weeks after the wedding, when Catherine was home alone, she was terrified to hear what sounded like a rain of large rocks on the roof. A look outside proved it to be just that; the yard and roof were cluttered with rocks large enough to do damage where they fell. When they began to rise up for another onslaught, she ran back into the house and cowered until Burchard returned. His inspection showed no unusual number of rocks on the property, and he teased her a little about her fears.

A night or two later, though, Burchard was aroused from sleep by the bedcovers being roughly snatched off him and thrown on the floor. It could not have been Catherine kicking in her sleep since she lay beside him as peaceful as an angel.

No draft could possibly have lifted so many quilts. He reorganized the bed, tucking everything in firmly at sides and bottom.

Just when he was almost asleep, Burchard's pillow was yanked from beneath his head. Quite sure now that Catherine was doing this to get even with him for disbelieving her rock story, he stood staring at her intently, for some sign she was actually awake. Thus, he got to witness her pillow being pulled away so rudely that she awoke screaming.

These attacks became routine with Burchard, who, predictably, became an insomniac. He was thankful that Catherine slept through everything after that first night. Finally, one event removed any doubt as to who the spirit was. While Burchard was reading in bed, the covers rolled slowly away from him as if by human hands, and on the sheet in front of him appeared a message. "These things will continue forever." The handwriting was that of his deceased wife, Harriet.

Turn That Music Down!

Here's an unusual story from Harold Eastman, a native of Iowa who taught at the College of the Ozarks for many years and now lives at Lenoir Village, a retirement community in Columbia.

Eastman told how he grew up next door to a family that included his future wife, Ruth Poe, and her brother Clyde. After growing up together as close friends, the two young men went into military service for World War II. Clyde died in action and at the first opportunity Harold went to visit his friend's parents.

After the exchanges usual for such a situation, they told Harold they'd been having a problem with Clyde's phonograph. "He's been gone for more than a year," said Mrs. Poe, "but it still plays almost every night. We must be doing something wrong when we turn it off. Would you come and show me how to operate it properly? We don't want to give it away or anything, for he loved it so, and there's always the chance ...."

Harold remembered the phonograph well. It was, when Clyde got it, the great status symbol of teenagers, and the lucky owner delighted in playing jazz records day and night. His parents did not share his taste in music and there had been the same conflict about volume that is so well known in today's homes.

Harold and Mrs. Poe went upstairs to Clyde's perfectly maintained room and Harold carefully showed her how each control worked. She said she had, then, apparently been doing all that could be done to turn the record player off. She had even been taking the disk from the turntable and laying it aside. How could a wind-up machine be playing by itself? Eastman could not offer a clue, so he advised them to pack the phonograph away or dispose of it. He knew Clyde would not want them to be so worried. Mrs. Poe repeated that they wanted to keep their son's treasure. Eastman never forgot the incident, though the Poes sold the house and moved away not long after.

A number of years later, Ruth Poe and Eastman, married, with three children, were visiting his own parents, who still lived beside the Poes' former home. Their oldest son, who had heard about the spooky record player, went to visit the house next door and with all the tact a teenager could muster, asked them if there was anything about the house they didn't like. They said they often heard footsteps overhead, and bits of music and conversation, but they didn't use the upstairs except for guests, so it didn't bother them.

"Stop now. Believe this," Eastman concluded in writing about his experience. "This is a totally true story. It is not a fabrication for entertainment."

Justice on Back Order

The book *Historic Haunted America,* by the same team who did the *Haunted Heartland* books, Norman and Scott, tells of a peddler named Samuel Moritz who stopped regularly in Laclede County, the Lebanon area, in years just before the Civil War. One time, when his pack was almost empty and he was heading home, Moritz arranged to spend the night with a farmer named Baker. Traveling in the dark would, of course, be foolish for a peddler who had obviously sold all his wares and would be carrying a tidy sum of money. Nobody thought anything about not seeing Moritz again, assuming he'd just gone on his way the next morning, and had found a more profitable route for subsequent selling trips.

A few years later, however, on a moonlight night, a local minister named Cummings was driving home in his buggy when he crossed a certain bridge and was surprised to see a man with a pack and a sturdy walking stick. The man was peering about anxiously, one version of this story being that he was under the bridge.

Cummings stopped and offered a ride. The man did not answer, but looked at him and pointed more emphatically with his stick. Thinking the peddler might be deaf, the pastor climbed from his buggy and leaned down to speak louder, but the man moved out of sight. Then the minister's reliable old horse unaccountably began to plunge about, obviously badly spooked. By the time he was under control, the stranger had completely vanished. Yet when Cummings looked back, the man had resumed his position, pointing under the bridge, though there was nobody there to see him.

This incident troubled the minister all night and next day he told a neighbor about it. Fearing the man he'd seen had been mute and was trying to point out someone in trouble, the two went to the bridge and there found farmer Baker hanged from one of the supports. As they clambered around on the muddy bank, trying to get him down, they dislodged a great deal of soil and rock and to their horror, found human remains had been buried there. Some clothing was left, or possibly the peddler's pack; they recognized Moritz.

The question then became whether the peddler had haunted Baker all that time, perhaps driving him to dig into the bank and make sure the body was still there, or whether conscience had just preyed on Baker until he went and killed himself at the scene of his crime. In any case, said the writers, the peddler had had his revenge.

First Responder

"There's no use to look for ghosts in cemeteries," a psychic investigator told me. "Why would they hang around there? By the time a body is buried, the spirit has left it and is occupied with doing whatever it needs to do. The place to look for new ghosts would be hospitals, or the scenes of accidents." Sounds logical, doesn't it? And, actually, a number of nurses have told me of strange — often very touching — things they witnessed as patients died. A couple of good EMT stories were offered for this book.

The first of the latter came from a woman named Shelley who called in when I was a guest on George Noory's radio show from KTRS in St. Louis. Shelley said she was a volunteer EMT in a small town and there, rather than have everyone take time to go to a central place and ride out in an ambulance, anyone close to the accident scene goes from home so victims will have someone with them as soon as possible.

One night, Shelley said, she was the first on the scene of a one-car accident and discovered immediately that the driver, the only person in the car, was dead. She moved to the safer side of the road and began the notations she needed to make on her clipboard. Gradually, she became aware, from her peripheral vision, that somebody was standing almost behind her at her right shoulder. When she turned to look, nobody was there.

This happened twice, and was very unnerving because the person seemed to be wearing blue, like the driver of the wrecked vehicle. Shelly said, "I actually went back across the road to make sure he was still in the car." She did not resume her original spot and some bypassers stopped. She was aware of the person behind her all the time she talked to them and she said she talked to keep them there, though the usual tactic would be to encourage the people to go on. Soon the members of her team arrived, and with the familiar activity, her feeling of having an elusive companion disappeared. But Shelley said that when she was alone again an eerie feeling hung around her, and of course she thinks of this each time she is the first to arrive at an accident scene.

An Ozarks Call

This experience comes in the words of an EMT named Mike, who wrote it down for us:

"One Christmas Eve in the mid 1990s, I was working for an ambulance service at a rural station in Barry County. There were two crews on duty. Late that evening the other crew was sent out for a possible cardiac patient in a densely wooded area in a remote part of the county. They were told that an orange pick-up truck would meet them at a highway intersection near the location and would lead the ambulance on to the patient.

"We were later told by the initial responding crew that while enroute to the call, they had come upon a fog bank across the highway. As they drove through this, all electrical systems failed and the ambulance engine too. The crew had a portable radio they were able to call dispatch on and request another ambulance to replace them.

"My partner and I were chosen to respond. As we approached the disabled ambulance, there was no fog and the sky was clear. We continued on and met the orange pick-up at the described intersection. Its windows were tinted black, so we could not see how many people were inside or who was driving.

"The pick-up led us way back into the woods on an old dirt road to a trailer house that looked like a log cabin. I exited the ambulance with my equipment and turned to see if the pick-up's driver could give me any information about the patient. I looked all around, but the truck was gone. I did not hear it drive off; it was just gone.

"Entering that trailer felt like going back into the past. Christmas carols were playing over an old Philco radio, but with no dj's voice ever coming in over them. No ads came on either, just music.

"The patient was sitting on the side of an old cast-iron bed, wearing long johns with a flap in the back, red like you see nowadays only as a novelty. The room was dimly lit with two old oil lamps and there was a Ben Franklin potbelly stove next to the head of the bed. I started the patient's IV with a little difficulty in the poor light and as I was assessing his condition, the hair on the back of my neck stood straight up. I turned around and there were two men and a woman. The men had on hand-made overalls, and the woman was in an actual potato sack dress. I had not heard them come in. I really expected Rod Serling to step out of the shadows with a his lit cigarette and say, "Mike's mind is the key to the door of imagination in the Twilight Zone." The people didn't speak and when I looked again they were gone.

I attempted to use my portable radio to call dispatch for a helicopter for the patient, who had a myocardial infarction and needed the fastest possible transport. My radio would not work, though the old Philco kept playing away. It must have had batteries better than mine. We loaded the patient into our ambulance and started with him toward the hospital. Once we were out of the area I was able to reach the dispatcher and request the helicopter. We met it and they took the patient on.

I never saw any of those people again and I never knew how the patient did at the hospital.

"I don't know if this is exactly a ghostly happening or just Ozark weirdness. That is spooky country."

A Farmer's Advice

The following story was provided by George R. Noory, previously mentioned as a late-night host on Station KTRS (550am) in St. Louis.

"One night a caller by the name of Jim phoned in to my talk radio show because we were discussing various mystical topics. He related what he said was a personal story:

"'I was once very depressed; nothing in my life was going well. My job wasn't what I wanted, I had broken up with my girlfriend and a number of other things had me extremely upset.

"'It was a pretty November day in Missouri, so, despite my depression, I got into my car and just drove, trying to clear my head. Eventually, I came to a small town and saw a park bench next to a small lake and park. I got out and sat there for awhile. "'A farmer in old coveralls came by and sat next to me, introducing himself as Gus. He was a delightful person and we chatted for an hour about the world in general and my problems in specific. His advice made me realize how important my life truly was. Afterwards, my depression completely gone, I thanked Gus and he wandered away. I got into my car and drove home.

"'About a year later, after things had turned around for me, I decided to go back to that small town and thank the farmer. When I arrived I did what most city folks would do, went to the local barbershop. I asked if anyone knew where I could find Gus.

"'The barber advised me to talk to Gus' daughter and pointed out where she lived. Sensing the worst, I knocked on the door. A woman answered and I explained who I was and what her father had done for me. I asked if he was there. She said no — her father had died. But I was the fifth person to

come by to thank him for his help and advice, even though
Gus had been gone for fifteen years!"

A Sticky-Fingered Ghost

Not many ghosts — apart from poltergeists, whatever
those are — ever get accused of taking anything away, or of
exerting any kind of physical force. They're not supposed to
be able to, since they lack a body with bones and muscles. But
once at a book signing, a woman told me about an unusual
experience she had in her early teens. When I tried to phone
her later, she had moved, so this account is only as memory
serves.

First, she told me she had been seeing ghosts all her life.
Reared near Sturgeon on a Boone County farm, she several
times saw a man walking through the house. He was dressed
in black, "with a little stringy tie, like they wore in Civil War
times. He made me think he was dressed for church or maybe
a funeral. He wasn't terribly old, maybe sixty, and he seemed
sad. I wondered if I might be seeing someone reliving over
and over his first homecoming after a funeral of someone
who had shared the place with him, his wife, probably. Once
I thought he looked right at me and his expression said 'What
are you doing here?' The house though, was only thirty or
forty years old, not old enough to have been used by someone
dressed as he was."

The other ghost she says she saw there more than once
seemed to be a Confederate soldier. "He was young and in
grey, but dirty and rag-tag. He wouldn't have been an officer
because his uniform was very plain. He didn't have a gun, and
I couldn't see any indication that he was hurt; he'd just come
to the door of the room and look in and then move away."

The ghost who meant the most to this storyteller was a little girl of six or eight she met while visiting in California.
"She was very cute, blonde headed. She wore a long dress
with a frill around the neck. She had on no jewelry. She was
always carefully carrying a big serving dish of some kind,

something that looked too big for her. She may have been a servant, but didn't seem at all downtrodden. She seemed proud that she could successfully carry the big covered dish. I could never figure out where she'd fit into the history of that particular house; she was so far before its time. She sometimes seemed to be aware of me. One time I smiled at her and she smiled back, sweetly.

"I had this plush toy thing, a dog that was actually a bag for pajamas, and I'd had it for years. It was always in the same place, and with the pajamas in it looked like any stuffed animal. Younger children who visited were always interested in it. I was attached to it because it was a gift, so I kept using it after I was actually too old such things."

When this object disappeared from the speaker's room, she said, the little ghost girl was naturally her prime suspect. The house had not been ransacked. Nobody with small children had visited on the day before the pajama dog disappeared. Nobody had been urging her to get rid of childish things.

This experience raises some interesting questions: Where would a ghost take a physical object? Where do ghosts stay when they're not wandering around? Could they somehow change what is real in our world into something different for theirs? This storyteller's last comment: "I always thought the least she could have done was to leave her tureen in exchange!"

From Historians

One great asset for books like this is seniors who have a special interest in history and take the trouble to record small bits that would otherwise fall through the cracks. Mary Elwell of Revere and Della Huff of Tipton, are two women who are in demand in their communities for history-based programs. Here's a story from each, each story about an unfortunate woman.

Mrs. Elwell recently did a program on the ghost town of Dumas, in the northeastern corner of our state, in Clark

County. Dumas, on the Des Moines River, once was a busy little place which had its mansion, church and school, stores — including a millinery shop — depot, post office, boarding house, a sawmill, rock quarry and pickle factory. An important facility was a water station for the steam engines of the Santa Fe Railroad, which crossed the river at Dumas.

Then came Diesel engines, and trains no longer stopped at Dumas; they just swept through. Businesses that had depended on the rails to take their products to markets were ruined and the town faded away. Now, Mrs. Elwell says, Dumas has only one house left.

She remembers the town as it was because her grandparents lived there and when she was small she often visited them. One of her vivid memories is of hearing repeated tales of a terrible train wreck that occurred in 1892. A wooden trestle, weakened by high water, collapsed. Several cars fell into the flooded river, killing a number of people. One woman was found with her head severed and the story grew of people seeing her in the area from time to time.

If there is anything to the theory that dying under traumatic circumstances makes for restless and pathetic spirits, this lady would have had good reason to haunt the area of her death. She died suddenly and horribly, away from home, her body not intact.

Mrs. Elwell says the accident had nothing to do with the decline of Dumas; the town had grown up simply because the Santa Fe Railroad crossed the Des Moines River there and when the railroad service stopped, the town could not sustain itself.

Some people believe that a town or store or school or church or business place has a kind of spirit formed from the human effort and concern that went into its creation and operation. If that were the case, then the spirit of Dumas would perhaps be sadly restless too, a ghost town with a ghost story.

Mrs. Huff's unfortunate woman was, by comparison with Mrs. Elwell's, quite fortunate. Both her father and her husband were prominent men and for many years, she was mistress of a mansion. Yet in life and in death, she apparently was very much ignored.

In 1990 for a Halloween appearance, Mrs. Huff told a story about a Pennsylvania woman who was apparently neglected during her lifetime and since, and now is said to haunt the Pennsylvania Bar Association's headquarters which was her former home, the William Maclay Mansion.

Mary Harris Maclay, born in 1748, was the daughter of John Harris II, the founder of Harrisburg, PA, and she was the wife of Pennsylvania's first state senator, William Maclay. She bore her husband nine children and died at the age of 61. Almost all Mrs. Huff could find about Mrs. Maclay was that she was said to often pace up and down on the street in front of their mansion, waiting for her husband to come home. Nobody now knows what she looked like except that she was said to be small and wear her hair in a bun.

Within the couple's former home there is a large portrait of William Maclay but nothing to indicate that he had a wife who once was responsible for running the huge place as a home for a family of eleven persons. Undoubtedly one of her duties was to entertain often and elegantly to help advance her husband's career.

At the cemetery a massive and impressive monument marks the husband's resting spot, but only a very small and simple stone memorializes his wife. According to Mrs. Huff's story, when a cemetery clerk was asked for Mrs. Maclay's death date, it could not be found. Only an X verified that she had died and been buried. The date, located later, was April 20, 1809.

For all we know, of course, Mrs. Maclay may have been a pampered daughter and wife, and a treasured mother, even though nothing exists to tell us that. But there must be some reason why the attorneys who occupy her former home blame these happenings on her discontent: photos that show a ghostly outline of a woman descending the lovely stairway; the sensation, when one is outdoors, of being watched from a window; doors that open and close of their own volition; people feeling sudden chills or finding sweat breaking out on their chests; sounds of humming and whistling.

The most specific story is from the executive director of the organization, Theodore Stellwag, who said that once when he was alone in the house, he heard a voice and went to investigate. He found a French door open, looked out and felt the door close behind him. When he tried to open it, it felt as if someone was holding it inside. He finally managed to yank the door open, only to feel a sudden drop in temperature, as if he were walking into a refrigerator.

Some psychics might advise the lawyers to assign one of their researchers to locate pictures and full data about Mrs. Maclay. Perhaps if a nice portrait and commemorative plaque gave her credit for her contributions as mistress of the mansion, the troublesome manifestations would stop!

A Message On Parting

One of the nurses who shared something poignant was Liz Bolin, who lives near Centralia. She told of a patient who had suffered several strokes and had not spoken for several years. When she was dying, the woman said, with joy:

"Absolutely sure! Absolutely sure! Absolutely sure!
God is everything! God is in everything!
God is in everyone...God is all.
When you are fulfilled, God is fulfilled.
God is in you. God is in you.
Absolutely sure! Absolutely sure! Absolutely sure!"

Haunted
Houses

Though we've already looked at a number of Missouri's haunted houses, the following are in a special class. All of them still exist and most are listed in the National Directory of Haunted Places. Three can be toured and one can even be slept in. One is a private home whose present owners say they've never seen, heard or felt anything unusual in it.

Chapter Twenty Two

The Lemp Mansion

*The energies left behind by suicides are not
able to displace themselves ... the ...
ironic punishment for taking your own life is
never being able to leave it.*
— Karen Novak character's speech in the novel,
Five Mile House

Surprisingly, the 33-room Lemp Mansion on De Menil Place in St. Louis, hasn't had its share of attention in annals of the ghostly, despite *Life Magazine's* 1980 designation of the house as one of the ten most haunted in the U.S. Here's what gives the Lemp Mansion its remarkable qualifications. Three members of the Lemp family killed themselves under its roof and a fourth elsewhere. At least one family member died a lingering death there and a favored and promising Lemp son sickened there of an ailment that would take his life at only 28. Within the walls of this house, a large and power-ful family dwindled to just a few and saw a great fortune lost. The home itself went from being a jewel in the city's crown to ever-cheapening apartments and rental rooms. It sold in 1974 for $40,000—less than a modest subdivision home— and was rescued just in time by an enterprising family. Their loving and respectful efforts have almost completely restored it. As it did in its glory, once again the Lemp Mansion has thousands of guests each year, though these pay to eat in its restaurant or to use its bed and breakfast offerings.

The house was bought in the 1880s by John Adam Lemp, who had brought the first lager beer to St. Louis in 1838. He developed the Falstaff line, among several others and his son, William, carried the dynasty forward to increasing prominence. The next generation, under leadership of William Lemp, Jr., brought the business to its peak. Its buildings covered eleven city blocks and the annual income grew to 3.5 million dollars for an output of 350,000 barrels of beer. But "Billy" Lemp apparently destroyed it all through his despair about prohibition. In 1919, he closed the brewery "to spite the government," according to Jeff Meyer, who wrote about the house and the family for the *Post Dispatch* in September, 1979. William Jr. sold Falstaff to the Griesedieck family for $25,000 and the brewery buildings for eight cents on the dollar to a shoe manufacturer.

This would have been enough to inspire his grandfather's suicide, had that not taken place in 1902 after Frederick's death. William, Jr. killed himself in 1922 in the same room by the same means—a small calibre bullet to the heart. Reclusive Charles Lemp committed suicide in the basement of the house, some sources say, after shooting his dog. A sister killed herself in her luxurious home in Hortense Place.

Meyer wrote that in 1979 the atmosphere of the Lemp Mansion was forbidding and sad from outdoors and unnerving inside. Pictures from *Post Dispatch* photographers reinforced that description, showing dark paneling and windows too clouded with dirt to let in much light.

Dick and Patti Pointer, who bought the house, immediately began work to create a distinctive restaurant. With help from their nine children, they reached their goal in three years. The first task was carting off debris, and they told Meyer that for seven months they did nothing but drag out and haul away trash. As they worked, they watched for anything that might have belonged to the house originally, both furniture and decorative woodwork. They investigated walls and ceilings added to convert the house for apartments and made many exciting discoveries. They could hardly believe how many of the mansion's beauties had survived its worst days. The Pointers then researched the house exhaustively, looking for pictures that might show them where their findings belonged.

As to feeling the place was haunted: members of the family experienced differing vague to acute discomforts, mainly sensations of being watched and unwelcome. For some, Meyer wrote, it was a daily battle at first, ignoring unearthly presences that "seemed to follow them from one dark corner of the house to another."

An artist brought in to restore a ceiling, knowing nothing of the house's history, fled one day after feeling relentlessly hostile eyes on him for an extended period. He told Pointer, "This place is crazy. You've got a ghost or something here."

Dick Pointer, who had been a paratrooper and felt he was "not scared of anything," admitted to Meyer that one day while painting in a bathroom, he began to feel someone watching him intently. He said it was "the most terrible sensation you can have. I get goosebumps now, just thinking about it." He turned around and saw nothing, but when it happened again, he said, "I cleaned my brushes and got the hell out."

The situation was not helped by people from the neighborhood and former renters telling the Pointers weird tales. One aged woman said the Lemps were reputed to keep a retarded child in the attic and people who saw it at windows said it looked like a monkey. The Pointers told each other that such stories were natural for those who had lived for years near a house with a history and appearance like theirs.

Meyer's story said a Pointer son, Dick Jr., lived alone in the mansion for four years after the restaurant was in operation, his parents and siblings living nearby, all working together by day. Dick, Jr., who insisted he did not believe in ghosts, shared basement quarters with his Doberman, Shadow. Only once did they have an unexplainable experience: awakened by what sounded like a kick to their door, they made a run through the house, but found nothing amiss.

Dick, Jr. reported no feelings in those years, of being observed and resented, and according to one writer, Shadow never displayed any unusual reactions. Another writer mentioned that the dog would not go above the ground floor, possibly referring to another dog.

The Pointer family found that the mansion's reputation had worked for its preservation; neighborhood children apparently never tried to explore it. Not until Meyer's story appeared did the family take time to check out features of the property that had inspired awe in those nearby: an underground pool and dance floor and access to what are called the Cherokee caves. These caverns, named for their location along Cherokee Street, had been a big reason for the Lemp patriarch's choosing the site. They provided natural refrigeration for storage of his beer.

Today the Lemp Mansion is a beautiful, non-frightening place and the renovation must please its spirits, if any, because nothing really unpleasant happens there. Things have moved about, says Paul Pointer, present owner and operator of the restaurant and bed-and-breakfast. They've done this both in poltergeist manner and just as seeming misplacements that turn up in remarkable spots. Lights and appliances sometimes behave strangely; doors may be unaccountably locked or unlocked. Candles on a mantel once lit themselves and once, while Pointer talked with guests about the Lemp ghosts, a wine glass rose up from a counter and dashed itself on the floor.

Here's a typical little episode from the Lemp Mansion nowadays. An employee saw an elderly man come in and sit down, obviously waiting for service, when the front doors were still locked and the restaurant was not yet ready for customers. She couldn't figure out where the early bird customer had come from, but turned aside for an instant to get him a cup of coffee to make it a bit more gracious, telling him he'd have quite a little wait. Turning back around, she saw nobody and he had been too close to her in the large room to have been lost to sight that fast.

Another event had a useful outcome; members of the family heard the sound of horse hooves at a side entrance. Nothing was there, of course, but their looking for tracks brought the discovery of a cobbled area lost in grass. This had apparently been laid to insure a clear and clean place for alighting from carriages. The Pointers used the cobblestone to make a floor for one of the basement rooms.

Most of what happens Pointer says he just considers "interesting." For instance, in going through his late father's papers, he found a letter someone had written him when the Pointers first acquired the Lemp house. A former tenant described an unusual man seen regularly while the Lemp Mansion served as apartments. He was of smaller than average size, always dressed nattily in vintage clothing, notable for always having on new-looking, wonderfully cared-for shoes. This apparently perfectly real and solid person bustled along on business of his own, not returning greetings. Nobody knew who he was or what floor he lived on, but he was seen constantly in the hallways and on nearby streets. Some of the Lemps were small people and all dressed very well indeed.

Paul Pointer said he had never discussed this remarkable letter with anyone who was writing about the house for publication. In fact, he had almost forgotten it until a guest came in and told him essentially the same story. This former tenant, however, had lived at the Lemp Mansion at another time entirely from that of the letter writer. Pointer says he went home and dug out the letter and was amazed to see how perfectly the two accounts matched.

The full story of the Lemp Mansion is told in a book called Lemp: *A Haunting History,* available from the Pointers or, perhaps at libraries. The author is Stephen P. Walker.

"A house is never silent in darkness to those who listen intently; there is a whispering in distant chambers, an unearthly hand presses the snib of the window, the latch rises. Ghosts were created when the first man woke in the night."

— James Matthew Barrie,
in The Little Minister.

Chapter Twenty Three

Ravenswood

Let no evil dreams disturb my rest
Nor powers of darkness me molest.
— Evening Hymn

This mansion seems to house a spirit who still cherishes her privacy and feels possessive about her clothing. We're told that on the day after Nadine Leonard's death, the door of her bedroom was locked and remained so for some days, defying all non-damaging ways to get it open. Fortunately for the door, it didn't have to be treated badly; it seemingly unlocked itself just in time to avoid force. Another instance: when Nadine's wardrobe was being reorganized for display and left lying about overnight in a rather disorderly manner, an employee came in next morning and found the clothing all neatly folded and returned to storage.

Ravenswood, more than 30 rooms and tourable, is in Cooper County near Boonville. It was built in 1880 of brick manufactured on its own property, 2000 acres owned by one family from 1825 to the present. The house was built for Charles E. Leonard, a Union captain, and his bride, Nadine Nelson, "the belle of Boonville," beautiful and pampered daughter of one of the area's first millionaires. A showcase of the technology of its time, Ravenswood had running water, gas lights, a fireplace in each room and, elaborate plasterwork ceilings. Nadine's initials as a married woman are etched into frosted glass of the front door.

The newlyweds traveled the world, she gathering lovely furnishings and ornaments for Ravenswood and he adding to his famous herd of shorthorn cattle, first of their breed imported west of the Mississippi. The couple returned with their treasures and made their home one of the state's most choice sites for entertaining. It was famous for its "fairy-lighted lawn parties," with a permanently standing dance pavilion. Parties of more than 100 people were no novelty.

Adding to the already prestigious Nelson social and business connections, Nadine's sister, Maggie, was married to Lon Stephens, Missouri's governor. This glittering couple gave Ravenswood gatherings special status, attracting state celebrities of the era to eat, sleep, and dance at the rural mansion.

Ravenswood's staff's capabilities were demonstrated when a certain dance ended and 100 or so guests started home, only to come trooping back because a stream was up and they couldn't cross. Nadine, who was almost ready for bed, put her dress back on, told the live musicians to continue playing until daylight, and with her husband she led resumption of the dancing. At dawn a hearty country breakfast was served to all guests and by the time that was over, the troublesome water had subsided.

One little detail could have caused marital problems that would inspire ghost stories. Despite all its attractions, Nadine didn't really like Ravenswood much. (One of her complaints: "Must the peacocks scream all the time?") She preferred the town house her father had given her, because she relished the social activity of Boonville and didn't like the constant carriage trips back and forth to Ravenswood. Leonard apparently adapted to this without annoyance, commuting between the farm and the townhouse.

At its peak, the house was full of Venetian glass and Italian tapestries, and it still has its suit of armor in the hall, its family portraits by George Caleb Bingham, an impressive library, and many of Nadine's exquisite dresses. These include her tiny ivory satin wedding gown, and a gauzy navy and grey creation made for Grover Cleveland's inauguration. She had at least one Worth gown, a great status symbol of wealthy women of her time, and a multitude of dainty long-sleeved little tops, short and tightly fitted, decorated with painstaking needlework—-embroidery, applique, braiding and fringe. These are lined throughout with delicate boning that guaranteed perfect posture. They were hand sewn for her in Europe from measurements taken on her wedding trip, reordered as she desired new ones.

Ravenswood's haunting reports have been the usual passersby accounts of floating lights and of music wafting faintly from the lawn, as well as many a visitor's firm statement: "you can feel her there ... not offended that we're in her house, just there." Guests and family members have reported a large metal disc music box in an upstairs hall spontaneously playing, usually after midnight. Family members also have reported hearing downstairs crashes so frightening they never dreamed of going to investigate until daylight, and then, without exception, finding no hint of what caused the disturbance. One description: "... like someone down there with a sledge hammer just taking things apart. It lasted for fifteen minutes ... left no trace."

Ravenswood has only a single tragedy to foster ghosts. Nadine lived to be past 90, but her one son, Nelson, collector of the library, died at the estate's entrance when his car slipped out of gear and crushed him against the gate he was opening.

Chapter Twenty Four

Longview

One day we will meet again those animal friends . . . by crystal streams in green pastures of heavenly beauty. A dream you say? Who knows?

— Loula Long Combs in her
autobiography, *My Revelation*

Near Kansas City, at Lee's Summit, is an estate that any horse-loving spirit would understandably be reluctant to leave. It was, when lumber tycoon, A. C. Long established it in 1911, called "horse heaven" and "American Versailles" — an international wonder of the equine world. On its 1,780 acres stood a literal village of stucco buildings with red tile roofs. Besides the 50-room family home, there were dozens of buildings to house staff, different kinds of animals and farm equipment, and Longview's own veterinary hospital with a full-time doctor. Long also built a chapel with a school in the basement for his employees' 60 children. He built a greenhouse and insisted that the farm have its own water tower, providing filtered water for all souls, human and non. A buried-wire electrical system provided for all needs without damaging Longview's beauty.

Where loveliness was concerned, there was a 20-acre artificial lake and everywhere were flowers, in beds, borders and pergolas, in arbors and sunken gardens. Roses grown at

Longview regularly won the highest prizes in flower shows, including national level.

In addition to its indoor riding ring and an arena that could seat 2,000 spectators, the estate contained seven miles of bridle path and driving roads. These were accompanied by so much white wood fence that Longview had a team of men who did nothing but keep its paint pristine.

At its peak, Longview had 400 employees but the family itself was only four, Long and his Quaker wife and their two daughters. Of these sisters the younger, Loula, became world renowned as an incredible winner at horse shows, both riding as a young person and driving in her maturity. She competed all over the U.S. and in Canada and England, from the age of 15 to her early 80s, winning hundreds of ribbons and trophies, as well as thousands of dollars in cash prizes. A memorable characterization of life at Longview came when she wrote "My father never refused to buy any horse I wanted, and I wanted many of them."

For horses was what Longview was really about, dozens and dozens of horses, though the farm also had all kinds of animals and the crops to provide their food. Long imported a Scottish driving ace to train the harness horses and John Hook of Mexico, Missouri, the country's top trainer then, to breed American Saddlebreds and prepare them for exhibition under saddle. Long and his staff assembled what was called "the biggest saddlebred nursery in the world," made up of the finest mares that could be bought and three great stallions, My Major Dare, Easter Cloud and Independence Chief.

Longview's ghost stories reflect the idyllic life of Loula Long Combs (for she operated the property as a mature married woman after her father's death and until her own demise in 1971). She wrote of how a ride or drive could lift her spirits instantly if she was tired or troubled and she boldly admitted praying for her horses if they were hurt or ill. People who worked at Longview have told how she drifted about with or without horses, accompanied by a cloud of dogs and other pets, including at one time a skunk and a pig. They tell of the charity shows she planned and executed, only Longview's

many horses performing. Former employees recount her endless kindness to all of them and her special interest in their children.

Predictably, what the ghostly Loula is said to do today is allow hoofbeats to be heard as she rides or drives by, to let people glimpse her sometimes in the half-dark of the indoor ring, or maybe see a sparkle of light flying off silvery-spoked wheels. Employees are reluctant to enter this place alone, some writers say.

Only one even mildly pettish thing has ever been attributed to Loula Long Combs' ghost. Once when for some special event the family home was open for several days for tours, people working there reported that her bed was in disarray each morning, as if it had been slept in.

Longview's acreage is greatly reduced now, partly flooded by the Corps of Engineers, partly sold off or given away by Loula and her sister Sally in their last years. Longview Community College occupies land they donated for the purpose. Part of the farm has become a luxury subdivision, with some of the horse facilities used by a local riding club. Other portions are utilized by horse people who travel from all over the state and beyond to enjoy the rolling expanses for cross-country riding.

Loula Long Combs' autobiography, *My Revelation,* might encourage us to imagine her still there, driving her best beloved, Revelation, over familiar paths. After recording her love and appreciation for the place and all its inhabitants — family, staff and creatures — Mrs. Combs shared her own conviction that "... one day we will meet again those animal friends ... by crystal streams in green pastures of heavenly beauty. A dream you say? Who knows?"

Chapter Twenty Five

Lilac Hill

The whole house now seemed to vibrate, with sounds just below the range of hearing, the air to quiver with unseen forces.
— Barbara Michaels in *Ammie, Come Home*

"We've never really been afraid, because we know if there is such a thing it can't hurt you, but gee whiz, it's just really weird." That's what Joe Jeff Davis told a *St. Louis Post Dispatch* reporter in 1977, while his family still owned and lived in Lilac Hill, near Fayette in Howard County. This three story classic Federalist house, built in 1832-33 by A. W. Morrison, sits amid 365 acres on a hill overlooking miles of hills, woodlands and farms. It is one of the oldest houses in Central Missouri, built by slave labor of handmade brick, its parts fitted together with pegs of wood and iron, its walls two feet thick in some places. The estate's name came from hundreds of lilac bushes which once surrounded the house and Marsha Davis says that when she lived there, more than 50 remained, white and French, as well as the old fashioned kind. She assumes that in the Morrisons' days, there may have been many other varieties.

Lilac Hill is listed in the *National Registry of Historic Sites*, the *Missouri Historic Sites Catalog* and the *National Directory of Haunted Sites*. The Morrison family occupied it until 1952 when the last descendant died there at the age of 50. Between then and 1974, when the Davises moved in, four families lived at Lilac Hill and so far as the Davises could learn, none of them complained of hauntings.

But here are some of the sounds the Davis family reported: firm footsteps in the night, sometimes coming into the parents' bedroom; rustling paper; muffled screaming that once went on for two hours in overhead space that had been the loom room where some female slaves worked; dragging sounds from upstairs for four hours; weeping that seemed to come from a corner of the parents' bedroom; distant, argumentative human voices. In addition, they saw flashing lights, smelled foul odors, and felt cold drafts. Their dog, too, at times behaved in unusual ways.

Some happenings were extremely perplexing, especially the prolonged weeping. When it began, the Davises first thought one of the children was having a nightmare, but checked and found them all sleeping peacefully. Then Davis went outdoors to look, thinking there could have been a car wreck or other accident. During an equally long session of overhead noises, they seriously thought of going to a motel for the night, but decided to remain. They had a great deal invested in the place and loved it. It was exactly the right size for their family.

Nothing personally threatening ever happened except for the time one son felt so certain someone was behind him on the stairs that he ran into his room and out the window and down the slanting roof to the ground. "It wasn't far," his mother says, "and he was fit and athletic; that was the closest we came to actual danger."

The couple told a newspaper reporter in 1987 of a son-in-law who was a total disbeliever, but on one visit wound up on sleeping on the family room floor with a blanket over his head because, he said, something walked around his bed. Then he felt the weight of someone sitting down on it and a woman's voice said, "Don't worry; I'll only be here a little while."

No one in the family doubted him, because the parents once had a similar experience. Davis had gone on to bed while his wife delayed to take clothes from the dryer and fold them. When she came into the bedroom, he asked if she'd come in earlier and lain down. He said somebody had entered the room, walked around to her side of the bed and he'd felt the weight as she settled down, had turned over to put his arm around her and nothing was there. He thought she'd got up again.

Because the Davises talked freely to the media about their house, a group of psychics from Kansas City asked for permission to visit and when they did, reported finding the main entity there was a woman named Minerva, known to the staff and neighbors as "Miss Minnie," and that she still considered herself mistress of the house. The Davises supposed this could have been either the last resident or the builder's wife, for both had that name. The latter lady's gravestone had been displaced by some previous tenant who cleared space and put outbuildings where the family cemetery stood. The stone said she was born in 1808 and died in 1858.

The psychics also mentioned that activity is often higher in a house where children live. It did abate for the Davises when two of their children left home and Mr. Davis' mother, in her 80s, came to live with them.

The next family in the house declared they saw and heard nothing, but after them, David and Joanie Wells, who had no children, moved in. They described things the Davises did not see as well as many of the same manifestations. These included crashes similar to plaster falling, or a chandelier, after which they could find nothing out of order. At times the Wells' said they heard male and female voices in urgent conversation. Their Cocker Spaniel, Buffy, sometimes chased things nobody could see.

The next and present owners, Ken and Carol Staten, declare that they have seen, heard and felt nothing unusual at Lilac Hill. An Air Force retiree, Staten says it is a great improvement over living in Washington, D. C. where they were before. They had wanted to get away from the city and bought the house after looking at it for less than an hour. "The acreage is just what I wanted for raising cattle," he says, "and the house is just what my wife wanted."

This picture used by gracious permission of its owner,
Bluegrass Horseman magazine, Lexington, KY.

Chapter Twenty Six

The James Farm

Perhaps they woke from the dreamless sleep of death only when their children and grandchildren remembered them.
— Barbara Michaels' novel *Be Buried in the Rain*

How could the farm where Jesse James grew up, near Kearney in Clay County, not be haunted? There Zerelda Cole James Sims Samuel lived with three different husbands and bore seven children. There she saw her ten-year-old son, Archie, killed by Pinkerton detectives and there she lost her own right hand. On that property she saw her husband tortured, never to recover. There she endured suspense about the well-being of her famous two older sons and gave them refuge when they needed it; there she fended off their foes, legal and illegal. Most of all, on this land she guarded the body of her son Jesse after his murder, his grave dug extra deep and in sight of her bedroom window.

Zerelda Samuel spent most of her widowhood on the farm, sometimes alone except for servants, as did her daughter-in-law, Annie Ralston James. Annie and Frank James' son, Robert, also spent his later life there, sometimes alone, sometimes with a wife. In addition to the emotional edifice these people would have created on the property, there were the joys and despairs of siblings of the famous "boys" and those of a family of slaves that remained on for generations as paid servants.

The James Family Farm has always had a reputation for being haunted, with the reports one would expect: moving lights in and around the house, sounds of pounding hooves, muffled shouts, shots and wailings. Yet surprisingly little has been written about the haunts, in comparison to the uncountable books and articles devoted to the brothers' exploits.

In January, 1982, the *Kansas City Star* reviewed a vigil kept in the house overnight to mark the 100th anniversary of the death of Archie Samuel, only person ever to die violently in the house. As mentioned earlier, this came about when detectives, hoping to flush out Jesse and Frank—whom the family has always maintained were not even there—threw some sort of incendiary device into the house. The impact or shrapnel killed young Archie and damaged Zerelda's arm so badly that her hand and forearm had to be amputated. Some sources say this was done without anaesthesia and there in the house, by her own husband, a physician. Officers of the James-Younger gang, which documents family history and helps maintain the house, believe another doctor was brought in for the purpose.

Despite all the psychic drama this event could have produced on its 100th anniversary, the men in the house that night felt nothing but a cold draft, which the late Milton F. Perry, then curator of the museum, laughed about as typical of any aged and unheated cabin in January. The other vigil keepers, two men from Chicago, with *Kansas City Star* writer, D. P. Breckenridge, said they spent most of their time, huddled around the fireplace, though they were warmly dressed.

However, people who work regularly in the house — volunteers and employees who take care of upkeep and exhibits — have had more interesting experiences. These are few and mild, considering all that happened there and those who tell of them are first to admit being so totally saturated in history of the family and so interested in it that they hardly regard the Jameses as gone.

They laugh about a summer day when several people together were rehanging freshly laundered curtains. They began feeling apprehensive as a sudden thunderstorm came up. When it sent drafts into the house that violently slammed several outer and inner doors in quick succession, they fled without exchanging a word or a look first.

A less explainable happening: the framed picture of Jesse on his grey horse, Stonewall, has never hung straight, no matter what new hangers and adjustments were tried. When it was sent away for reframing, and to be treated for museum preservation, everyone assumed that problem would be solved, but the picture still hangs at the same angle as before.

Reports continue of lights seen in the house when it is locked and of movements to which its monitoring system does not react. Another type of security system activates by itself several times a year, never in daytime, never earlier than midnight.

At times the feelings of "something" being present are so intense that no guide wants to be alone in the house. A sensation several have shared is that someone else has entered, after a tour group is admitted, even though the door is always locked then to prevent anyone's coming in and wandering around unsupervised.

A guide, taking a group of people through on a night tour held in connection with some special event, was startled to hear overhead a frantic scrabbling, as of some animal, one as large as a raccoon, in the attic. Almost immediately, from two sides of the room, came loud, substantial rustling in the leaves outside, reminding her of the fact that the Pinkertons surrounded the house on the night of their attack. A wild animal sheltering in the attic in the James era might well have heard their approach and taken flight, making the same noises.

In the "death room" which displays the feather-duster, picture and stool that saw Jesse's death, as well as one of his coffin lids, light bulbs burn out at a remarkable rate, far faster than anywhere else in the house. Staff members all try to avoid being the person who puts in the new bulbs.

One staff member says she has more than once, on foggy mornings, when sound carries strangely anyhow, heard the hushed voices of men from woods fairly near the house, and restless movements of horses, which reminds her that Frank and Jesse were said to sometimes wait in the woods for a sign that it was safe to come on to the house. Later in the day, with others, when she goes to look, this worker never finds any tracks.

Some of the staff were experimenting one day with grave witching, a variation on water dowsing in which two wires replace the traditional willow wands. As an earlier chapter explained, dowsing is commonly used by genealogists and others looking for grave sites, principle being that the wires' ends will move toward each other when held over soil that has been disturbed to a depth of more than six inches. Over Jesse James' twice dug-up gravesite, they said, these wire ends first crossed each other, then vibrated so strongly that the operator dropped them.

Just across the road from the James farmstead is a nice antebellum house called Claybrook, which was the home of Jesse and Zee James' daughter, Mary, and her husband, Henry Barr. This house, where their baby daughter, Henrietta, died, and a later resident hanged himself, is said to be haunted by a child's cries, by the sound of someone clearing his throat, by steps going up and down the divided front staircase and by the sound of a ball bouncing down those stairs. On one occasion, staff members say, a female member of a tour group came running down the stairs, white faced, and raced out to her car and away, with no explanation to anyone, ever. Today Claybrook, fully restored, is maintained by the county as an historic site.

Despite the causes for their fame, all biographers agree that the James family maintained a loyal and loving closeness. They would probably agree with Mark Twain, "The spirits of the dead hallow a house ...."

A Haunted Household

Chapter Twenty Seven

Family Phantoms

Be careful not to conjure up
more phantoms than you can put down.
— Old Proverb

Here's another story — cluster of stories, actually — that seems exclusive to Missouri: it's a haunted family, a group of people who experienced varied strange events together and apart and in more than one location. The person who recorded the most interesting aspects was Sylvester Marion Jones (1836-1917), a Methodist minister. For part of his career, he was a circuit rider. By horseback, he traveled about among small rural churches, holding services for congregations that could not afford a full-time pastor of their own. His manuscript was titled *The Spirit Biography of S. M. Jones.*

Though a few odd things had happened on the Montgomery County farm where Jones grew up, he wrote that manifestations became more frequent and much more serious after he and his six brothers held a seance. Skeptics might laugh at the idea of farm boys of that era even knowing what a seance is. However, this was in the time of the famous Fox sisters, three women from New York who had greatly stimulated interest in the occult, mainly through publicly-held seances.

The sisters have been credited by many with starting what was then a fad called "spiritualism" but extends into our own era with more credibility and acceptance. It was many years before the Foxes were debunked as creating their own remarkable effects. Meanwhile, they were much written of and people flocked to see them perform in public. Many other people decided that they, too, were "mediums", go-betweens for those with bodies and those without. No doubt the Jones brothers had read in newspapers about these women, and had heard their parents and neighbors speculating about them. Maybe somebody from their area had even gone to see the Fox sisters. Almost certainly the boys had heard ministers earnestly entreating their congregations not to dabble in the unknown, lest they meet terrible danger.

At any rate, one day, when their parents were gone from home, the brothers decided to have a seance. After all, the two youngest Fox sisters were only fifteen and twelve years old. Sylvester Jones would have been twelve years old when the craze began, about 1848. Reasoning that spirits were more likely to respond to the most mature of them, the two oldest boys sat down together and invited visitors from the other side. When nothing happened, the next older brother joined them, and then the next. Not until the youngest, just five years old, sat down did the table move and knock.

Nothing significant came to the sitters, and the parents, when told, seemed to find it all more amusing than alarming. Jones' manuscript sounds as if the parents sometimes joined in on seances and did not discourage neighbors coming over to hear bedroom thumps and other phenomena that came to be common in the house. Perhaps they thought it was all just a clever game their sons were contriving.

At some point, however, the sounds and other manifestations became disturbing enough that the father decreed a stop to all seances. What he previously labeled "imaginations of the brain," he now called "work of the devil." One incident with a neighbor may have brought on this decision. The adult men and at least one of Jones' sons were together when sud-

denly the floor seemed to lurch under them and a great blast
of noise filled the house.

All were struck dumb for a moment, but the senior Jones
had a quick mind. When the neighbor asked "What was that?"
Jones pretended nothing had happened, and when his son
started to echo the question, gave him a stern, silencing look.
Later he explained that if such things got around, their property would be valueless because nobody would want to live
on a haunted farm, and the father was thinking he might need
to sell out and move his family elsewhere.

Some of the most interesting events that S. M. Jones
reported involved other family members. He wrote of his
mother's complaining about the heavy thuds that often came
at night from overhead. She felt compelled to get up each
time and make sure that none of the children had fallen out of
bed. They would invariably be sleeping soundly. One morning she described how her own sleep had been badly dis-

turbed the night before by things falling on her in bed, soft, fluffy little things that reminded her of kittens. She said they "fretted" her all night, because she knew the cats had been put out. She said, "They were the softest things I ever felt," and then, "I just kept pushing and throwing them off of me, but never heard anything hit the floor and this morning there was nothing to be found in the house."

At least three times, family members together or with servants witnessed the ghost-of-a-living-person or doppelganger effect. The most memorable was when two or more of the young men were working outdoors together and saw a servant woman approaching along a fence row. They wondered to each other why she was outside at that time of day, instead of in her usual housework routine, but went back to their tasks until she should reach them, perhaps with a message from their mother. To their surprise, the woman never arrived, and sometime later, looking up, they saw her again approaching beside the fence, not much closer than when they first saw her. When they asked their mother about it at night, she told them the servant had been with her all day, but she "walked the floor the whole time, with a terrible toothache, terrible pain."

This servant woman and another, doing laundry outdoors one day, saw Mrs. Jones coming to them across the field, wearing a kerchief on her head and eating something from her hand. Intent on being busy when their mistress reached them, they both became deeply occupied with their work. She never appeared, however, and the servants thought she had perhaps stepped into concealment, to watch and see if they were really working.

Yet the incident seemed so strange to them that they could not resist asking Mrs. Jones about it. She told them "I wasn't outdoors today except to go to the smokehouse and cut off some ham for supper. I sliced myself a little piece and ate it as I came back in, but I went nowhere this morning except from kitchen to smokehouse doors and then back again. I was never in the field at all. I did have a kerchief on this morning."

One chilly night, when their father had been to town and was expected home at any minute, all thought they heard the familiar cadence of his horse's hooves coming up to the house, then the jingling of metal as their father dismounted. One of the sons put on his coat, ready to go out and take care of the horse. His father would be cold and tired and eager to get to the fire, but it was imperative that the horse be made dry and warm at once, then fed and watered. This was a son's taken-for-granted duty at the time.

To the boy's surprise there was no father and no horse in the yard or at the barn. The whole family shared his puzzlement, Jones tells us, and together they heard their father's arrival soon after. It's probably a safe guess that the dutiful son made two or three of his brothers brave the barn with him that night just in case they might find there unearthly duplicates of their father and his horse!

The Jones manuscript contains many incidents similar to these and a few that were quite frightening.Here's one of the worst stories: Jones writes that once when he was enroute home from St. Charles he needed to stop near O'Fallon and spend the night. It was the custom then for travelers to stop at any convenient house and ask for "a night's lodging." Most people were pleased to provide supper and a bed in exchange for a small amount of money, some help on whatever work projects were underway, or some sort of little gift. Just the novelty of having a visitor was cherished by most rural people. Maybe he would prove to be a good story teller, or would be carrying a musical instrument and could play and sing for them!

Jones was received cordially where he stopped and was told that the family had plenty of space. On one end of their house were a couple of unused rooms, one-over-one, former servants' quarters, which had a separate entrance and no interconnecting door to the family rooms. The householders told Jones, however, that if he'd rather not be so isolated, he was welcome to stay in their section of the house, or they would have one of their sons sleep with him.

This concern seemed a little odd to Jones, but he opted for privacy and felt no qualms about being alone, despite the fact that the host and his wife asked at least four times if he was sure he'd not be afraid.When the host took Jones into the guest room, he built up a good fire in the fireplace, which seemed odder still, since it was not at all necessary for comfort. The man then climbed the ladder that led to the upper room, and standing where his head was well above the upstairs floor, spent a long few moments studying the room.

What Jones experienced after his host departed was ushered in by his writing: "But hark, hush!" and then he told how he heard soft footsteps overhead. Puzzled about who could be there after all the hosts had said about his being alone, Jones lay quietly debating what to do. He finally decided he should make himself known to his fellow lodger, in order to avoid frightening or offending him, so he called out, climbed the ladder and shone the lamp all around. The place was completely empty. When the steps were repeated, Jones got up again, but still found nothing. There was reassurance in a sight familiar to his childhood, a roll of "sole leather". This was leather that had been stiffened to use in cutting soles for shoes. His father, among whose skills was making and repairing shoes, always had such material around.

But after Jones returned to bed, the leather became anything but comforting. The footsteps came closer to the ladder than they'd ever been and were joined by the sound of someone beating on the leather with something heavy. Jones noted that as the fire flickered and rose up, sounds would stop. As it died down, they recurred and, of course, the fire would soon die completely. Would the being above then come down?

The sounds continued as a set sequence, first foot steps, then footsteps approaching the ladder, then the beating on the leather, and the beating sounds gradually lengthened into periods of as long as 15 minutes. Jones though that surely his hosts could hear all this and would come to his aid!

The minister's explanation as to why he did not simply bolt from the room? It had also occurred to him that the sounds could be made deliberately by some group of people who were intent on teasing him, in which case "to flee would denote great cowardice and disturb the family." If the sounds meant some plot was afoot to attack him, the family could be in on it; one did hear stories from time to time about how lone travelers were set upon and robbed and killed. "If I am to reach the family, I shall have to go out of doors and thus expose myself to the mob, if there is one," Jones realized. He decided he could do no better than to stay where he was and hope to deal with whatever happened.

Despite his fervent prayers for relief, an even worse element was added to the series of sounds. After the beating on the leather stopped, came the noise of a large party of horsemen riding at speed toward the house. "I heard like eight or ten men ride within about fifteen feet of the house and dismount. I could hear, as it were, the old time stirrups striking against each other and ringing. And the men appeared to rush to the door in a gust of wind, but the moment I expected the door to be broken in, all became silent again." So the whole sequence repeated over and over and because sounds had grown progressively threatening, with each onslaught of horsemen, Jones expected them to intrude upon him. He said these sounds continued until daylight.

When his hosts asked how he rested, Jones says, "They would better have asked me how I died, for hell was a paradise to my spirit prison of unceasing torments. If there ever were a haunted house, which we do not doubt, this was one. Did guerrillas in time of war one night ride up, dismount, rush into the house and beat some poor Negro to death? If not, what caused the haunt?"

It would be hard to top Jones' unique account of a haunted family whose experiences also included foreseeing deaths and less grim events. Jones' papers are documented as much as anything can be: his descendants have pictures of Sylvester Jones and some of his siblings. They have his will and other historic materials, several with his known handwriting which matches that of the manuscript in which he shares his "spirit biography." They have documents pertaining to his military service and have located the property on which he was reared.

S. M. Jones did exist; his book is not a clever piece of fiction, unless we must believe that, somehow, a man who gave his life to the ministry in apparent total sincerity, could also fabricate a detailed lie and present it as truth.

Descendants have published Jones' paper as a book, combined with other historical material from the minister and his family. It can be ordered from Sunset Publishing Co., 6916 State Rd. C, Fulton, MO 65251. Title of the book is "A Voice from the Past."

Haunted Horses

Chapter Twenty Eight

They're All Spooky

And still of a winter's night, they say,
When the wind is in the trees ...
The highwayman comes riding, riding, riding;
The highway man comes riding ....
— Alfred Noyes, *The Highwayman.*

Missouri is fifth in equine population among all the states, so it's only natural that horses should be outnumbered by no animal but dogs in our ghost stories. Also, Vance Randolph and other folklorists tell us that horses will show us ghosts, if any are near. We need only look straight out between our mounts' ears.

Even horsepeople too young to have heard of this belief jokingly attribute to equines an ability to sense ghosts, or to think they do. The language of horse people is full of it. "She's young and spooky yet," they'll say of a colt who has not learned to take the unexpected in stride. "Oh ... spooky looking!" they'll say of an area containing sights that might alarm horses.

But this can be a serious issue, for horses, being prey animals, are always alert for danger and ready to run from it. They often make their own sudden decisions in this matter, to the peril of their rider.

One of my friends warned me the south end of her ring is haunted, "Every horse who comes here wants to shy in that spot, even when they've not seen another one do it," she says. Could the answer be that one horse did experience a legitimate fright there and exuded something that stays around, like what bloodhounds pick up on? Maybe, other horses noticed and added their own fear until the place became heavy with warning.

Or, maybe horses really do see apparitions of the traditionally attired variety, for they certainly have an almost universal aversion to moving white objects. A piece of paper blowing across the road, a plastic bag caught in a bush, a bed sheet flapping on a nearby clothesline: it takes most horses many safe passages by such things before they can ignore them. Some never can. For this reason, owners often make a point of keeping live white things around their horses, goats or barn cats or dogs of some large European guard breeds. A horse who lives with white things moving around in his space all the time is less likely to shy or bolt when he meets one on the road. I know a certain rotund barn cat who is named, appropriately, White Thing. So on to stories of horses and white things, visible or not.

The Horse Who Came to Church

Probably our best horsey ghost story came from an event at a little settlement named Sand Springs, which was between Rolla and Springfield, not far from the Roubidoux Creek. During the Civil War, this church supposedly had a minister named Maupins who was not very well liked. His morals regarding women were in question, and he was rumored to ride with the Jay Hawkers, who in the counties bordering Missouri and Kansas terrorized people loyal to the South. But having any kind of a minister was a luxury in those days, and people tried to overlook the fact that Maupins often devoted his sermons to rebel-bashing. A Confederate officer, Charles Potter, retired because of war injuries, lived in the area and was not alone in wishing Maupins were elsewhere. Finally he told friends that he would face the man down in the church and send him packing.

When Potter appeared, he was in uniform and on his fine black horse, an animal who had shared his war experience and had injuries of its own. They came down the aisle and stopped in front of the pulpit, but just as the officer began his speech, someone shot him in the back. The shot came from outside, through an open window.

Potter slumped in his saddle and then slid to the floor. The horse bent its head to him, hesitated for a moment, and then turned and walked slowly back down the aisle, out the door and across the porch, its shod feet very loud in the silence. Maupins, probably prepared for what had happened, knelt and commanded the congregation to join him in praying for their safety. This enabled the shooter to escape.

Haunted Heartland and Judge Moore both extended this story elaborately, going into the matter of who the shooter was, her relationship with the preacher, and what became of them all. For our purposes, the main details are that forever after this night, many people claimed to hear a shod horse's hooves on the wooden floor. These sounds came by day or night, during services or when individuals were in the church alone.

In time, the building deteriorated beyond use for worship, but was utilized by travelers who needed shelter. It was these people who gave the story most credibility, because they knew nothing of what had happened earlier. Wayfaring strangers frequently asked local people about the horse who lived in the old church.

A determined debunker might point out that the story tells us nothing about when the horse himself became eligible for ghosthood. They might ask whether this is a case of a live animal being a haunt, or what. Regardless, the tale has found its way into many books for more than a century after it was said to have happened.

Haunted Homecoming

In the 1960s a group of Lebanon High School students made a collection of ghost stories and other folklore. From this material, for several years, they produced a magazine named *Bittersweet*. Here's the group's best ghost story in which a horse participated.

Near Plad, around 1910, lived a farm family with a son named Lowell who worked elsewhere, but usually joined them on weekends. When Saturday mid-morning came and he had not appeared, nobody was concerned, for he was a reliable person. They put in their usual hard day's work, which for his sister, whom we'll call Mary, included preparing Lowell's bedroom. She went to bed and to sleep early and was too drowsy to more than note with relief the sound of her brother's horse trotting up the lane and across the yard to the porch.

Familiar sounds brought her wide awake, however. She heard her brother dismount onto the wooden porch, his spurs jingling, heard him speak softly to the horse as he untacked it and leaned his saddle against the wall. As usual, he gave the horse a little slap and a word or two to send it off to graze, and he came into Mary's room and paused. Not turning over to look at him, because it was too dark to see, anyhow, she said, "Go on up, Lowell. Everything's ready."

He didn't answer, just climbed the stairs accompanied by the sound of his spurs, went into his room and closed the door. Next morning when Lowell didn't come down to breakfast, someone went to rouse him and found the bed untouched. Mary's story was checked out: no horse in the yard, no hoof-prints anywhere, no saddle on the porch. The family spent an anxious day, believing, in the attitude of the time, that Lowell had made his final homecoming. In late afternoon, however, the boy rode in, hale and hearty, having been delayed by pleasant events. All were left to wonder, who, if anyone, had spent the night in their house!

A White-Hat Guy

Another of the Lebanon students' horse stories took place at Oak Grove School, site of the tale given earlier in another chapter about the grinning ghost who could be seen only from outdoors, and who inspired a group of horses to bolt enmasse. Quite a few years later a young man returning from a rather distant party, stopped under the largest of the oak trees that gave the school its name; he needed to rest his fancy new horse — equivalent in his era to a sports car in ours — and perhaps he wanted to revel for awhile, in memories of what a sensation he'd been among his friends with his enviable horse and his own big, new, white western hat.

Rustlings drew the rider's eyes up and he saw someone sitting on a branch just above his head. The man wore a silly expression, suggesting that he might be drunk, which could mean he should be helped down from the tree and pointed toward home. This personage did not respond to friendly conversation, however, and at some point the party-goer decided that he, himself, might be the one in danger. The story does not tell us exactly what led up to it, but in panic he fired his gun. The man on the branch leaned down, plucked off the white hat and flung it in front of the horse, who reared in panic and set out at a dead run.

No doubt the rider urged him on, for the animal was badly spent when they got home. His owner was in worse condition emotionally, however; he jumped off, leaving the expensive status symbol standing in its sweat and tack, and ran upstairs to bed, spurs and all. His family found him next morning with his head still under the covers. We might like to know the horse's fate, but like so many ghost stories, this one ends where it ends.

A Horseman Who Wasn't

Another story from the Lebanon students told of two young brothers who had walked five miles one afternoon to attend evening church services. When they got there, they found the meeting had been cancelled, so tired and disappointed, they started the long trek back home. Twilight found them still trudging along a narrow country road. When they heard a horse coming fast from ahead of them, they separated, one to each side of the road to give the rider plenty of room to pass. They heard and felt all they expected, from experience of such passings — clicking of bridle rings, creak of leather, rush of air. But there was no horse and no rider. The boys stood staring at each other as the hoofbeats began to fade away and then, with no need for consultation, started running as hard as they could. Their fatigue was forgotten; they only hoped the ghostly horseman would not turn around and pass them again. The story says the boys didn't stop running until they were in sight of home.

Colts and Butternut

More than one anthology tells of a strange horseman who haunted a certain portion of a road near Bolivar. Residents of the area thought he was the spirit of a horse thief unknown locally, who had been hanged and hastily buried nearby. However, this was one of those apparitions appearing so real that on encountering him, nobody thought anything about it until later. Anyone could see that he wore two good Colt revolvers, that his boots were battered but had been fine ones, that his trousers were of the sturdy butternut fabric many a rebel soldier took years to wear out after the war. The horse he rode was strong and handsome.

Most who saw this rider considered him just a traveler who did not reply to their greeting or move aside politely to let them pass. And strangely, nobody's horse ever greeted the unknown one or even looked at it. A few claimed to have been chased by this horseman when they met him at night. One man claimed to have been shot in the back by the eerie horseman and he displayed bullet holes in shirt and jacket, but there were none in his flesh. It also was whispered that someone in the area knew the horse thief, because flowers sometimes were placed on his unmarked grave.

Randolph's Spin on Horses

Here are some of the horses Vance Randolph wrote of, in his book, *Ozark Magic and Folklore:*

🕊 A tall white charger ridden by a military man appeared silently at the gate of a farm house where a large family had gathered at the bedside of their aged patriarch. Several men, sitting outdoors, greeted the newcomer and complimented his horse, supposing he was another kinsman. However, in only a moment they recognized something sickly about the pair, and watched them both disappear just as someone came to the door to announce their elderly relative's passing.

🕊 Near Dead Man's Pond, a few miles from Reeds Spring, a young man named Palmer E. Sharp had a strange experience with an "empty" horse. He had taken the animal for a young lady to ride to a dance he'd invited her to. Having delivered her safely to her parents, he was homeward bound himself, when he noticed the extra horse was lagging in an odd way. Scolding it and jerking the lead did no good, and when he looked back, he saw, momentarily, a man sitting on its back. The image faded so quickly he said he could not have given any detail of how the phantom looked or what he wore.

The body of water they were near had a reputation for being haunted because during droughts, when it got very low, human bones could be raked out of it. May Kennedy McCord, a well-known Missouri radio personality of the 1940s, was native to the Reeds Spring area, and she said on air that she'd not think of going near that body of water at night. More data about Deadman's Pond came to me for use in *More Missouri Ghosts*.

A Haunted Horse Farm

A few miles north of Columbia is a 100-acre farm called Skyrim, which has for many years teemed with horses and horse activity; Alice Thompson and her late partner, Dick Cook, bred, raised and trained American Saddlebreds there and coached show horse exhibitors. Many of their pupils, human and non, have been outstanding in the show ring and their favorite stallion, Skyrim's Bourbon Stonewall was for many years one of the highest ranking of his breed, nationally, for begetting show winners.

Thompson's parents, John G. and Mona Neihardt originally owned this property. She was a musician and sculptor and he was a teacher and writer. Before coming to teach at the University of Missouri-Columbia, he'd been prominent among Nebraska's writers and had been named Nebraska's poet laureate, Some of Neihardt's work focused on the Lakota Sioux. Being of mystic bent himself, Neihardt was fascinated with the tribe's religion and its spiritual leaders. One of these men was the subject of Neihardt's most famous book, *Black Elk Speaks*, in the 1960s called "the bible of the young." This book was Nebraska University Press' all-time biggest seller.

While he lived at Skyrim, Neihardt led, for a group of people who shared his interests, a series of "psi" experiments. Several of the people in this circle taught at the university. Some were local writers. They worked in the scientific way, doing all experiments as a group, repeatedly, and documenting each event carefully. The group did successful telekinesis, apportation, and various types of channeling.

During this period — and since — a number of remarkable things happened at the farm. Alice Thompson has compiled a book that records it all. The late Maurice Schwalm, psychical investigator from Kansas City, was present in 1984 and wrote about one particular gathering for a regional Mensa publication. He said people from several states attended and that results were some of the most powerful and unique he had ever seen. The most memorable, he said, was a sound like a locomotive moving through the house, producing almost unbearable noise and vibration. Some others who were present said they did not hear or feel this at all.

Neihardt's granddaughter, Lynn Frazee, grew up at Skyrim, as noted before, and feels that perhaps the study done there created an atmosphere for unusual possibilities. For example: when her grandmother died suddenly from effects of a traffic accident, the children were devastated, for she had been a vital and loving anchor in their lives. Lynn's bedtime was always enhanced by hearing the small sounds her grandmother made in nearby rooms as she moved about barefooted, in a rustling long robe. When Mrs. Neihardt ended her evening's reading, she always went to check the furnace, then performed her last act before bed, a kiss for each sleeping grandchild. Lynn usually managed to stay at least partly awake until she received her grandmother's affectionate goodnight.

For a few weeks after the death, Lynn says, while she and her sister were trying very hard to adjust to this big change in their lives, the soothing night sounds continued as usual and kisses were delivered on schedule. "They felt like bubbles breaking against my skin," Lynn remembers.

Many of the unusual things that happened at Skyrim, however, centered on the horses. An aroma that Thompson called "the sweet burning," heralded events, good or bad, pertaining to the animals. In an interview for *Saddle & Bridle* magazine, Thompson described this scent as both pleasant, like fresh plant tissue, and unpleasant, like decayed organic material, with an element of ashes and scorching. She and Cook became so accustomed to it that if either smelled it anywhere on the property, they would seek out the other to report it, so they could be prepared for something to happen. If they were together, they would look at each other and one would say, "Yes, there it is again." Two incidents that followed the sweet burning:

🐎 A fine mare, bred to their great stallion, had delivered a lovely foal and seemed to be doing fine, but in a few hours began hemorrhaging. Before they could go in to

call the doctor, he drove up, saying, "I just felt like checking the mare again before going home." Thus, he was on
hand to give what help he could, and though the new
mother died, her owners were spared the pain of wondering if immediate medical attention might have saved her.

A foal was born during a thunderstorm, injured before he
was found, and for his lifetime he seemed prone to accident and illness. But Thompson said his spirit was so
optimistic and joyous in spite of all he went through —
so responsive and trusting in spite of all the things his
people had to do to try to help him — that she felt privileged to know him. She said it was as if the sweet burning, that time, announced arrival of a blessing, something
endlessly inspiring and touching.

Scared Of What?

S. M. Jones, in his *Spirit Autobiography,* discussed in
chapter twenty seven of this book, gives one of the most dramatic accounts to be found anywhere of a horse's reaction to
something the rider could not see. It would be hard to dismiss
what Jones described as merely a sensitive equine's response
to its rider's apprehension.

Jones wrote that after the Civil War he was teaching at a
country school where a "spelling school" (spelling bee) was
planned for a certain evening. To get there, Jones had to travel a route he dreaded taking in the dark on a cold night. The
road forked and though he could reach the school from either
branch, each one passed by a cemetery. He said this would not
have bothered him in daylight, but at night the road would be
empty. In one of the cemeteries rested several former neighbors of Jones, people he termed "eccentric and wicked", and
the other cemetery was the site of a spirit who was said to
walk about a great deal.

"As I have a peculiar gift of seeing and hearing strange
things, I hesitated much as to which fork I would take," he
wrote, reasoning that he'd just as soon take neither. To this

point and a little beyond, we might still say that Jones' own dread influenced his horse. When they reached the fork, the animal refused to proceed.

Jones likens it to the Biblical story of the balking of Balaam's ass. That animal, seeing in their path an armed and vengeful angel, refused to move, which presumably saved Balaam's life. In this touching story, the ass finally turned its head to its owner and said, "Why have you struck me these three times? am I not your ass, who has always done your bidding?"

Jones writes that his mount, too, refused his instructions, despite "persuasion and the lash being applied freely." The goading only made him advance a few paces, "tremulously as

though stepping on unholy ground, meanwhile looking to the left at some object invisible to me." The animal's next tactic was to spin and try to bolt back up the road. "I applied the rod excessively, but to no purpose." Jones writes. "The animal reared and pitched, trembling from head to foot and seemed willing to die rather than press forward."

Jones decided that some frightful barrier stood before them, so he "exclaimed in an authoritative tone of thunder 'Get up! Get up there! You infernal, hellfired, son of a b. horse. Confound your infernal continental tripe! Get up there!" These words might well be memorized by anyone who hopes to see a supernatural display, for Jones says they seemingly inspired a long streak of ice in the center of the road to become animated, contracting into first a little spotted dog and then, rising into the air, a "long-legged unearthly looking calf." It was still rising and growing when Jones decided not to remain as witness. "This was enough for me and too much for my steed," Jones writes. The horse reared one last time, almost erect, and they pounded off for home.

His last paragraph says Jones later learned that he might have been murdered had he reached his destination, though he does not explain why. He concludes with "thanks to the Angel of Mercy for his kind and timely protection."

Other Haunted Creatures

The Hudspeth Hounds

by Solomon Wise

The Hudspeth Hounds are loose tonight
And their bay is long and shrill;
As over the ridge and through the fields,
They thread the dusky hill.

They follow the fox through leafless woods,
With a full mood riding high,
Over the brow of Wendelsham
Under a windless sky.

There's a plaintive sound in their lonesome cry,
For the master's ghost lies still;
In his lonely grave, he sleeps in peace
On the crest of Harden Hill.

Time was when he followed the hounds' long trail,
Through the brakes and far away,
But a wraith grows weary after awhile
And clings to his cloak of clay.

. . . . . .

Now a phantom cry is on the air
As the fox treads spectral ways;
And Hudspeth sleeps the sleep of death
And dreams of the good old days.

(Author's note: Wendelsham and Harden Hill were hills in
north central Jackson County.)

**Thomas Benton Hudspeth (1849-1926) of Sibley, Jackson
County, developed a breed of fox and wolf hounds that was
known by his name. This poem appeared in the *Independence
Examiner* in 1942.**

Chapter Twenty Nine

Dogs

"... Deep love endures to the end
And far past the end.
If this is my end, I am not afraid.
I am not lonely. I am still yours."
— Robinson Jeffers, *The Housedog's Grave.*

Considering how easily and deeply humans bond with dogs and cats, we might expect to find endless stories of pets who seemingly return from the other side to protect or comfort or warn those they loved here. No such stories have come to me from Missouri, but there are others. We all know, of course, that cats see ghosts. Who has not felt a little chill to see demure Fluff staring intently at something in midair or high up? Sometimes we can detect a minute dangling spider, or an out-of-season mosquito, but usually we see nothing and can only take reassurance in the fact that the cat soon desists and goes cozily back to sleep.

Most of the animal stories Vance Randolph recorded were unpleasant ones. He told of a group of ghostly pigs who guarded the grave of their owner, who had been buried with all her jewelry. He told of the remains of a long-gone slaughter house near Southwest City which still resounded with the despairing and agonized cries of cows and pigs. One Randolph tale was of a phantom fox whom hounds would

chase until they were exhausted and then it would turn into a white and black "feist" dog (Ozarks term for a playful little mixed breed dog with no particular talent, good for nothing but "feisting around with the kids").

Randolph's dogs were usually big and black, sometimes headless. Night travelers were often frightened by the sudden appearance of hellish black hounds who accosted them and panicked their horses. Hunters and farmers reported seeing these spectral dogs harassing livestock or game; bullets passed through them with no effect. So did whips and sticks. Some war veterans told Randolph of a large black dog who appeared to their group before any battle in which one or more of them would die.

One doctor, however, had a different experience. In a certain area, he was always joined by a large black dog who loped companionably along beside him for a mile or so, then stopped and turned back. The doctor didn't know who the dog belonged to, but considered it a nice animal. His horse was not disturbed when it appeared. Then one night, as they forded a little stream, the doctor happened to look to the side and notice that the friendly dog was running on the water's surface.

Another doctor, this one in St. Louis, claimed to have been helped by some ghostly dogs. *Historic Haunted America* reported that Dr. John J. O'Brien had a very sick patient he felt compelled to see again before he himself went to bed, so he set out on a night of blizzardy snow. The doctor soon realized he had no chance at all of finding his destination, in a part of town without street lights. He was not even sure he could find his own home if he turned back!

The doctor's reliable mare, for the first time in her life, strongly registered resentment of his leadership. Then, in the swirling white, the doctor became dimly aware of two huge mastiffs joining them from the front. They took up positions on each side of the mare and led her through the snow to the street the doctor needed.

He meant to relate this stunning event as soon as he got into the house, but his patient was so ill he had to work steadily with her. By the time he left, the snow had stopped and light was breaking. As a member of the patient's family brought his mare out, the doctor finally got to ask, "Who do those mastiffs belong to? I never saw them around here before." The resident shook his head, saying he knew of no dogs of that description. Subsequent visits to the neighborhood shed no light on them, and the doctor was quoted as saying he watched for them all the time.

But now for two dog stories from our own time:

Who Woke the Dog Up?

Terry Frazee of Wildwood Farm near Centralia has an interesting story that seems to confirm the idea that dogs may sense unseen presences. He says that during his late teens he often spent weekends at a house owned by his aunt and uncle and rented to one of Terry's favorite hunting companions. This was a place Terry had visited often as he grew up. He says he had slept in three different bedrooms and felt nothing in any of them except the one called "the girls' room".

Three sisters had shared this large and pleasant upstairs corner room, which had many windows on two sides. All three girls were now gone from home. Terry says he had at times felt in that room as if he were being watched but not in a way that oppressed or frightened him. No trauma was connected with this house so far as Terry knew. There had been a fourth daughter, born within a month of Terry and then lost in infancy, but the tragedy of losing a child had not been compounded by the circumstances of her death.

On this night, Terry was unusually tired and so was Brandy, his bird dog and cherished companion who always shared his bed. Terry was awakened suddenly from deep sleep by Brandy's leaping to her feet on the bed. She did not jump down as she might have if she just wanted a drink or a cooler sleeping surface. Terry sat up and saw by the moonlight that she was rigid, hackles up, teeth showing, lips fluttering in a soft growl. Brandy was staring into the center of the room, not at the windows. Terry felt a strong sense of danger, and not just from the dog's reaction; he felt something more. By the time he had calmed his dog, however, the feeling was fading. They did not return to sleep easily. Brandy was restless, not leaving the bed, but moving around a lot and curling closer to Terry than she usually slept. He puzzled for a long time about what could have happened, why the room would seem malignant on this one night when it had not before. He says such feelings never came to him and Brandy in that room again, though they slept there repeatedly.

Years later, at a family gathering, he was able to ask a cousin, one of the girls who had occupied the corner room, whether anything unusual had ever happened in the house. She said she knew of nothing except that someone who lived there before her family had lost four children, all under the age of four years.

What Happened to Bruce?

While the Joe Jeff Davis family lived at Lilac Hill in Fayette, they had a large and much-loved German Shepherd named Bruce. Having been with the family since puppyhood, he was devoted to their children, jealously keeping strange people away, putting his body between them and anything he considered possibly dangerous.

Bruce slept mainly on the porch, except for bad weather and times when the children brought him in to play. However, he occasionally scratched urgently on the door to get in and then stayed as close as he could to the family. Bruce was far too polite and well trained to ever get up on furniture, but one day, Marsha Davis says, she heard strange, distressed sounds from a room that was ordinarily unused. It contained a tall old bedstead and matching furniture which had been in the house when they moved in; they had bought all this with its fragile antique velvet bedspread and draperies.

Mrs. Davis did not associate the new sound with Bruce, being so different from anything she'd ever heard from him. But it was not a part of the ghostly repertoire she was accustomed to (described in chapter 25) either, so she went to look. There was the faultless dog in the center of the bed, priceless old spread wadded into a shredded pile under him.

"He was glassy eyed, like in shock," she says "and there was jellyish green slime all over everything. We just threw the bedspread away. But poor Bruce; he wasn't himself for half an hour or so. Then he seemed perfectly all right."

A veterinarian I asked about this said the only logical explanation she could hazard was that Bruce had eaten something toxic that made him deathly sick, but he managed to rid himself of it. She said drinking anti-freeze could produce green vomit, but a dog would not survive it; she knew of nothing else that would produce gelatinous vomit with no identifiable body or plant parts in it. Another doctor found it unusual for a mature dog to eat something strange and for a well-loved, trusting dog to go off alone with his problem, rather than to someone who had always helped him in the past. She also thought it remarkable that a dog in extremity would take the trouble to climb up on a high bed where he had never been before. So perhaps we can wonder, with the Davises, if Bruce chased something otherworldly into that room and had some sort of confrontation. His successor at Lilac Hill, as we've noted in the earlier chapter, often went in wild pursuit of things nobody else could see.

Bruce lived out the Lilac Hill experience with his family and moved with them to a new home where he died when he was almost fifteen, devoted as ever. Perhaps Sir Oliver Lodge, a pioneer psychic investigator, said it for many of us about animals and ghosts: "We human beings live in a world teeming with sounds we cannot hear, colors and light we cannot see, odors we cannot smell and presences we cannot feel. It is a world in which animals repeatedly demonstrate that they possess what to us is an unexplainable sixth sense."

Jim the Wonder Dog

An all-time demonstration of this sixth sense is one of Missouri's great mysteries, Jim, the Wonder Dog. Joel M. Vance, writing about him for *The Missouri Conservationist* in 1990, said "... the dog's abilities were inexplicable and somewhat frightening." Jim inspired production of a book and hundreds of magazine articles, which continue to appear.

Jim was not a ghost, but many people said their hair rose at seeing him "answer" complex questions correctly and make predictions that came true. A frequent reaction to Jim was "That dog is spooky!" Some people who feel that spirits can attach themselves to the living and function through them have a special question: could Jim have been the vehicle for some St. Francislike entity who hoped to change humankind's disregard for the value of animals?

Jim was born March 10, 1925 in the state of Louisiana, descended from Llewellyn setters with top rankings for field performance. His breeder, a man named Taylor, sent him to Sam Van Arsdale, then living in West Plains, as a sort of joke gift. Jim did not meet standards for his breed, being less active than his littermates, possessed of too-big front feet and eyes so expressive and near-human that they made people uncomfortable.

Van Arsdale, an avid quail hunter who traveled all over the United States and into Canada for his sport, did not at first take to Jim. Before investing in a trainer, he gave the puppy to a little niece to play with, to see how Jim's temperament might be. The games the two youngsters devised were remarkable, the owner said — without specifics — and Jim was sent to be trained as a hunting dog.

In his first outing, in a hot, dry field, he was not promising. Instead of eagerly seeking birds, Jim just moved from shady spot to shady spot and rested. When Van Arsdale heard this, he said he would give Jim away, but the trainer objected, saying there was a lot to the puppy and he should have his chance.

On their next outing, Jim redeemed himself handsomely, working like an experienced dog. The mystery was solved: birds were present there. The trainer knew there had been no birds the first time, just their scent. The other puppies didn't know that, but apparently Jim did.

For a couple of years Jim was only an outstanding hunting dog, his remarkable eyes continuing to bring comment from everyone who saw him. Van Arsdale's wife often remarked that he seemed to understand everything she said to him, and one day when they were on a picnic, she asked him to show

her a certain kind of tree. He went and put his foot on it, looking back at her as if relieved that he finally had an opportunity to show what he could do. When the couple asked Jim to
identify other types of trees he went from one to another, correct each time. He even found a tin can, on request.

After these revelations, Jim gradually became a celebrity.
At first his owner just demonstrated to neighbors and hotel
guests how the dog could pick out a man wearing a vest or a
woman in a blue dress. Then he demonstrated that he could
also point out who had two chow-chows at home and who
had never stayed at the hotel before. Van Arsdale discovered
that Jim could locate cars by color or by being shown a
license plate number. He could do this even if the car was in
the next block.

Van Arsdale began putting questions in more complex
form: he'd ask "Jim, if we want to keep our money safe from
Al Capone, where do we put it?" rather than "show us the
safe." Jim even proved that he understood questions put to
him by other people, in other languages and, most important-
ly, he did so when Van Arsdale was not present. This last
point is vital, since "wonder" animals of the past have usually been found to depend on cues from their owner, or the
guidance of subtle body language, not always intentional by
the owner. Some newspaper stories describe Jim performing
when his owner's back was deliberately turned, or when Van
Arsdale stood with hands in pockets and an unlit cigar in his
mouth, making cues impossible.

Many people consider Jim's predictions conclusively
supernatural. Using pictures or written words placed before
him, he correctly foretold the outcomes of sporting events and
elections as well as the gender of unborn children. Jim was
examined by expert and skeptical trainers and by many vet-
erinarians, all of whom admitted they could see no explanation for what he was doing. They speculated that perhaps Jim
had some special kind of intelligence humankind does not yet
understand.

National magazines featured Jim and at least one major
movie studio filmed him for its newsreel. This publicity
brought Van Arsdale many generous offers to buy Jim, or to

take him on tour, or to participate in such stunts as having him photographed with Franklin Roosevelt, whose election he'd predicted. The couple preferred that their aging dog enjoy a quiet life, just as beloved pet and friend. When he died, on March 18, 1937, of heart attack, they had a coffin built to fit Jim and tried to bury him in the family plot in Marshall. This was denied, despite a huge amount of flowers testifying to public opinion about the famous dog. The cemetery board suggested burying him right outside the entrance where those who wanted to see his grave could find it easily. Ironically, the cemetery has grown so much that Jim is now inside it, with his modest monument. For almost 65 years now, people have come from all over the country and beyond, to see his grave of Jim the Wonder Dog.

Since this was written for the first edition of *Missouri Ghosts,* a memorial park has been created to honor Jim and preserve memory of him. The site is a downtown Marshall lot where Van Arsdale's hotel — Jim's home — stood. A decorative wall and flower garden provide a suitable setting for a life-sized bronze likeness of the unforgettable dog.

Evelyn Counts, a Marshall woman who took a leading role in immortalizing Jim says she has been contacted by several people interested in doing something more with the dog's story than has been done up to now. One of them is a California film producer.

The useful thing about all this is that each time Jim's story is told, it will remind us, as the best ghost stories always do, that we mighty humans still don't know everything.

Now thy fled spirit
Delicate and suave,
Thy virtue's core
Above the grave must soar.
— Stevie Smith,
Death of the dog Belvoir

Chapter Thirty

MoMo

I don't know what the thing's proper name is,
but if I meet one, I'll just call it 'Sir.'
— Statement of a deputy sheriff in 1972.

The time was July, 1971, and the place was a pretty rural spot in Pike County, near the city of Louisiana. The participants were Joan Mills and Mary Ryan who had stopped for a picnic as they traveled to St. Louis. *Fate Magazine*, in November 2000, told their story and what came after.

"We both wrinkled up our noses at the same time," Ryan said. The women agreed that they'd never smelled anything so disgusting, calling it worse than a whole family of skunks. Naturally they looked all around, no doubt already certain that they should leave quickly. What they saw was more frightening than skunks.

"This thing was standing in the thicket," Mills said. High weeds hid its lower half, but the two agreed it was bigger than a human and had hair all over its body like a gorilla. "But the face was definitely human," Mills said. "It was more like a hairy human." And it was staring at them with great interest. When the creature moved toward them, the frightened women ran to their car, a Volkswagen, and locked all the doors. Mills had unfortunately not thought to snatch up her purse, which held the car keys.

The intruder made a gurgling sound they compared to "someone trying to whistle under water," and then went all around the car, "caressing it," the women said, and peering into windows. This gave them the chance to see that the palms of its hands were bare of hair. They said nothing about claws, though some later witnesses mentioned them, but the women did say his arms were quite long in proportion to his body height.

The creature whom the press would christen MoMo (Missouri Monster), tried to open the doors but could not. He did not lift up the back end of the car and shake it, as the women were afraid he might. When Mills accidentally hit the horn, he jumped back in alarm, but seemed quickly to grasp that the sound was not dangerous. For no reason the women could guess, this strange individual gave up on them, explored their picnic spread briefly, ate a sandwich, and went back into the woods. Needless to say, Mills and Ryan ran and got the car keys and roared off home with no regard for speed limits. They immediately reported their experience to the highway patrol.

Almost a year passed before MoMo or one of his relatives appeared again and set off a frenzy of newspaper coverage and community hunts. Two young boys were playing in their yard on the outskirts of Louisiana when an older sister heard them screaming and looked out. What she saw was something "six or seven feet tall, black and hairy." Under its arm was a dead dog. "It stood like a man but didn't really look like one," she said, describing little if any neck, and hair curtaining its face.

All summer came more reports, first in the area of Louisiana and then farther away, even in nearby states. These were varied. The creatures described ranged from six to twelve feet in height. Odors ranged from "moldy horse smell," to "like garbage, and growing stronger when MoMo spotted watchers, as if to repel anyone's approach" "rotten flesh ... foul, stagnated water." The monsters' covering of hair was usually black, in one case "erect", in others flowing and of every shade including white. Eyes were said to be big, round, and glowing orange, different eyes than anyone had ever seen on any creature or human. One viewer said the face was actually "almost pleasant in its expression."

A very young man named Harlan C. Hewes came from Oklahoma City, OK to lead a search for MoMo. Hewes had founded an organization called International Unidentified Flying Objects, and among the group's speculations about MoMo was that he was the lost pilot of a crashed UFO, or an experimental animal placed on earth to aid aliens in testing our planet for livability.

Police Chief Shelby Ward put up signs warning people away from the area where MoMo was believed to be "to keep them from shooting each other." Nevertheless, searchers did find a footprint. From its size and depth, they estimated an animal who weighed at least 300 pounds. They also found what they thought might be a hand print. Hewes made casts of these and took them for analysis to Lawrence Curtis, director of the Oklahoma City Zoo. Curtis pronounced the prints "not natural, not made by an animal, possibly a hoax done using a mitten," but he added that if MoMo should be captured, he'd like to have him and his mate for the zoo and breed little monsters.

Meanwhile, the media had a fiesta, as one might imagine. The *Post Dispatch* and *Globe Democrat* sent reporters to the scene, and the Associated Press kept people all over the Country — and beyond — informed of developments. Letters to editors poured in, mainly speculations about what MoMo was, but some demanding relentless hunt until everyone was safe from him.

A few letters pled for mercy for MoMo and these brought the revelation that the U.S. Fish and Wildlife Department had long since set up a protective protocol for any Abominable Snowman/Yeti/Bigfoot/Sasquatch specimen who might ever be captured. "After 120 days protection under the Endangered Species Act," The Associated Press said, "Bigfoot would undergo humdrum processing for long-term safeguarding." The government would want to find out whether the environment for these creatures was still adequate, how many existed and how fast they reproduced.

The MoMo furor gradually diminished, and became something to joke about. When asked what the creature actually should be called, one deputy sheriff said "I don't know what it's official name is, but if I meet one, I'll just call it 'Sir'." A Louisiana restaurant operator, when asked by a traveler what the whole matter meant said, "Maybe we didn't learn all we could have, but we had a lot of fun." AP, however, signed off by reminding us that for many years before they ever were proved to be true, reports persisted of the existence of animals later named gorillas, pandas, and komodo dragons.

Three
Great
Mysteries

We may or may not believe in ghosts, ESP, UFOs, or anything else beyond our everyday experience, but Missouri has three well-documented happenings besides Jim the Wonder Dog that defy explanation. They are found in numerous internationally published books about the otherworldly, books done shallowly for sensation and others incorporating scholarly study. One event, involving what is today called "channeling" has too much substance and complexity to be laughed away. Another is an incredible variation on what our species presently understands; for now, it is just an enjoyably scary novelty. The third phenomenon seems to demonstrate some of the worst the unknown can do.

Chapter Thirty One

Patience Worth

Oh, lost
and, by the wind grieved ghost,
come back again!
— Thomas Wolfe, *Look Homeward, Angel*

"The most tantalizing case in psychical research ... and the greatest of all literary riddles." This is how something that happened in Missouri early last century has been described by writers about the paranormal. It was contact, via Ouija board, from an entity who said her name was Patience Worth, that she was born in the 1600s in England and died in our country in an Indian raid. She then proceeded, for more than a decade, to produce millions of words of conversation, maxims, poetry, prose and drama. People flocked to St. Louis to witness sittings by her channeler; they eagerly bought printed versions of her work. Patience Worth's pronouncements were read in the United States and elsewhere as magazine articles and as books from one New York book publisher, Henry Holt.

It all began in July, 1913, when two St. Louis friends, Pearl Curran and Edith Hutchings, joined a fad then current for "Weedj," a game board painted with letters and numbers. Supposedly spirits would use the board to spell out answers to questions, if two human operators provided physical means by resting their fingers lightly on a little wooden marker.

A few weeks of effort had brought the ladies nothing but some sentence fragments, garbled material that seemed to be vaguely religious in content. Then, suddenly one night, the marker began moving decisively and it clearly spelled out "Many moons ago I lived. Again I come. My name Patience Worth."

Mrs. Curran's mother copied down the string of letters that followed, and when these had been divided into words and sentences, they promised that important messages would soon arrive. Over the next several weeks, Patience Worth became a strong presence for this group of friends and their friends' friends and neighbors. A popular newspaper writer, Caspar Yost, heard of Patience and *The Globe Democrat* carried a series of his articles which relayed what the mysterious entity said about death and the hereafter. Yost also gave samples of Patience Worth's poems.

Another St. Louis literary personage, William Marion Reedy, became intrigued. Reedy edited a widely respected magazine of prose, poetry, essays and book reviews. He was credited with "discovering" — giving their first sales — to a number of writers who became famous. Though he accepted nothing Curran relayed about Patience's origin, Reed said what was being produced there was "near genius" and needed to be preserved. His endorsement, with growing public interest in the Patience phenomenon, influenced Holt to publish a book Yost wrote about her, and then two of the novels which came, purportedly, from Patience through Curran.

Long before this, Patience Worth had begun manifesting without need for Edith Hutchings' help, or even the board's. Curran found herself uttering letters and then words as fast as she could speak, and she said that with the fiction, Patience sent colored pictures depicting its scenes. Mrs. Curran visited New York and Chicago and other cities to accommodate crowds interested in Patience. Audience members included Amy Lowell, Hamlin Garland, Fannie Hurst, Upton Sinclair, Edgar Lee Masters and other celebrity writers of the time. Ethel Barrymore and Mr. and Mrs. Douglas Fairbanks were only three of the famous entertainers who came to hear her.

The Currans and some supporters started a magazine devoted to Patience Worth's work, but it lasted for only a few months because interest in the riddle inevitably faded. In 1922 John Curran died, leaving his wife with a young daughter and another child on the way.

After a short period of traveling about, presenting readings in clubs and private homes, Pearl Curran moved to California, where one dedicated Patience supporter offered her financial help. Curran tried to make more money by writing, but with little success. Critics compared her work unfavorably to what had come through her from Patience. Pearl Curran died in California in late 1937, her last reading on Thanksgiving day having been a moving prayer of gratitude from Patience, for being given the opportunity to reveal helpful truths. Though Curran had told her friends that Patience had warned her of imminent death, they still were surprised. Mrs. Curran's health had not seemed seriously delicate.

To the world, Patience Worth ended with Pearl Curran, but in reality, we're told, she continued channeling through one of Mrs. Curran's daughters. This woman apparently worked reluctantly, and only with a small group of friends. One Missourian, Dr. Irene Hickman of Kirksville, was in this circle. She recorded and published poetry dictated by Patience Worth in California. Hickman, a long-term Worth devotee, collected and studied Curran's channeling materials for years.

Patience Worth drew many to share a conviction stated in 1927 by Walter Franklin Prince, a respected investigator whose *The Case of Patience Worth* is the most complete study ever done on the subject. In 1927 he wrote, "Either our concept of what we call the subconscious must be radically altered .... or else some cause operating through, but not originating in the subconscious of Mrs. Curran must be acknowledged. In the former case we normalize what has always been deemed 'supernormal'; in the second case we admit the supernormal."

At least once in each generation comes a revival of interest in Patience Worth. The half dozen or so books and vast other work written about her are studied anew, as are her own apparent writings. Findings of past investigators are pondered and still nobody, no matter how determinedly unbelieving, has been able to present a theory, let alone evidence, as to how Patience Worth could have been a hoax.

Nobody has proposed a motive or described how the Currans could have faked the Patience readings. The couple was well off when Patience Worth first manifested, but not at all secure at the ends of their lives. The fact that Pearl Curran was hard put to support herself as a widow proved that they had not profited from Patience Worth. Indeed, the husband once said in an interview that they lost a great deal on the magazine and that he'd spent at least $4,000 just on the comfort of people who came, free of charge, to the Curran house for readings. Additional expenses were incurred for stenographers and typists hired to help handle the Worth materials.

It is doubtful that the Currans did all this for attention, since much of the attention Patience brought them was negative. Pearl Curran told an interviewer that she was looked at with distrust by some of her friends, and with awe by others, in both cases losing relationships. Also, she was ridiculed in both the printed and the spoken word. The schedule of readings she kept, often many nights in a row, was fatiguing and stressful.

While none of the three literary figures in Curran's life — Yost, Reedy and Holt — ever conceded Patience was exactly what Curran said she was, they gave vital support.

Yost pointed out that any writer who could produce such work would not be likely to present it as another person's and in obscure language that made public enjoyment difficult. Reedy remarked that with writing being so time-consuming at best, nobody would opt to compose in secret and memorize everything and then sit and transmit it to the relatively few people who could and would come to listen.

Investigators, Prince tells us, found nothing in Pearl Curran's background that suggested capability for doing such writing. As a schoolgirl she had little interest in anything but music and she was allowed to end her education at the age of

13. She had never cared about history or England and no later change in attitude could be found. Religion had only a small place in Curran's childhood and none in her adult life. No interest in serious literature or writing could be uncovered. What she did read was light fiction and not much of that. The Curran home contained no books pertaining to anything Patience talked about and there was no evidence that either of the Currans had checked such materials out of libraries. Their home included no area set up for research or writing.

Prince himself conducted some of the investigation he described in his book and a detail much dwelt on was that Mrs. Curran did not spend the time in seclusion that would have been required for the quantity of memorizing she would have had to do to stage her lengthy channelings. She kept her usual schedule of socializing, shopping and managing a house that was, while not luxurious, more than just comfortable. According to those who wrote about her, Pearl Curran was considered by her friends to be a pleasant, uncomplicated, unpretentious person. Her step-daughter said Pearl Curran was not capable of conceiving a hoax or carrying it off.

Even if Mrs. Curran had been a recluse, protected from all distraction, the question remained of how anyone could memorize and deliver, without errors and at conversational pace, the amount of material Pearl Curran relayed in sittings often lasting two hours. Nobody could do it, even by devoting the whole of each day to what would be recited that night.

An additional question from Prince: how could polished, graceful poetry be produced impromptu when audience members suggested topics Mrs. Curran could have no way of anticipating? This was a frequent feature of her sittings.

Also baffling was the general quality and content of the PW work, declared by various experts of the time to be superb. Today's critics would be much less impressed, because it is wordy and flowery, but that was the admired mode in her era. Few of today's readers would stay with most of the prose, laboriously reproducing speech patterns and difficult vocabulary of another time and place. Those who knew, though, said that facts presented in the Worth material were exactly correct for the 1600s in the area where the entity said she grew up. This was true also for the Eastern and Bible Land settings of her fiction and drama. One religious expert said Patience Worth's attitudes were typical of the liberal Quakers of her era. Her messages are explored in some detail in Appendix A.

Perhaps next year someone will be able to explain Patience Worth. Maybe as more science fiction comes true, all the great untapped brains of the past will be channeled. For the present, Missouri holds its position in annals of the supra-normal for having what Dr. Prince called "the most amazing case of its kind in history."

Chapter Thirty Two

The Spook Light

"There are no unnatural or supernatural phenomena, only very large gaps in our knowledge of what is natural .... We should strive to fill those gaps of ignorance."
— Edgar D. Mitchell, Apollo 14 Astronaut

Technically, this phenomenon of moving, varicolored lights is not Missouri's, for its main activity is just across the state line on Oklahoma soil, but Missouri roads have given uncountable people quick access to an unaccountable sight. These roads can be picked up near Hornet, a hamlet south of Joplin. Though the Spook Light is not what we usually think of as a ghost, it inspires in viewers the same sort of disbelief and uneasiness as ghost sightings, sometimes great fear. Some people declare that they've found spiritual inspiration in the lights. Like the whole subject of ghosts, it seems to be just one of those things we do not, at this time, understand.

Here are a few of the many Spook Light (also called Indian Light or Hornet Light) descriptions, from hundreds of articles written about it:

🐿 a ball of orange-yellow fire that radiates — or does not radiate — heat as it goes by

🐿 a blue-silver ball or a ball made up of many balls of many colors

🐿 two greenish, bluish balls that spin against each other

a purple bubble, sometimes diamond or oval shaped
light concentrating itself into the size of a golf ball, too
blindingly bright to look at

Most commonly, the light swings or bobs back and forth
across the road, its formations varying in size from about that
of a basketball to that of a bushel basket, its altitude varying
from ground level to tree-top. However, when under intense
observation, the light has been reported to come speeding
down the road and just before seeming inescapable impact
with a car or person, lift up, fly over, come down behind them
and continue on. It's said to usually retreat from whatever
advances toward it. If shot at, the light may burst into a fire-
works-like blizzard of tiny sparks or bubbles and then
reassemble, but it has also been reported to do this without
being shot at.

Some people have declared that the light followed their
car as they left the scene. Residents of the area have reported
it coming onto their property. One said it spent an evening on
his porch and at times seemed to be looking in the front window. Another described its appearance in the barn door one
night when the family was milking and said it blocked their
exit for an nerve-wrackingly long time. It's been called "very
consistent, performing almost every night in all weather at all
times of year." It's even been reported in daylight.

Of course many explanatory stories have been created
since 1886, the date usually given for the light's first being
described in print. Because Choctaws originally held the land
where the lights appear, people created explanatory legends
involving Indians. The lights were the spirits of young lovers
kept apart by cruel elders, or one light was a lost chieftain trying to find his way home.

Because the light's area of activity includes some mining
sites, there were stories on that theme too. For instance, a
miner looks for his children stolen by Indians or for something he has lost along the path. There's even a Civil War
story, about a deserter executed by cannon fire. The most
thoughtful story is that the light somehow commemorates
sufferings of exiled Cherokees on the infamous Trail of Tears,

struggling through the general area in the winter of 1838-39, forced from their homes in the south to Indian Territory in what became Oklahoma.

Many qualified people and groups have applied scientific methods to their study of the Spook Light. They have accomplished little more than to disprove some of the easiest theories, that the light is swamp gas, St. Elmo's fire, will-o-the-wisp or refracted car lights. Swamp gas requires presence of more water than exists in the Hornet area, they tell us, and it gives off a distinctive sulphury odor. St. Elmo's fire does not move about freely on its own, but must attach to something which is electrically charged. Will-o-the Wisp is seen over extensive masses of decaying organic matter, not over a dry road or open fields such as the Spook Light apparently chooses for its abode.

The idea that car lights are refracting from highways or airports out of sight of the viewing road called Devil's Promenade might be accepted except that the Spook Light was written of long before cars, highways or airports existed.

To see the Spook Light, instructions from Joplin City Hall say "take I-44 west from Joplin to 43 Highway. Drive South on 43 approximately six miles to BB Highway. Turn right and drive approximately three miles to the road's end. Turn right and drive another mile to the second dirt road on the left. You will see a little building on the right and are now headed west on Spook Light Road also known as The Devil's Promenade. Park anywhere along the side of the road and wait. Approximately 1 1/2 miles down the road is best and darkest."

Experiences of Missourians with less ambitious lights than the one near Hornet might also be worth a little analysis. Judy Grundler of Columbia tells of lights seen by three generations of her relatives on their farm. These mini-spooks are small and bluish white, usually seen across a certain field, in pretty much the same spot, only occasionally approaching closer, observed only one time on the lawn of the house. She says that they were consistent in showing up, when she knew of them, consistent about disappearing as cars went by.

Among the *Bittersweet* collection of Ozarks lore was a brief story of two men driving home in a wagon after a hard day's work at logging. Unaccountably their tired horses became agitated enough that the men leaped out, each going to a horse's head to quiet it. From that position they could see, from some distance behind them, a large, brilliant light in the road. As they watched, it sped forward and finally overtook them. They had time only to lower their heads against the horses' necks before it swept over them and on down the road ahead and out of sight. This happened somewhere in the Ozarks, but was presented as a one-time oddity, unconnected to the Hornet Spook Light.

One interviewee who preferred not to be identified repeated a family story from her mother's time, when the family lived on a farm near Braggadocio, far down in Missouri's bootheel. Almost every evening, a single ball of orange fire would roll down a particular tree trunk, across the ground and under the porch. It never did any harm, but it frightened the children and made neighbors unwilling to visit after dark. Far-fetched as that may sound, it could lead us to a possible explanation, for another part of the story is that a friend who was a woodsman told this family he'd often seen a similar phenomenon. He said it happened only in one kind of tree and that was the very kind they had by their porch.

Eugene Brunk, Assistant State Forester for more than a decade with the Missouri Conservation Commission, says that trees which are rotting inside can produce quite a lot of methane gas. In taking core samples, he has heard the gas escaping from pierced trees and has known of instances when enough escaped that it could be lit and would burn for ten minutes. Methane may escape less dramatically through cracks in bark, and it can reflect light shining on it, Brunk says. Is it possible then, that with temperature changes, a tree cracked down its length could release gas that would reflect the light of lamps in a house as it followed a crack down exposed roots that went under a porch?

"Maybe ...." Brunk says. This would be a very long shot and is far removed from antics of the Hornet Light, but may indicate a principle that will someday be found to apply.

One theory about Spook Lights is that they are caused by something contained in the ground beneath them. A classic example is the locality in Texas state where the incredibly profitable Spindletop Oil Well was developed. Weird lights were said to have danced over the terrain there for as long as anyone could remember.

Still another possibility might be underground movements associated with earthquakes. In the summer before Missouri's great quakes of 1811-12, strange lights and odors were widely reported in the area of New Madrid where the quakes occurred. Missouri's famous Spook Light appears in a fault area.

"Dears, I am so sorry for you ...
God bless you, you poor darlings ...."
They smiled at her
with shy little baby smiles ....
They grew faint, fading slowly
away like wreaths of vapor
in the frosty air.

— E. F. Benson Story,
"How Fear Departed
From the Long Gallery"

Chapter Thirty Three

An Unpleasant Exclusive

Hence, horrible shadow! Unreal mockery, hence!
— Shakespeare, *McBeth*

Missouri's fourth exclusive in annals of the supernatural inspired a book and a movie, both named *The Exorcist*. Most people have seen or heard of both. Main differences between fact and fiction are that the victim of apparent possession was a boy instead of a girl and that nobody died as a result of combat with demons. The real-life episode lasted for about three months and was resolved. The victim, now in his sixties, was freed and lived a normal life. Here's what happened, according to *Possessed, The True Story of an Exorcism,* by Thomas B. Allen.

In 1949, the life of a Maryland family named Mannheim (for purposes of the report) living in a suburb of Washington, D. C. was disrupted when their son became the focus of strange happenings. Robbie (again, not the true name) was almost fourteen and had been spending a great deal of time playing with an Ouija board. He'd been introduced to this by a recently deceased aunt. Robbie's parents didn't monitor his game. They said later they had no idea what he was asking the board or whether he thought it was giving him contact with his aunt.

First happenings were puzzling and mildly annoying sounds. Sounds of dripping water came where faucets were tightly shut and some animal seemed to be clawing wood, but no source could be found. The next eerie occurrence was what sounded like someone marching back and forth in squeaky shoes beside Robbie's bed. Several family members heard this. Sounds became more disturbing, as the clawing seemed to come from within Robbie's mattress. Then a large, heavy chair lifted itself from the floor, tipped sideways and dumped Robbie out. His father and uncles were unable to tip the same chair when exerting all their weight and strength to do so. At a friend's house, a rocker Robbie sat in began spinning wildly. At school his desk-chair moved out into the aisle and glided about as if on runners.

Understandably, Robbie became upset. He was allowed to drop out of school, but this didn't help. He began to wake up at night screaming, and his family sometimes heard him muttering in his sleep in strange voices, often spouting obscenities. Sometimes the voices threatened harm to family members. Scratches began to appear on Robbie's body, sometimes suggesting a taloned paw, sometimes spelling out "NO".

The Mannheims could not dismiss this as a mentally ill child's hoax. They had seen such things as a dresser moving under its own power across the bedroom to block Robbie's bedroom door. Its drawers zipped in and out as if someone were frantically searching through them. The parents sought help from doctors, psychologists and ministers, but nobody knew what to do. Their own Lutheran minister prayed regularly with the whole Mannheim family. Friends and church members organized a special prayer circle. When every effort seemed fruitless, the minister suggested getting help from a Catholic priest, since that denomination does not dismiss the idea of devils.

The local priest who agreed to help sent Robbie to a nearby Catholic hospital where he would be surrounded by dedicated Christians and by symbols of religion. He had Robbie put in restraints to control growing violence which included spitting on people and kicking at all who approached him. In spite of this, Allen writes, Robbie somehow got a piece of bedspring loose; he raked it with such force down the whole length of the priest's arm that the wound took more than a hundred stitches to close.

In early March, about a month after their problems began, the local priest admitted defeat, and advised the family to take Robbie to St. Louis, where there is a concentration of Jesuit priests. Tradition says that The Order of Jesus retains some of the ancient books and rituals that can be used for exorcism. St. Louis University was founded by the Jesuits and at that time they operated it.

In St. Louis, a team of three priests spent many nights with Robbie, praying around his bed, commanding possessing demons to depart. Despite these measures, all symptoms grew worse. Robbie flailed about as if doing strenuous exercises, and for longer than seemed humanly possible. He laughed wildly. He destroyed the priests' prayer books and attacked anyone who came close enough, breaking one priest's nose, causing another's to bleed. Robbie threw his food around the room and sang for hours at a time, often obscene songs from long-gone eras of history.

At one point, however, according to Allen's book, one of the boy's strange, deep voices said Robbie would not be free until he, himself, called on Jesus for help. This seemed to be the turning point. The priests adapted their efforts to using Robbie's few rational moments to make baptism possible. The actual ceremony took place only after four hours of physical struggle, with Robbie protesting and cursing throughout. Amidst it all, however, the priests heard Robbie say, as if to himself, "I do renounce Satan and all his work."

Problems didn't end immediately, but at 10:45 next morning a clear, rich voice said through Robbie, "I am Saint Michael and I command you, Satan, and the other evil spirits to leave this body in the name of Dominus. Now! Now! Now!"

After a few minutes more of struggle, Robbie grew quiet and announced in his own voice, "He's gone." A great explosive sound ripped through the hospital, heard by all who were there. A little later, Robbie took communion, ate, and had a deep sleep. He awoke asking where he was and seemed to have little memory of the ordeal he and so many others had been through.

Though the priests working with Robbie had been told by their superiors not to make any record of the experience, some of them did. Earlier, the Mannheims and others had written down what they saw happening with Robbie. Allen was grateful for this, saying it made Robbie's the best-documented case of exorcism in our time. And it happened in Missouri.

Regardless of one's feeling about the supernatural, the fact remains that Missouri has four of the most studied and most written of mysteries in history, the case of Patience Worth, the Hornet Spook Light, Jim the Wonder Dog and the "Robbie Mannheim" Exorcism. As study continues, our state may become world famous for being the place where major questions were answered.

When A Body ...

Chapter Thirty Four

Meets a Nonbody

Vex not his ghost; O! let him pass.
— Shakespeare, *Hamlet*

*Then a spirit passed before my face;
the hair of my flesh stood up.*
— The Bible, *Job*

Anyone who collects ghost stories soon sees that most of them fall into categories. Some are obvious fabrications, spun out for fun by good storytellers; those told by my cousin Ed surely are examples. Some ghostly doings are pranks such as the one at Christian College; some are drama created and enacted for a serious purpose — like the Ozarks patriarch who, on his deathbed, had a young descendant brought to him and said, "It's time for me to tell you how to do the h'ant that keeps people away from our still." Some ghostly encounters related in perfect sincerity are illusion. We all know that extreme stress, sleep deprivation and some drugs — all of which can change body chemistry — may be the real cause of hallucinations of sight, sound and smell.

Some encounters accepted as supernatural are honest mistakes or uncertainty. A perfect example came as the first edition of this book was almost finished, from a relative who adamantly disbelieves in ghosts, ESP, UFOs and whatever else can even remotely be termed occult or supernatural. But she told me this, about a ride she took on her Arabian mare, accompanied by a very large white dog.

"There were only a few more nights left to see the Hale-Bopp Comet, so I got on Crissy bareback and we went down the road a half mile or so to that open field that gives a good view of the sky. Emma Rose was the only dog who came along. When we passed the house where the pointers live, I was watching for them, though Crissy is never alarmed by dogs and Emma Rose is enough accustomed to these particular ones that none of them make more than a token challenge to each other. They didn't come out, which is unusual.

"Just past there, at that brushy curve, I saw a dog standing looking across the road. In the poor light, I didn't recognize it. It looked something like a chow, only taller. I wondered if it might by a coyote. Then it started across the road and I could see that it had a peculiar gait, as if crippled. All this time Crissy did not turn her head toward it or move her ears. Emma Rose didn't look either, and the dog never looked at us. It was really creepy, as if no dog were actually there or we were not there for it. That dog had to have heard us coming on the gravel. It made a sort of half circle out in the field, and then moved into the trees. I would never have thought animals could be so close together and none of them acknowledge the others, especially when one of them was not moving normally."

We talked about the fact that a neighbor, considerably farther away on an intersecting road, used to have a pair of chows, but we'd not seen them for so long we doubted they were still there. We wondered if someone had dumped out an injured dog, or a stray had been hit by a car. We agreed to watch for the chows or for any new dog in the area and for a limping coyote. Within a week we passed the crossroads and saw the two chows with a taller companion who looked like a chow mix and appeared to have a missing hind foot.

So much for what could have been a good story, the limping ghost of Hartley Road! And so much for the commonly accepted idea that if animals don't react to other animals, some of them are not physically present.

What explains this incident? Maybe the air was moving across all souls at a right angle, not dropping any clues. Maybe the lame dog is deaf and sight-impaired. Maybe all the animals involved are well acquainted in their nighttime life which we humans know nothing about, so that meeting on the road was a non-event to them.

Natural happenings, though far-fetched, explain another category of ghost stories. An 1895 *The Missouri Patriot* reprinted a Des Moines newspaper story telling of the end of a "peg-legged ghost" that had haunted one of the city's hotels for a decade. Many guests and hotel employees had heard, through many nights, the sound of a normal and a strange footstep in sequence down one particular hall. Rooms on that whole floor became hard to rent, so the proprietor finally decided to replace the floor of the hallway.

When the boards were taken up, he found a remarkable explanation for the peg-legged walking. One joist had been grooved out along its whole length to accommodate a line for gaslights, but had not been used that way, for some reason. Rats, however, had found it a most convenient conduit for travel, so much so that their moving bodies actually rounded off sharp edges of the groove. Rats are heavy enough that their passage caused the imperfectly seated joist to raise up and down against other boards, and this created sounds that frightened people for years and cost the hotel owner quite a lot of money.

Categories of Ghosts

Just as stories have categories, so do the ghosts. Different types of spirits do different things. Banshees vocalize in an unearthly manner; poltergeists make noises, throw things around and sometimes get credit for starting fires. Any dictionary or thesaurus gives an incredible number of synonyms for ghost: apparition, phantom, wraith, revenant, visitant, entity and doppelganger are just a few. An apparition is something we can see, and perhaps phantoms and wraiths are too. Revenant just means one who comes back, and some boats are given this for a name. Visitants and entities are indefinable presences or perhaps any of the other types of ghosts. Doppelgangers, as we saw with Mark Twain, are the doubles of living people.

Psychic investigators also speak of "thought forms," the apparent explanation in Maries County when a couple reported regular visits in their home of a pleasant looking elderly woman. She was no threat to anyone and caused no disturbance; they would just see her at the kitchen counter, in the rocking chair, at the front curtains, looking out. Finally they described her to enough people that someone said "she sounds just like a woman who used to live in your house; she's still alive, in a nursing home near here." The couple went to see her, and indeed the image they had seen was exactly like the woman before them. This aging lady told them how very deeply she had loved the house, built for her when she was a bride of eighteen and the only home she had known since then. She said she spent a great deal of time reliving her happy life there with her husband of more than sixty years. The couple said nothing about seeing her and resigned themselves to sharing the house.

Complicating the matter of ghosts is the fact that two of the synonyms commonly given are "spirit" and "soul." Even in the Bible, the three words are often used interchangeably, and we hardly notice: Holy Ghost, "... he gave up the ghost;" "... the spirit returned to God who gave it;" "tonight thy soul will be required of thee." It's interesting that airlines and ships speak of their passenger lists in terms of souls aboard and different groups attribute different qualities to some of these terms. For instance, Jehovah's Witnesses feel that our bodies and souls are inseparable, that each of us is a soul, not a body serving as vehicle for a spirit. They feel that all living things are souls, animals as well as human beings. The religions of most Indian tribes attribute spirit to every element of nature.

Why Does It Matter?

We who collect ghost stories soon become aware of just how intensely interested people are in all that pertains to the hereafter. As mentioned earlier, we're told that some of the most used — and most stolen — library books are those featuring ghosts. The popularity of mysteries turning on the supernatural is undying. As the first edition of *Missouri Ghosts* was written in 1997, a whole new category of romance novels was developing, those in which living people are in love with ghosts; this trend continues. It's a big surprise to see in books of quotations how many prominent and respected people, over the centuries, have speculated about ghosts and how many have said they believe in them.

Why does our species care so much? Some of these quotations explain it clearly. Robert Blair, a British poet of the 1700s, wrote in a poem called "The Grave":

"Tell us, ye dead! Will none of you in pity
To those you left behind disclose the secret?
Oh! that some courteous ghost would blab it out!
What 'tis you are, and we must shortly be."

From our own generation comes this statement from a movie director named John Carpenter: "The most important question each of us has to answer is what happens to us after death. We don't want to accept it as finality. Ghosts are proof that there is a spirit inside that survives death."

Pronouncements of skeptics are equally thought provoking. The British writer, J. B. Priestly, commented on the fact that so little of what comes from the supposed hereafter in seances and various psychic readings has any real importance for our lives. He asked why those in spirit form, who should be in a position to give us invaluable information, apparently choose not to. He speculated that we can hope for nothing that is beyond the medium's knowledge. Priestly argued that if spirits have any power to do anything or communicate anything, our departed loved ones would use their ability to protect and guide us.

This takes us back to that Missouri exclusive, Patience Worth. A few instances of channeling have offered elaborate descriptions of the hereafter and suggestions for how we should be living, but what Pearl Curran gave us, as from Worth, seems the most concise, logical and usable. Some of it appears in Appendix A.

But What If We Meet One?

This is the bottom line with many fans of ghost stories: regardless of what ghosts are or what their intentions are or what they know, how do we protect ourselves against them? Fascinating as ghosts are, most of us would join Alfred, Lord Tennyson is questioning whether we really want our departed loved ones hovering around all the time, watching us, tuning in on our thoughts.

For advice on dealing with ghosts, Missourians are lucky. We have three widely recognized experts, psychical investigators from three parts of the state, Bevy Jaegers of St. Louis, the late Maurice Schwalm of Kansas City and Dr. Irene Hickman of Kirksville. Their outlooks vary, but are mainly reassuring. Jaegers and Schwalm see most discarnate (bodiless) entities as basically harmless and not especially interested in us; Dr. Hickman takes the demonic side of the supernatural more seriously but tells us how to avoid it. More data about each of these people appears in Appendix B.

Jaegers has studied psychic phenomena for decades, has written extensively about them and conducted seminars and classes. Her view is that most so-called ghosts have agendas of their own and only occasionally are interested in us. "They have no power over us except the power to frighten, and I don't believe many of them try to do that," she says. She points out that most injuries reported from ghostly encounters come from someone's falling or otherwise getting hurt in a panicked retreat, and less often, from collapse or heart symptoms. Taking a calm view of ghosts can prevent dangerous reactions and Jaegers' viewpoint helps us.

She says that if the apparition appears aware of you, or perhaps makes an entreating gesture, it's best to say something like "I'm sorry I can't help you, but if you put out your hand and look for the light, you will find a better place than this." Jaegers says a great many manifestations are from spirits of people who died under circumstances that left them confused about whether they are dead or alive. Some are fearful of going to another level of existence. Some are deeply attached to living people or to earthly places or possessions and cannot readily give them up. When she works with a team of psychic investigators, their procedure in houses reputed to be haunted is just to give the message of looking for the light and going to the better things available. In most instances that seems to work. Jaegers adds that praying can give courage in such situations; she and those in her group frequently pray, alone or together.

Jaegers repeats that dangers from evil spirits are minimal, saying, "It's more a matter of being *obsessed* than *possessed*." She reminds that it's easy for someone in a vulnerable emotional state — from bereavement, perhaps, or another crisis — to undermine their physical and mental health by dwelling on the idea of communicating with the departed. As many charlatans operate in the field of parapsychology as anywhere else, she says, often offering help that is impossible to produce and preying on those who believe them. People tend to accept the expertise of these people much more easily than they would accept it in another field. Jaegers says that anyone who wants help from a psychic or parapsychologist should go at it in the same way they'd look for any professional services, drawing on the experience and referrals of people who have some way of knowing who can be trusted. Local law enforcers often know who, in the area, works in a professional way and gets tangible results. Doctors may know, too, especially psychologists.

Bevy Jaegers warns against looking for answers from ouija boards, seances and such; resuming and retaining the best of ones normal life is usually a far more effective cure for problems.

Schwalm said "... if you meet a ghost, you should feel honored, for not very many people have this experience." He warned though, that chances are you'll never know you've met one, because most apparitions look perfectly real. He agreed with Jaegers that few ghosts have any bad intent toward us. Sometimes they just want to be noticed, and like a tiresome child, can be deflected by being ignored. "If you feel a touch, or see or hear or smell something, just go ahead with what you're doing," he said.

For those tempted to experiment with the occult, Schwalm's main warning was to realize that something troublesome may come home with you from a seance. He said that one should not go into deep meditation in a place reputed to be haunted. In such a setting it's best there to do nothing more than close the eyes briefly to see what impressions may come. Schwalm emphasized that people with tendencies to be obsessive should entirely avoid the occult.

Schwalm believed that wearing or holding a cross has a protective effect for many individuals, and he suggested that any kind of religious symbol, even from a faith not your own, can give this benefit. He, too, suggested prayer, remarking that Silent Unity, a program of perpetual prayer sponsored by the international group called Unity, is a good refuge in these cases. He often asked for remembrance from the Kansas City prayer unit when he felt he might be going into something potentially dangerous. Another self-protecting move, he said, can be simply to visualize oneself surrounded by white light.

At the same time, Schwalm had a cheering thought that is new to most of us: "Remember that you have around you, at times — maybe most of the time — spirits with a supporting or protective interest in you. These may be relatives or just someone attracted from elsewhere because they'd like to have a part in something positive you're doing."

Like a guardian angel?

"If you want to think of it that way," he said, and added that there's nothing wrong with invoking protection and help from such beings. One last remark: "their responses aren't likely to be dramatic messages, more likely just feelings or ideas that seem to be your own."

The Dark Side

Dr. Hickman, while agreeing in many ways with the others, feels that most of the world's suffering stems from the attachment to humans of malevolent entities, or of fragments of energy from those who were confused, frightened or emotionally disturbed. She feels that the spirits of people who had various vices or obsessions often seek out living humans through whom they can continue to experience the things they enjoyed in life. For instance, someone who died from smoking, or the abuse of alcohol or other substances — or even food — may attach to a person who is fighting the same compulsion, increasing that person's pleasure in the vice and thwarting efforts to stop. Sadists will seek out individuals whose activity they can share and encourage.

Dr. Hickman also speaks of "the dark ones," fragments of power engendered by such destructive emotions as hate, greed, vindictiveness, cruelty, and various vices. These forces are less organized in what they try to do, but can cause a great deal of confusion and other problems.

In Dr. Hickman's philosophy, we're at our most vulnerable when we indulge in activity we know we should avoid. Thus, the greatest element of self-protection is just avoiding going to the places and doing the things that would be enjoyed by evil beings. But, Dr, Hickman warns, the best of us are vulnerable when exhausted, ill, under anesthesia, depressed or highly stressed, so we should try to live in the most healthful way possible. Particularly, she says, we should avoid drugs and alcohol.

One other recommendation from Dr. Hickman: "Be militantly independent! Resolve that nobody and no thing is going to dictate to you what you should do or feel or think." She gives an example of her view of how entities may work: "In a period when I was using an ouija board, an entity kept announcing itself as Saul of Tarsus. I knew it was an imposter, so just admonished it and put the board away." She says, "Too many people who try these things will welcome the indication that some celebrity from the past is seeking them out. This is intended to flatter us into accepting all they then try to tell us to do. If anything like that happens to you, declare forcefully that you don't buy it and don't want to hear from them again. Then try never to give them another opportunity to come close to you."

Afterword

So here ends the revamping of the first edition of *Missouri Ghosts* with a great deal of material added; at least 1/3 of this second edition is new. MG probably will never be rewritten for great care was taken to be comprehensive and accurate. What seemed like a great burden in earlier stages takes on nostalgic preciousness as the last pages are typed. This task has been a demanding companion for several months, but we're not so eager as we thought we'd be to push it out into the world and turn to other projects.

Will one of these undertakings be another collection of ghost stories? The files are almost exhausted. Yet for this book, incredible new stories were offered from unexpected sources, and perhaps that could happen again. Apparently Missouri's ghost reservoir is bottomless. If you have experienced or know of something unexplainable that happened in our state, or was told of by a Missourian, send a note to Box 200, Hallsville, MO 65255, and we'll add it to the files and hope there some day will be enough for *Missouri Ghosts III*. If you shared an experience at a signing and were surprised never to be called, write us a reminder. It's easy to lose what is hastily jotted down in the hectic atmosphere of book promotion.

Thanks and best wishes to all readers: your kind reception has made these two books the major joy of a lifetime.

Joan Gilbert

Appendix A

What Patience Worth Said

The apparent entity, Patience Worth, was quoted at great length for her clever conversation, her jokes, and for her testiness with people who asked trick questions or otherwise treated her lightly. But predominantly, especially at first, she seemed to want to talk about religion, and her audiences asked many questions about life after death and the nature of God.

Of the next world, Patience Worth said, "Believe me, good souls, life is there as here." Later she said one difference is that there are "days and days and days in what thou wouldst say was hours." She indicated that we still have work to do in spirit form, because one short earthly life does not allow for full development. She admonished that peace and salvation come only from "work and work and work alone." But Patience Worth dismissed the idea of reincarnation, saying "Once uttered, man is forever. Once we cast the flesh, the spirit is free, untrammeled forever."

Her picture of God: "He is our father and his name is Love." She went on reassuringly that like the best human fathers, God sympathizes with his childrens' pain and sorrow, consoling those who allow him to. She said God does not condemn, and that he wants to be loved, not feared. Patience

Worth said God never forsakes us, here or in the next world, that when we pray he listens not to our words, but to our spirits, and that his love extends to the tiniest of his creatures, "... e'en the midge whose wing-whirr be all its voice." Finally, of God, Patience Worth said, "Nae walls can hold him. Thy heart is afull of him, Brother."

She was encouraging about death, too, calling it "Our Mother," describing it as "... a yawn, a blink and the wakin'." She said that on any terms death "is small price to pay" for the pleasures of life here and the life to come. When asked if we will be reunited on the other side with those we loved here, she replied, "Farewells are something of Earth that must be unlearned."

What Patience Worth said in her poetry was sometimes humorous, always appreciative of nature, very often focused on social comment far ahead of her time and of Pearl Curran's. For instance, in an era when the inevitability and gloriousness of war was unquestioned, she presented several stanzas graphically showing its horrors. Each stanza ended, "Father, is *this* thy will?" She compared the potential of individual women with the restrictions forced on all women; she pointed out the injustice of inescapable childbearing in a poem with this ending:

> *"For womankind goeth through the valley of death*
> *In darkness, with no taper for to lighten,*
> *Leading man to the brink of day*
> *And he, finding the day made perfect*
> *Through the agony of womankind,*
> *Struts!"*

Patience Worth always showed great compassion and appreciation for children, and she proposed a replacement for the standard child's prayer which reminds them each night that they may die in their sleep. She offered these touching lines:

"I, thy child forever, play
About thy knees, this close of day.
Into thy arms I soon will creep,
To learn they wisdom while I sleep."

Often, when Patience Worth wrote about nature, her voice did not sound as if it came from another century. Two samples:

"I think of the hushing of leaves ...
And of the weaving of the wind, in and about,
Or the rustle of some field folk, or the shuttle of a wing.
I think of a deep, dark shadowed place, besplotched of
     sunlight and shadow;
And I, Oh my beloved God, in such a place
     feel at one with thee ...."

"I love waters and dew and frost
And thorn and young buds, befurred buds.
I love forsaken nests. I love paths
Bebriared, leading to deep thickets ....
I love to find a fallen feather or a down-trod bloom,
... I love cliffs where the fern clings
And there is moss, thick, and snails.
... these things ... are seeds to my soul."

The novels Patience Worth wrote, are to most of us, far less interesting than her poetry. The language is too hard, action too slow, conversation and description too drawn out. One of her greatest fans, Dr. Irene Hickman, has commented that some judicious editing might regain for Patience Worth's fiction some of the popularity it had in the 1930s. At that time her novels were much respected for the historical details of life and setting they revealed. Experts said this information was eerily accurate, but only dedicated scholars of the periods Patience wrote about could fully appreciate that fact. The total bulk of Worth's knowledge of history, they said, was unbelievable to have been absorbed and retained by one individual. That of course raised other questions, because the Patience Worth entity had not represented herself as anyone who ever had opportunity for extended education or deep study and research.

Patience Worth's most successful novel, probably, was the one called *A Sorry Tale.* It described parallel lives of Jesus and a man born on the same night. The two grew up in the same area; their paths crossed casually occasionally, but they did not really meet until Calvary, where they were crucified together. The language and pace of this novel are — unlike most Worth fiction — not far from what we are accustomed to reading.

In total, the writings of Patience Worth now occupy almost 30 books, some still in typescript. Her most popular books and those written about her are out of print and hard to find — except for the one Dr. Hickman produced — but to whoever is intrigued by this remarkable phenomenon, the search would be worth it and the Internet could help.

Rather than being studied further, Patience Worth, whatever she was, might prefer that we just remember what she said about serious things, especially in this poem:

> *"My hand, behold it – God's implement!*
> *With the touch of its flesh I am quickened*
> *Into a creator;*
> *Thereby am I a part of him, given*
> *An infinitesimal portion of His power ....*
>
> *Behold my hand, the link between earth*
> *And that splendor which is Eternity;*
> *For labor is the path unto Redemption."*

The book by Walter Franklin Pierce, *The Case of Patience Worth,* contains a great many of her poems. Dr. Hickman's *I Knew Patience Worth,* records mainly poems from the California channelings. This and Hickman's other books are available directly from her at 660-665-1836.

Appendix B

Three Mentors

Beverly Jaegers

Beverly Jaegers of St. Louis is probably the best known of Missouri psychic investigators, having figured in a number of interesting police cases in her own area and beyond. One of the most memorable was a murder case in which she correctly described for law enforcers where a victim's body would be found. On another occasion, she predicted a coffee shortage, benefitting an importer so richly that he gave her a house in gratitude. Even more impressive, she remote-viewed the Challenger tragedy before it happened, her findings registered in advance through an agency that exists for this purpose.

Jaegers now spends her time mainly on free-lance writing, much of it focused on antiques and other subjects far from the supernatural. One of her most recent major undertakings is a series of books on fingerprints and how they may be used for character analysis as well as identification. Some of these, published by Berkley: *Beyond Palmistry, the Art and Science of Modern Hand Analysis; Beyond Palmistry II, Your Career is in Your Hands;* and *The Hands of Children.* Mrs. Jaegers has, however, published a number of books and articles about the paranormal and she has made many media appearances and presented many lectures and seminars. She has been quoted and interviewed in publications here and in other countries; she is frequently consulted for her expertise.

Jaegers' approach is always low-key, her view of the supernatural mainly matter-of-fact. Her primary interest is how we all can enhance our lives by understanding something of what lies beyond the ordinary.

Dr. Irene Hickman

Dr. Irene Hickman of Kirksville, an Iowa native, was featured in a 1975 book, *Psychic Women,* with five others who had discovered unusual abilities they could use in positive ways. From childhood, Hickman has told interviewers, she "just knew" certain truths which led her to study the supernormal from about the age of twelve. At sixteen, she was working her way through college by palm reading in a tea room.

As an osteopathic physician, Hickman specialized in psychosomatic cases, with hypnotism as one of her tools. Spontaneous past-life regressions of some patients confirmed her own feeling that reincarnation is a fact and that past lives may affect present ones.

While living in California, Dr. Hickman was part of the group which regularly witnessed the work of one of Pearl Curran's daughters, apparently channeling Patience Worth. As mentioned earlier, Dr. Hickman recorded and transcribed some of this material, particularly the poetry, and published it in a small book called *I Knew Patience Worth.*

Experience and study led Dr. Hickman to confirm the age-old belief that many problems of physical and mental health come from what history calls possession of demons, and what she calls "predatory and parasitic spirit attachments." Dr. Hickman reminds that the Bible repeatedly shows Jesus "casting out demons."

Dr. Hickman has written other books and her writings have been anthologized. She also has lectured and participated in seminars in most of the states and in eight foreign countries.

Maurice Schwalm

Maurice Schwalm, who died in January, 2001, was prominent for many years in most reports of hauntings, mainly from Kansas City and its surrounding area, but also throughout the state. His role was most often that of psychical investigator, but he often appeared on radio or television; he claimed more than 100 media appearances for sharing his experiences. For a year he hosted his own show, reporting what he termed "earth mysteries" as well as hauntings.

Schwalm held office in his area's chapter of Mensa and was published widely in both general and professional magazines. His work appears in several anthologies. In October, 1999, he brought out his own book, *MO-Kan Ghosts, The Casebook of a Kansas City Psychic Investigator.* This is available from Belfry Books. A book Schwalm recommended to those interested in the paranormal is *ESP, Hauntings and Poltergeists: a Parapsychologists' Handbook,* by Lloyd Auerbach.

Native to Kansas City, Schwalm earned a BA in History at the University of Missouri-Kansas City and later added certification in banking and insurance law. In the insurance industry until retirement, he then worked full time as a physical investigator. Schwalm's resume says that he visited more than 100 haunted sites.

Appendix C

Order No. 11

The people interviewed for chapters 18 and 20 feel that their counties, Cass and Bates, have an unusually high level of paranormal activity because such intense suffering took place there during the Civil War. Most Missourians do not realize how many innocent civilians of all ages met misery and untimely deaths in Bates, Cass, Jackson and northern Vernon Counties because of a cruel military ruling, the infamous Order No. 11. Its results have been called the greatest government abuse of U. S. citizens except for the confinement of Japanese Americans during WWII. It also has been compared for cruelty to the ejection of Native Americans from the Southeastern states in the 1820s and 1830s.

Order No. 11 came about because Union forces allotted to commanders on the Western border of Missouri were not adequate to cope with the guerrillas from Kansas and Missouri who were fighting each other and the Union. After William Quantrill led 450 men on a brutal raid at Lawrence, Kansas, killing 150 people and destroying 185 buildings, Missourians on the border lived in terror of reprisal.

Because they knew Union forces in the area could not protect them, they felt they had to rely on Missouri guerrillas, most of whom were, in fact, long-time friends or family members of many residents of the border counties. Thus a great many of these people supplied the guerrillas — as generously as their means allowed — with food, money, horses, clothing and anything else the men needed.

Union military leaders could not stop this support, since they had no means of sorting out who was and who was not providing it. They obtained from the national government the right to create and enforce a military order — the brutal Order No. 11 — which decreed that everyone in the three counties and north Vernon must leave their homes and the area.

As written, the rule exempted those who had certification of Union loyalty and it gave people fifteen days to locate refuge, gather up their belongings and make travel arrangements. Enforcement, however, was left to James Lane, a Kansas counterpart of William Quantrill and the target of the Lawrence Raid. Having aligned himself with the Union, Lane seemed to take satisfaction in indulging his hostility to people of the border counties. He enforced the order harshly, evicting people without giving them time to prepare or obtain supplies and he allowed looters to travel with the enforcers. Residents of the border counties often saw their most loved and vital possessions taken by others and many saw their hard-won homes set on fire.

Border residents' belongings were already badly depleted by Kansas raids and by military confiscations. Good horses, mules and vehicles were largely gone from the area. Few people had anywhere to go on such short notice, and all knew that friends and relatives in nearby counties were unlikely to welcome them, having so little left to share.

The result was that, as with Native Tribes forced onto what the Cherokees called "The Trail of Tears," children, the aged and the infirm suffered greatly and died quickly during the winter that was soon upon them. They had not only to contend with their own lack of shelter and food, but with physical danger from raiders and from anyone they might encounter whose loyalty opposed their own.

Order No. 11 was enforced, beginning on August 25, 1863, and in November of the same year, a countermanding order — benefitting only those who could prove loyalty to the Union — went into effect. Even those people usually found their homes gone along with their livestock and farming equipment. Little was left for them to rebuild their lives around. The area had become known as "The Burnt District" because both Union Army and guerrillas had systematically destroyed crops and property to prevent the other side's having use of them.

It was much longer than two months before others who had been evicted were able to go back to what was left of their homes. Most had to wait until the war was over, and a great many of these, having learned of conditions where they formerly lived, never made the effort to go back.

To this day, many people in the border counties that were so unfairly afflicted feel great bitterness for the suffering and losses of their ancestors. If emotion really can affect the paranormal atmosphere of an area, the border counties certainly had far more than their share of fear, anger, and sorrow, and of unleashed greed and brutality.

Two novels about this era: *The Burnt District,* by Ellen Grey Massey, an e-book from Hardshell.com, also available in print from fax# 417-532-5155; also *Another Spring* by Loula Grace Erdman, published in 1966 by Dodd Mead, out of print, worth searching for through rare book sources.

Appendix D

The U.S. Psi Squad

In 1971, Bevy and Ray Jaegers helped to found an organization for people who wanted to learn how to enhance their extended senses and employ them in useful ways. This group has grown in numbers and in acceptance with law enforcement, scientists and the military. Bevy, who began in the 1960s to develop her abilities has often been asked to lead training for police officers and military intelligence personnel. These groups no longer laugh at the idea that someone might delve into his or her own mind and by a procedure called "remote viewing" discern facts vital to solving a crime or important in military activity.

A great deal of information about the Psi Squad is available on an impressive website, www.uspsisquad.com. Just one sample of what can be seen online, is the group's findings about the Russian submarine, Kursk, which went missing on August 12, 2000.

During the night of August 14-15 and after, members of the Psi Squad applied themselves to this mystery and their findings, had they acted on immediately, might have saved some lives. The Missourians — and members in several states and in Canada — determined that men were still alive on the sub through August 17, that the two heavy explosions from within doomed the craft, not a collision; they saw that openings in the double metal hull flared outward.

Psi Squad members found more people on board than had been reported, not all of them military. A number of other items from Psi Squad viewing of the sub are too technical to interest most of us, but were proved true when conventional investigation took place. Email verifies the time and date when each person's remote viewing findings arrived at their point of collection. They were monitored and stored there by people outside the organization.

A few of the findings that are easy for any of us to visualize: greenish material that one described as "goo" floated on the inside water surface, giving its color to all that could be seen by dim lights still burning in parts of the vessel. Both inner and outer hulls had been breached and great damage inside the vessel was obvious, but its nuclear apparatus was not involved. The ocean was seeping into rear compartments, where the crew took refuge because these enclosures were supposed to be water tight; doors apparently had not been able to seal completely. A considerable number of men survived the blasts, but their number decreased steadily as more and more of the sub flooded and air got worse and worse. The men suffered greatly from cold.

Though the Squad tried to make contact with agencies that might have used their findings in time to save the trapped sailors, Russia was refusing any help and there was no way any outside group could take action.

Someday, surely, help of remote viewers will be sought at once when other means of discernment cannot be used. The Psi Squad report on Kursk ended with this reminder: "at least four submarines, two or more of them nuclear powered, lie in deep waters around the globe. Sea water, as is well known, is corrosive."

The following statement is a part of the report: "Remote Viewing is not a new skill. It was brought to operational and tactical targets during research at Stanford Research Institute and culminated in the U, S. Army's Stargate Project at Fort Meade, MD. The Kursk-viewing group is the only non-military remote viewing team in the U.S."

Appendix E

Another Patience?

One of the most complex and puzzling experiences offered for this second edition of *Missouri Ghosts* came from a fellow Missouri Writers Guild member, Wanda Sue Parrott of Springfield. Her book about a visitant similar to Patience Worth, *There's a Spirit in the Kitchen*, was published last year by Galde Press, Inc. In it is described the visible and audible arrival of an entity similar to Patience Worth in many ways and different in many others. Calling herself Amy Kitchener, she said she had come to make Parrott rich as a food columnist and in the process to serve Kitchener's own purpose, telling people what they most need to know about nutrition, homemaking and child rearing in our changing world. Kitchener had many other concerns, including protection of the environment and citizen responsibility for monitoring government.

Parrott was living in Pacific Palisades. California, at the time – 1973 – writing for the *Los Angeles Herald Examiner.* Though she had no particular interest in writing about food and did not even consider herself a good cook, she followed Amy's suggestions and did establish a syndicated food column. Not until her retirement did Parrott feel like writing anything about the entity who described herself as "a humble housewife" who was born in 1820 and by the year 1846, had become the mother of two young children. Her husband, Charles, she said, operated a store and they lived in a two-story wooden house with the great luxury of running water as that was defined in the era: water piped into the house from an outdoor cistern and delivered into one sink by a hand-operated pump.

Amy described in fond detail her new coal-burning cook stove. She also described that stove's present home with an antique collector who uses it as a decorating conversation piece. There is very little else in the book about Amy Kitchener as a person and Parrott's efforts to prove that she existed have so far been unsuccessful. Census taking at that time was haphazard and handwriting often unreadable. Parrott once thought she was close to the data she needed, but is not sure.

Parrott's book is hard to describe, for it is not organized in the traditional way. Certainly it has a great many recipes and household hints, and some of this material sounds old, but some involves products of our own day, even convenience foods. Is Amy demonstrating that once out of the body a spirit is aware of everything in all times? Now and then Amy discusses the state of American society and she has a concern we can hardly follow about color as therapy and revelation. Maybe Parrott is giving us a forerunner of what all books will one day be, compendiums to glean in a random way with minimal direction from the author. To sample *There's a Spirit in the Kitchen*: About our world, Amy said that Earth is "a spiritual experiment," The United States of America being a separate and somewhat different spiritual experiment. She pointed out that our country has given people the best opportunity so far in human history to pursue "the greatest of all freedoms, to find and be your higher self. This is the ultimate attainment of your earthly life."

Of the group of beings she belongs to, Amy says, "We are the ascended race, wearing, sometimes, human face." This sounds like reinforcement of an idea repeatedly presented in paranormal lore, that spirits and beings from elsewhere are among us all the time to learn for their own benefit, or to do what they can to help us. Since they wear such good human disguise, we never suspect their real identity. Elsewhere Amy says, "We are male and female, yet neither and both" and "no soul is ever lost, only changed."

The reader must be warned that the voice of this book shifts around often and usually without warning. Sometimes it is presumably Amy who speaks, sometimes about Parrott and sometimes Parrott talks about Amy.

Sometimes surprising others, such as Abraham Lincoln, speak out. Recipes are not always separated from philosophy or child-rearing tips. Insights Amy offers about life after death is not all in one place. The Patience Worth material is much simpler and more logically arranged than Amy Kitchener's and it deals with fewer topics. Patience answered questions directly, though sometimes in rather paradoxical fashion. Parrott says Amy did not; she merely offered what she chose to when she chose to and usually could only be listened to. Parrott was seldom able to summon Amy. Patience Worth apparently was available anytime Pearl Curran sat down and invited her. Like Curran, Parrott employed some automatic writing initially, but also like Curran, soon began to feel the entity's words in her mind.

After completion and publication of the book, Parrott had little contact from Amy for some time, but she reports that recently Amy has resumed contact, in a "storyteller" role.

Bibliography

Books

Archer, Fred, *Exploring the Psychic World,* 1967, William Morrow and Co.

Allen, Thomas B., *Possessed, The True Story of an Exorcism,* Doubleday, 1993.

Atkins, Meg Elizabeth, *Samain* (novel), 1976, Ballantine Books.

Auerbach, Lloyd, *ESP, Hauntings and Poltergeists: A Parapsychologists' Handbook,* .

Bartlett, John, *Bartlett's Familiar Quotations,* 1955, Little Brown & Co.

Bayless, Raymond, *Experiences of a Psychical Researcher,* 1972, University Books, Inc.; *Animal Ghosts,* 1970, University Books, Inc.

Blackman, W. Haden, *Field Guide to North American Hauntings,* 1998, Three Rivers Press.

Blattner, William Peter, *The Exorcist,* 1971, Harper-Row.

Boswell, Harriett A. *Master Guide to Psychism,* 1969, Parker Publishing Company.

Buckley, Doris Heather, *Spirit Communication for the Millions,* 1967, Dell.

Caldwell, Dorothy, Editor, *Missouri Historical Sites Catalog,* 1963, State Historical Society of Missouri-Columbia.

Cohen, Daniel, *The Encyclopedia of Ghosts,* 1984, Dodd, Mead.

Coleman, Nadine Mills, *Mistress of Ravenswood,* 1992, *Columbia Daily Tribune.*

Combs, Loula Long, *My Revelation*, 1947, Longview Publishing Company.

Courtaway, Robbi, *Spirits of St. Louis*, 2000, Virginia Publishing Company.

Ebon, Martin, ed., *Communicating With the Dead,* 1891-1968, The New American Library; *True Experiences With Ghosts*, 1968, The New American Library.

Edwards, Frank, *Strange People,* 1961 Popular Library.

Ellis, Jerry, *Bareback*, 1994, Thorndike Press.

Enright, D. J. ed., *The Oxford Book of Death*, 1983, The University Press, Oxford.

Erdman, Loula Grace, *Another Spring,* 1966, Dodd, Mead & Company.

Evans, Hilary and Hugghe, Patrick, *Field Guide to Ghosts and Other Apparitions,* 2000, Harpercollins.

Gaddis, Vincent H., *Mysterious Fires and Lights,* 1967, David McCay Co. Inc.

Gilbert, Joan, *Missouri Ghosts,* first edition, 1997, Pebble. *More Missouri Ghosts,* 2000 MoGho Books.

Glancy, Diane, *Pushing The Bear,* 1996, Harcourt Brace & Co.

Guiley, Rosemary Ellen, *The Encyclopedia of Ghosts and Spirits,* 1992, Facts on File, second edition, 2000.

Hale Allean Lemon, *Petticoat Pioneer,* 1956-1968, North Central Publishing Co.

Hauck, Dennis William, *The National Directory of Haunted Places.*

Hickman, Irene, *I Knew Patience Worth,* second edition, 1995, Hickman Systems New Age Books; *Remote Depossession,* 1994, Hickman Systems New Age Books.

Hill, Douglas and Williams, Pat, 1965, *The Supernatural,* Hawthorn.

Holzer, Hans, *Ghosts,* 1997, Black Dog and Levanthal.

Jaegers, Bevy C., *Psychometry, The Science of Touch,* 1980, Aires Productions, Inc.; *Ghost Hunting, Professional Haunted House Investigation,* 1988, an Aires Production.

Jarvis, Sharon, Ed., *Dead Zones,* 1992, Warner Books.

Jones, Linda Newcomb, *The Longview We Remember,* 1991, Storm Ridge Press.

Litvag, Irving, *Singer in the Shadows, The Strange Story of Patience Worth,* 1972, Popular Library.

MacDonald, Margaret Read, *Ghost Stories from the Pacific Northwest,* 1995 August House.

Macklin, John, *Casebook of the Unknown,* 1974, Ace Books.

Manley, Seon and Lewis, Gogo, *Baleful Beasts,* 1974, Lothrop, Lee & Shepard Co., 1994, Athanor Press.

Massey, Ellen Gray, *The Burnt District,* 2001 Hardshell.com.

May, Antoinette, *Psychic Women,* 1984, Hickman Systems.

Mitchell, Clarence Dewey, *Jim The Wonder Dog,* 1942-1989, Jim The Wonder Dog, Inc.

Moore, Thomas, *Mysterious Tales & Legends of the Ozarks,* 1938, Dorrance, and Co.

Myers, *The Human Personality and Its Survival of Bodily Death,* Dutton.

Neider, Charles, Ed., *The Autobiography of Mark Twain,* 1975, Harper and Row.

Norman, Michael and Scott, Beth, *Historic Haunted America,* 1995, TOR.; *Haunted Heartland,* 1985, Dorset Press.

The Oxford Dictionary of Quotations, Oxford University Press, Second and Third Editions, 1953 and 1980.

Packard, Vance, *The Human Side of Animals,* 1961, Pocket Books.

Prince, Walter Franklin, *The Case of Patience Worth,* 1927-64. University Books; *Noted Witnesses for Psychic Occurrences,* 1963, University Books.

Randolph, Vance, *Ozark Magic and Folklore,* 1947 by Columbia University Press, 1964 facsimile by Dover.

Rogo, D. Scott, *An Experience of Phantoms,* 1974, Taplinger Publishing Co.

Santesson, Hans Stefan, editor, *The Locked Room Reader,* (fiction), 1968, Random House.

Schurmacher, Emile C., *Strange Unsolved Mysteries,* 1967, Paperback Library.

Schwalm, Maurice, *MO-Kan Ghosts,* 1999, Belfry Books.

Sherman, Harold, *You Live After Death,* 1972, Fawcett.

Smith, Alson J., *Immortality, The Scientific Evidence,* 1954, Prentice Hall.

Steele, Phillip, *Ozark Tales & Superstitions,* 1983, Pelican Publishing Co.

Steiner, Rudolph, *Reincarnation and Karma,* 1962, Anthroposophic Press.

Strong, Julia Bernard, *Letters 1836-1839,* unpublished, Joint Collection Western Historical Manuscript Collection/State Historical Society of Missouri Manuscripts, Ellis Hall, University of Missouri-Columbia.

Switzler, William, *The History of Boone County, Missouri,* 1882, reprinted now by Ramfre.

Tweedale, Violet, *Ghosts I Have Seen and Other Psychic Experiences,* Herbert Jenkinns, LTD, London, 1920.

USA Weekend, *I Never Believed in Ghosts Until...100 Real-Life Encounters,* 1992, Barnes & Noble.

van Ravensway, Charles (intro),*The WPA Guide to 1930s Missouri, 1936-86,* University Press of Kansas,

Walker, Stephen P., Lemp, *The Haunting History,* 1988, The Lemp Preservation Society, Inc.

Zbinden, Rosemary, *A Voice from the Past,* 2001, Sunset Publishing Company.

Magazines

The Almanac for Farmers and City Folk, "Ghosts in the Country," by Christine Shannon, 1993.

The Alumni Magazine, Northwest Missouri State University, "Roberta Hill: a Grand Lady," by Dave Gieseke, Summer, 1991.

Columbia Senior Times, "The Historic Lure of Ravenswood Mansion," by Joan Gilbert, September, 1996.

Delta Queen Steamboat Company, catalogs for 2000 and 2001.

Fate, "Agathas' Dutch Oven,", by Eva Marie Woodward, undated clip. "Life and Death on the Mississippi River," by Dr. V. Fred Rayser, October, 2000; "The House the Ghost Loved," by Joan Gilbert, January, 1988. "Print Expert Checks Bigfoot Tracks," by Tom R. Kovach, November, 2000,

The Harbinger Magazine, "The Hornet Ghost Light," author and month of publication not listed, 1970.

Life, "Terrifying Tales of Nine Haunted Houses," author and month of publication not listed, 1980 November.

Missouri Conservationist, "A Couple of Well Known Dogs," by Joel E. Vance, December, 1990; "Spooklight," by Suzanne J. Wilson, January, 1997.

Missouri Historical Review, "Missouri's Turn of the Century First Couple, Lawrence Vest and Margaret Nelson Stephens," by Marian M.Ohman, April 1997.

Missouri Life, "The Ghosts of Missouri, Past and Present," Joan Gilbert & Jacki Gray, December, 1984; "The Hornet Spook Light," Larry E. Wood, September/October, 1977; "Mistress of Ravenswood," Nadine Mills Coleman, September/October, 1973; "Ravenswood," by Carmen Kennedy, December 1985.

The Oats Wheel, "Ravenswood, Reflection of Times Gone By," no byline, January 1987.

Old Settler's Gazette, Legends of the Ozarks, edited by Melinda Stewart, undated, in the 1970s.

Ozarks Mountaineer, "A Few Ozarks Ghosts," by Joan Gilbert, September/October, 1991.

Ozarks Senior Living, "Ellen Gray Massey, Romancing the Ozarks", by Vicki Cox, September, 1994.

Parade Magazine, "Have You Ever Seen a Ghost?" Prince Michael of Greece, August 20, 1995.

Rural Missouri, "Patience Worth, Ghostly Writer," by Joan Gilbert, January, 1981; "Specter, Spirit or Spoof," Heather Berry, October 1989; "Steamboatin'", by Jeff Joiner, July, 2000.

Springfield! "The Legends of a Haunted Bridge," by Tom Mason, October, 1985.

St. Charles Living, "The Ghosts of Main Street," by John Dengler, February 7, 1997.

Yankee, "The Man Who Saw Bigfoot" (fiction), by Rebecca Rute, February 1990.

Newspapers

Columbia Daily Tribune: "Realtors Seek Haunted House Guidelines," no byline, June 6, 1991; "Breadtray Has a Slice of History," Tom Ladwig, undated clip; "Spirits in the House," Joe Bargman, October 25, 1987; "Bleak House," Sara Summerhays, April 14, 1991; "A Haunting Season," Betsy Krause, July 25, 1988; "Born of Compromise," Scott Charton, August 11, 1996; "Stephens Spirit," Steven Bennish, August 20, 1986; "Haunted Acres," Ashley Frantz, October 30,1998; "Voyage of Rediscovery," by Hugh A. Mulligan (AP), February 4, 2001

Columbia Missourian: "Ghostly Romance," Lee Ann Bowles, September 14, 1986; "Is Columbia Haunted By G-G-Ghosts?" Susan Flanigan, October 28, 1984; "Ravenswood," Kirk Curnutt, May 17, 1987; "Haunts, Horrors or Hoaxes," Dee Stiffler, October 30, 1992; "Well Known Boonville Ghosts," Tom Ladwig, September 27, 1987; "Party Benefits Heritage," Sara Bell, June 26, 1996.

Daily Gateway Guide: "Murdered Traveler's Ghost Is Said to Haunt Local House," Roger Scarborough, October 31, 1980; "Bloodland's Residents May Still Linger," no byline, October 30, 1975; "Ghosts Roam Pre-Civil War Mansion," January 1977; "Is there No Cure for MOMO's BO?" "MOMO Footprinted?" "MoMo in Rubber Gloves? Must be Dishpan Paws" all undated clips, UPI releases, late July, 1972.

Hannibal-Courier Post: "Ghostly Town," November 4, 1996.

Kansas City Star: "Mrs. M., A Spirited Guest at KC Hotel," Jennie Armstrong, April 10, 1985; "Ghostly Prey Elusive at James Farm," D. P. Breckenridge, January 26, 1982; "Ghosts:

A Dark Quest for the Unearthly," Brant Houston, October 30, 1981; "Ghostly Things Keep Feet, Tongues Moving," Myron Levin, May 27, 1979; "Tales of the Truly Weird," John Hughes, Star Magazine, October 25, 1987.

Marceline Press, "Death Rode the Rails," Clifford Funk-houser, July 23, 1973.

Mark Twain Lake Guide: "Garth Mansion, one of Twain's Favorites," Juanita Yates, June 4, 1984; "Rockcliffe Mansion," Juanita Yates, June 6, 1984; *The Missouri Patriot,* "A Haunted Hotel," no byline, September 9, 1875.

St. Louis Globe-Democrat: "History is Alive and Well in St. Charles," no byline, July 1, 1978; "Ozark Spook Light: Fact or Fantasy?" Peter Hernon, November 15-16, 1980; "St. Louis, Happy Haunting for Hallowe'en," no byline, October 27, 1978; "Thing Could Be a Hairy Biped, says UFO Watcher," Carles J. Oswald, July 22-23, 1972.

St. Louis Post-Dispatch: "The Haunting History of the Lemp Family," "By a staff member of the P.D.", March 18, 1990; "Where Spirits Walk," Harper Barnes, Jan. 26, 1977; "Vestige of a Genteel Past," Arthur Whitman, May 17, 1964; "The Splendors and the Mysteries of Ravenswood," Ellen Futterman, May 11, 1986; "Bingham's Arrow Rock," Robert LaRouche, October 30, 1996; "New Blends With Old in St. Charles," Robert LaRouche, October 6, 1968; "Psychic St. Louis," Jim Creighton, Nine part Series ending in late September, 1977; "Ghosts in St. Louis Lack Character," Jim Creighton, April 6, 1975; "Spirit of Lemp House," Jeff Meyers, September 2, 1979; "Weird Tale of Ghost in West End," June 1, 1906, no byline; "The Chase Hotel: the Tradition Lives On," May 3, 1985; "The Castle: Mystery in the West End," Georgia Sauer, September, 3, 1989; "West End Family Thinks Ghost May Inhabit House," Joan Foster Dames, January 11, 1967; "Mark Twain's Home Town," Al Foster, April 19, 1981; "X-Rated Hannibal of Twain's Day," Jack Rice, July 22, 1973; "Hunting Real Ghosts," no byline, May 4, 1988; "Out of This World Theory on Elusive Monster,

Robert J. Kelly, July 24, 1972; "The Thing: It Could BE a Yeti or Biped," Ed Wilkes, late July, 1972.

Springfield Daily News, and *News, Leader and Press:* "Ethereal Figures Vanish as Ozarks' Past Fades," Joe Clayton, October 12, 1981; "Spook Story Explained," Helen Botel, October 16, 1968; "Ghostly Stories Abound in Ozarks," Max Hunter, October 31, 1980; "Do Ghosts Like You?," no byline, undated clip, October, 1978; "Over the Ozarks," column ed. Jean Davis, June 2, 1977; "Things That Go Bump in the Landers," Jean Maneke, September 15, mid-70's, undated clip; "Haunted Hills," Traci Bauer, October 27, 1996; "Vance Randolph, Lowlander, Collecting a Legacy," August 17, 1975; "Ha'nts of Old Still Float Through Ozark Mountains," Mike O' Brien, October 28, 1996; USA Weekend: Hannibal, Missouri, Leslie Ansley, August 16-18, 1991.

Index

W

Y

Z

To Order More from MoGho Books

Send the form below to:
MoGho Books, P.O. Box 200, Hallsville, MO
with $19.50 for each copy of **Missouri Ghosts 2nd Edition** and $18.00 for each copy of **More Missouri Ghosts**. Postage, tax, and handling is included in that simplified price. (Sorry, no credit card facilities yet.)

Also available from MoGho books is **The Extended Circle, a Dictionary of Humane Thought**. This 436 page collection of quotations about animals contains the thoughts of everyone from Minnie Pearl to Abraham Lincoln, thoughts from all times and all places. Published in 1985 in England, its discounted prices now are $12.50 hardback and $9, paperback. This book has been called "The Animal Lovers' Bible."

Name_____

Address_____

Names and quantities of books_____

_____

_____

To Order More from MoGho Books

Send the form below to:
MoGho Books, P.O. Box 200, Hallsville, MO
with $19.50 for each copy of **Missouri Ghosts 2nd Edition** and $18.00 for each copy of **More Missouri Ghosts**. Postage, tax, and handling is included in that simplified price. (Sorry, no credit card facilities yet.)

Also available from MoGho books is **The Extended Circle, a Dictionary of Humane Thought**. This 436 page collection of quotations about animals contains the thoughts of everyone from Minnie Pearl to Abraham Lincoln, thoughts from all times and all places. Published in 1985 in England, its discounted prices now are $12.50 hardback and $9, paperback. This book has been called "The Animal Lovers' Bible."

Name_____

Address_____

Names and quantities of books_____

_____

_____